Strictly Legal

Also by Michael G. Cochrane

Class Actions: A Guide to the Class Proceedings Act,
Family Law in Ontario for Lawyers and Law Clerks
For Better or For Worse: The Canadian Guide to Marriage
Contracts and Cohabitation Agreements;
Surviving Your Divorce: A Guide to Canadian Family Law
Surviving Your Parents' Divorce: A Guide for Young
Canadians

Strictly Legal

THINGS YOU ABSOLUTELY NEED
TO KNOW ABOUT CANADIAN LAW

Michael G. Cochrane, B.A., LL.B.

INSOMNIAC PRESS

Library and Archives Canada Cataloguing in Publication

Cochrane, Michael G. (Michael George), 1953-   Strictly legal : things you absolutely need to know about Canadian law / Michael G. Cochrane.

ISBN 978-1-897178-38-6

     1. Law--Canada--Popular works. I. Title.
KE447.C62 2007   349.71   C2007-901109-8
KF387.C62 2007

The publisher gratefully acknowledges the support of the Department of Canadian Heritage through the Book Publishing Industry Development Program.

Printed and bound in Canada

Insomniac Press
192 Spadina Avenue, Suite 403
Toronto, Ontario, Canada, M5T 2C2
www.insomniacpress.com

Cautions

1. The goal of this book is to provide you with legal information, not legal advice about your case or situation. If you need more information or an explanation of how the law may apply to your particular situation, please consult a lawyer. Always ask for thirty minutes of free advice. Most Canadian lawyers are more than happy to meet with you to discuss your case—no charge for at least the first half hour. We want to meet you and hear about your needs.

2. The book has been written so it can be read by people in all provinces (except Quebec) and the territories. The law may vary, however, depending on where you live in Canada. If you need some specific guidance, do not hesitate to use some of the other resources that I mention in the book or to speak with a lawyer in your province or territory.

3. The views expressed in the book are not those of BNN, CTV or Ricketts, Harris LLP. It is just me, giving you my take on Canadian law. I hope it is of use to you and your family and that, in the future, should you encounter legal problems, this book will help you not only to focus on the real problem that you face, but also to save some money, should you be forced into the justice system.

Acknowledgments

The TV show *Strictly Legal,* and now this book based on the TV show, could not happen without the support of a lot of people. Jack Fleischmann at BNN gets credit, not only for giving *Strictly Legal* a chance on television, but also for thinking up the name!

On the TV producing side at BNN, much credit goes to the show's producer Mike Omelus, the broadcast associates Dan Pasqua and Adam Cohen and (more than she probably knows) to Susan Timewell-Jeffs, who does my makeup each week. On the operations side, the technical producer Robert Frizzell, the technical director Ian Ireland, production assistant Carla Harman, the audio operator Gil Masuda, floor director Steve Copek, robotics operator Zdenko Milic and studio technicians Ilysha Richardson, Peter Bolt and Phil Loftus all make sure that this program goes live on national television every Thursday at 8:30p.m. Eastern time, 5:30p.m. Pacific. As I mention on-air sometimes, they are a terrific and skilled team and make my life a lot easier as I make the transition from the courtroom and my law office to the TV studio each week.

My literary agent, Daphne Hart of Helen Heller Agency, deserves credit for partnering me as an author with Insomniac Press as a publisher. They have been very responsive and supportive in a lightning fast turnaround of this book.

A special mention needs to be made of Kim Parlee, who co-hosted *Strictly Legal* with me during its first season. Kim is a very accomplished professional, and she taught me a lot about what it takes to host a live national television program.

Lisa Henry, my assistant at Ricketts, Harris, deserves special thanks for helping me meet the demands both professionally at the office and for my extracurricular activities in writing and television. She makes sure I am where I am supposed to be, when I am supposed to be, and more.

My most important thanks, however, go to my wife Rita, my daughters Emma, Erica, Renée and Hanna, who (while they may not see every single show) never fail to be honest critics. Let's just say they keep me humble.

— Michael G. Cochrane, B.A., LL.B.

Table of Contents

Introduction

Why You Need This Book

Strictly Legal is now in its second season on BNN (Business News Network, formerly ROBTv), and every week the calls and emails flow in from across Canada. Canadians enthusiastically ask questions about their wills and estates, about their divorces, about starting their businesses, about collecting debts and protecting their inventions. They are interested in criminal law, business law, real estate, employment law and hundreds of other areas. They are interested not because they have a deep love of the law, but rather because this is a part of real life. This is a part of having families, homes, jobs and of "bumping into each other" in a society that gets busier and more complicated every day. I think that their interest in these areas illustrates just how important the law is to the lives of average Canadians.

After dozens of shows, something became evident; a pattern emerged. Whether viewers live in British Columbia, Saskatchewan, Prince Edward Island, Ontario, Nunavut, or any other province or territory, they have the same questions and interests in specific areas of Canadian law. Callers, and those who email questions to the show, have been asking very smart, very sensible and practical questions, and I have noticed that they do not want legal mumbo-jumbo or weaselly fine-print answers. They want accessible, understandable, practical answers. They want legal information they can use in their personal lives. That's what the show and this book are about: information about the law that Canadians can use.

Each week, I try to focus *Strictly Legal* on three things: at the beginning of the show I provide a few minutes of useful information about the topic for the evening. Sometimes, there is an expert guest, and we try to demystify some aspect of Canadian law; I then take telephone calls and emails and try to answer as many questions as possible on-air, again with the focus on demystifying and making the law useful and last I take a moment to engage in what I have called LawyerSpeak©. I take a legal term that is, perhaps, acting as a barrier to understanding Canadian law, and I explain it to show viewers how it fits into real life. It is sort of a translation of mumbo-jumbo legal terminology.

I have organized this book around ten of the most popular areas of interest and ten of the most common questions that viewers have about each. The title of the book is *Things You Absolutely Have to Know about Canadian Law*, and there are actually thousands of pieces of information in the book, all of which will be useful to Canadians. Each chapter is, of course, not meant to be an exhaustive examination of a particular area of the law. It is meant to be enough law for you to use. I try to provide straight answers and information that will help you solve problems and save money. After reading the book maybe you will have more questions, maybe you will want to speak with a lawyer, maybe you will want to call me at *Strictly Legal* and ask another question. Call BNN or email your question to me at strictlylegal@bnn.ca.

I hope you enjoy the book and find it useful.

Chapter 1

10 Things You Absolutely Need To Know About "The System"

A few years ago, a client met me at my office prior to heading off to court. We had a morning appointment with a judge. This client was not from Canada. He had grown up in another country and had moved here seeking a better life. As we packed up my briefcase and got ready to head up the street to the courthouse, he turned to me and said, "How much do you need for the judge?" I did not quite understand what he meant, and I asked him to repeat the question. He winked at me and said again, with a cynical smile, "How much money do you need for the judge?" I told him that I did not need anything for the judge, but he went on to say that he had ten thousand dollars that I could use to bribe the judge, if needed. I explained to this fellow that, in Canada, that was not only illegal, but also quite unnecessary and that he would be assured of an impartial hearing. We went off to court. He received an impartial hearing and I think he left the courthouse convinced that we had a wonderful court system, governed by the rule of law. It was a concept previously utterly unknown to him.

In Canada, the "rule of law" means that all of us, regardless of how much money we have, where we come from, our religious background, our level of education and so on, will be treated equally under the law. There is one law, and we are all ruled equally by it. This concept is the foundation of a civilized society like the one we enjoy in Canada.

Now, all of that sounds quite rosy. We do have a rule of law, and we do have an impartial justice system, but that "system" can also be a confounding maze of red tape, bureaucracy, inefficiency, expense, legal mumbo-jumbo, emotional turmoil and mind-numbing delay. So, "the system" is based on a beautiful concept, but some days it can certainly feel like someone has made it as difficult and as expensive as possible to have access to the rule of law.

In this chapter, I want to demystify at least ten key features of "the system" (and by "the system," I mean the justice system in Canada), in the hope that it will be easier for you to use it, easier for you to solve your problems (or defend yourself from problems other people have created for you) and to do so in a cost-effective way.

Canadians should not fear lawyers. We should not fear our courts. We should not fear judges and juries. We should not fear financial ruin because we have a legal problem. In this chapter, I want to remove any fear and replace it with a healthy dose of consumer smarts.

Part 1 — Lawyers

I am not ashamed to admit that most people would rather have a root canal at the dentist's than be forced into a lawyer's office in order to deal with some problem. I know exactly why this is the case: lawyers are associated with conflict, and that conflict is associated with spending money. People do not drop in to see a lawyer just to shoot the breeze. It is not uncommon to meet clients who constantly check their watch to make sure that they get as much advice as they can in as little time as possible. I do not blame them because in Canada lawyers can be very, very expensive. However, we are often unavoidable partners for you. You need us sometimes. So, it is better to learn how to manage the relationship than to fear it or avoid it.

The lawyer-client relationship is a unique one. The lawyer is part psychologist, part hand-holder, part teacher, part gladiator and part priest (for those who finally get an opportunity to confess their "sins" in confidence). One of the special features of the lawyer-client relationship is secrecy. Everything a person tells a lawyer must be kept in absolute confidence. This is known as lawyer-client confidentiality. Other than revealing facts necessary for representing a client, there are only two circumstances in which a lawyer may be justified in breaching lawyer-client confidentiality:

- If the client is about to commit a crime, the lawyer has an obligation to speak up to stop it. So, if a client tells a lawyer that they are going to kill their neighbour, the lawyer has an obligation to report that to the police. No one will fault the lawyer for breaching lawyer-client confidentiality.
- The same is true if a lawyer learns that there may be some danger of harm, either emotional or physical, to a child. We have a professional obligation to contact child protection authorities.

From time to time, you may see ads on television from lawyers who will negotiate a settlement with Canada Revenue Agency on behalf of people who have not been paying their taxes. This can happen through a lawyer's office because the lawyer and the client have lawyer-client confidentiality. The lawyer will contact Canada Revenue Agency and say that a person whose name they cannot reveal because of solicitor-client privilege has hired them. The person, the lawyer says, would like to voluntarily agree on a settlement with Canada Revenue Agency to pay taxes that should have been paid earlier. Canada Revenue Agency then negotiates a settlement with the lawyer. If the settlement is confirmed with Canada Revenue Agency, then the lawyer reveals the client's name to Canada Revenue Agency, and the taxes are paid pursuant to the settlement. If the lawyer and Canada Revenue Agency cannot come to terms, the lawyer thanks Canada Revenue Agency for their time and does not reveal the individual's name. Usually, Canada Revenue Agency is more than happy to make an arrangement to have some taxes paid, rather than forego the possibility of getting anything at all.

To find a good lawyer, you need to search out someone who has experience in the area in which you have a problem, someone who is honest and a good listener, is respected by their peers and, I think, someone who has a sense of humour. A good lawyer is punctual, considerate and professional in dealing with the client.

I am always amazed when someone asks whether it is permissible for lawyers to have sex with their clients. There is no specific rule that states that a lawyer will be disbarred (kicked

out of the profession) for having sex with a client. If the intimate relationship jeopardizes the lawyer's ability to represent
the client, however, then the lawyer runs the risk of being suspended for a period of time. (It is not the same with doctors. If
a doctor has a sexual relationship with a patient, it means an
automatic loss of licence.) A truly professional lawyer would
not become involved in an intimate relationship with a client
because it would create a clear conflict of interest and hinder the
lawyer's ability to provide objective advice to the client.

A good lawyer is also someone who will tell you things
about your case that you may not want to hear. After spending
thirty minutes with a potential lawyer, you should ask yourself
three questions:

• Do I feel comfortable with this person?
• Do I respect their opinion?
• Do they respect my opinion?

These questions are important because whether the lawyer
is now going to be your psychologist, your gladiator or your
priest, they are going to be your guide through the justice system, and you need to have someone in whom you can have confidence. I recommend that clients avoid blowhards (people who
talk about big wins or big cases). Stuffed shirts are, more often
than not, just that. You do not need the most expensive lawyer
in town. You do not need the oldest lawyer in town or the
lawyer who has the toughest reputation as a "gunslinger." You
need somebody who has experience and who will get the job
done in a cost-effective way.

How do you find such a lawyer? You are not going to find
them by flipping through the telephone book. Each province
has a law society and each law society is more than happy to
facilitate connecting people with lawyers who have experience
in a particular area. Ask around, because the best references are
from people in whom you have confidence. Ask your business
associates. Ask your neighbours. Ask people whom you
respect, and then go meet with the lawyer to make sure you can
answer those three questions positively.

In Canada, all lawyers are both barristers and solicitors. In Britain, for example, barristers focus more on courtroom work, and solicitors focus more on the office work. Here, while we are all both barristers and solicitors, some lawyers will focus more on one aspect of it than the other.

You are entitled to a lawyer without a conflict of interest. In other words, if you are seeing a lawyer because you are unable to pay your mortgage, you can be assured that in the past the lawyer will not also have represented the bank to whom you owe money.

When you hire a lawyer, you know that you are dealing with somebody who is insured, so that if there is a mistake made, you will be protected. You also have the comfort of knowing that the lawyer is supervised by a law society. Lawyers are guided by a set of rules of professional conduct, and we face the possibility of being disciplined by our law society if we do not follow those rules. I can tell you that there is no more anxious moment for a lawyer opening their mail in the morning than finding a letter from the law society marked "Personal and Confidential."

When you find the right lawyer, you will want to make sure that you enter into a contract in writing to hire them. This contract is discussed in more detail in an upcoming chapter (see Chapter 6—Contracts, Part 5—Lawyer Contracts). In this contract, which is called a Retainer, you will set out in writing exactly what the lawyer is going to do for you. The lawyer will commit to charging a particular hourly rate, and the retainer should explain the law firm's fees and disbursements policy.

Lawyers can be important professionals who assist you in resolving tough problems. They are your guides through the justice system. Make sure you have a guide that you like and a guide that you trust.

Part 2 — The Courts

Let me see, how can I put this? The courts are a maze. Not amazing—a maze. Civil courts, criminal courts, appeal courts, traffic courts, family courts, federal courts, provincial courts and, of course, the Supreme Court of Canada. Every province has its own court system. Every court system holds trials, where live people actually sit in a witness box beside a judge and give evidence, and every system has appeal courts, where judges higher up the ladder take a second look at the decisions made by the trial judges to see if they made any mistakes in the evidence or in their interpretation of the law. In Canada, there are hundreds of courts across the country and thousands of judges. Now you know why I call it "a maze." In an upcoming section in this chapter, we are going to look at judges, juries and justices of the peace, but for now let's focus on the courts themselves. The best way to find your way through a maze is to get a little higher and look down on it so you can see the path through. That is what I would like to do in this section.

The best way to visualize the court system in a particular province is to imagine a giant triangle with the point at the top. At the base of the triangle are the "trenches" of the justice system— hundreds of courts dealing with thousands of cases. At the top of the triangle is the province's top Court of Appeal. In between are other courts that also deal with matters and deal, in some cases, with appeals. Cases work their way up from the bottom to the top, if they are being appealed. The vast majority of cases, however, are not appealed and are simply resolved by judges and courts with only one or two appearances by those involved.

As we look at that giant triangle holding all of the provincial courts, we should imagine it as having two halves. One half of the triangle deals with criminal cases and the other half deals with civil cases. The criminal side concentrates on charges that have been laid against people under the Criminal Code and under provincial laws such as the Highway Traffic Act. The civil side of the triangle deals with cases involving such things as breach of contract, people suing each other for negligence, family law cases and other situations where private citizens sue each other. On the criminal side, we see Highway Traffic Court. On the civil side, we see Small Claims Court. On the criminal side, we see murder trials and other serious criminal offences. On the civil side, we see divorce cases, commercial litigation, injunctions and other serious matters. On the criminal side, we also see, at the very bottom, courts that have been created by municipalities. These are the courts that prosecute people for violating bylaws, building code infractions, not shovelling their sidewalk after a snowstorm and, lately, violating non-smoking bylaws.

Day in and day out, the courts process tens of thousands of claims. We tend to think only of judges making decisions, but, in fact, there is a vast network of people working at each of these courthouses, helping the cases to flow through the system. Courthouses are filled with clerks and public servants making sure that the paperwork for hundreds of thousands of claims is being processed through the court and tracked, filed, kept secure, delivered to the judge's office on time, and packed up and sent on to the appeal court, if necessary. This network of public servants plays a fairly thankless role.

No discussion of the courts in Canada would be complete without mentioning the Supreme Court of Canada in Ottawa. If you are ever in Ottawa, you should visit this beautiful, impressive place, where so many profoundly important decisions are made every day. The Supreme Court of Canada is the final stop for any case. There are no appeals after the Supreme Court of Canada has dealt with a matter. The Supreme Court of Canada deals with appeals from the top courts of the provinces. So, if someone has appealed a case up to the Provincial Court of Appeal and is still dissatisfied with that decision and if the matter is of national importance, then the Supreme Court of Canada may consider the case. Some of the cases considered by the Supreme Court involve criminal matters and some involve civil matters, but no matter what, this court has the final word.

The purpose of the court structure is to provide a forum in which disputes are resolved—reconsidered if necessary—but then resolved once and for all. Whether you are representing yourself or using a lawyer, understanding how to find your way through this maze of courts is of critical importance. Now that you know the basics, don't be afraid to ask for directions.

Part 3 — Self-Representation

There is no law in Canada that says a person has to have a lawyer for a dispute. I have seen people do a very capable job of representing themselves in Small Claims Court, in Traffic

Court and even in Family Court. It can be risky to represent yourself when an important asset, your freedom or your children are involved. For any criminal issue that may result in a significant fine or a jail sentence or a criminal record, it is essential that you consult a lawyer before trying to represent yourself. If you are in a family dispute and the custody of your children or division of your property and income is at stake, again, consulting an experienced lawyer is absolutely critical. If you are involved in a dispute that may result in an award of damages against you or could affect your property in some way (for example non-payment of your mortgage), again, speak to an experienced lawyer to obtain at least an hour or two of advice before going ahead.

On any given day in any province in Canada, thousands of people are representing themselves before the courts. In many cases, these individuals cannot afford to hire a lawyer, or they have lost confidence in lawyers and simply feel that they must go it alone. If you find yourself in such a position, I hope that this section demystifies (or at least opens your eyes to) some of the advantages and disadvantages of self-representation.

On the advantage side, if you represent yourself there are no legal fees. There will still be disbursements because the court system will charge a fee to issue a claim and to take certain steps when you are in a civil proceeding. Preparation is easier—no one knows the case better than you. And last, and certainly not least, if the case does not turn out well, you have no one to blame but yourself.

On the disadvantage side, if you are successful, you are not going to obtain costs of any significance against the other person, because costs (as we will see in an upcoming section) are designed to reimburse you for legal fees and disbursements incurred in bringing your case. In preparing, while it may be an advantage that no one knows the case better than you, it can sometimes mean that you lack perspective on your case. You become so immersed in it that you cannot see the forest for the trees. In addition, just because you know the facts of your own case it does not necessarily mean that you will understand how the law is applied to those facts.

Another disadvantage of self-representation is that you are going to find the system a little hostile. Lawyers do not like dealing with people who are representing themselves. Let's face it; people in the justice system are not going to welcome you with open arms because they will see you as making trouble. I know that doesn't sound fair, but that is the reality. Here are some guidelines for anybody considering self-representation:

- Be reasonable. Self-representation can be very frustrating and you are going to be tempted to lash out from time to time at the people on the other side of your case, the court staff, the judge and others. You are going to find yourself asking people for help from time to time, but do not be one of those people who turns around and is difficult the minute you think you can take advantage of someone else's mistake. What goes around comes around in the justice system, just like in real life.

- Representing yourself does not mean that everyone is going to give you the benefit of the doubt. People are not going to ignore deadlines, paperwork requirements, legal procedures and so on. The fact that you have decided to represent yourself means that things are going to slow down in the system. You are going to be making it harder for people to move your case through the system. You are going to be stopping to ask for advice frequently. In order to avoid any disappointment, do not expect anyone to do favours for you. I am not saying that no one will do you a favour, but don't expect it and you will never be disappointed.

- If there is a lawyer on the other side of your case, they are not going to be very willing to talk to you. Every lawyer has had an experience of dealing with a self-represented person. Perhaps, they had a meeting with them in a hallway and discussed the case for a few minutes. Later in the day, or weeks later, that same self-represented person jumped up in court and told the judge "Mr. or Ms. so and so (the lawyer) told me that I was supposed to..." The person may or may not have understood what the lawyer was saying. They may or may not be repeating it accurately, and what they are telling the court may or may not be in compliance with the rules. The only way for a lawyer to avoid this kind of incident in a courtroom is to insist that all communication with a self-represented person be in writing. That's why lawyers don't like dealing with the self-represented.

• Many self-represented people do not understand the meaning of a discussion that is "off the record" or "without prejudice." When lawyers are talking to each other they can, more often than not, determine when a discussion is without prejudice. In other words, the lawyers can have the conversation and both of them know that neither is going to mention it in court at a later date because it is confidential. This allows lawyers to discuss settlement scenarios without the fear of having either party mention it to the judge if the settlement does not materialize. Self-represented people can be confused about what it means to have a discussion "without prejudice" so, naturally, lawyers are reluctant to talk to them. If you write something to a lawyer in a letter, and you want that letter to be used in court, do not mark it "Without Prejudice." However, if you want to raise a possible settlement discussion in a letter with a lawyer, and you do not want that letter to be shown to the court, mark it "Without Prejudice."

• You may find, as you represent yourself, that you do not trust people. This will tempt you into taping telephone calls with lawyers or with other people involved in the case. First, this can be illegal, depending on the circumstances and, second, it just makes everyone even more reluctant to talk to you if they find out that you are taping telephone calls. Judges rarely have time to listen to these tapes, and most of the time everything on the tape is inadmissible. I was once involved in a case where I was asked by a judge to view a videotape that was produced at the last minute by a self-represented client. Reluctantly, I sat and watched it. The self-represented person on the other side of the case had presented terrific evidence—in favour of my client! I readily agreed that the judge should see the tape, so the videotaping backfired.

- Be polite and respectful with everyone in the system. Do not send outrageous, inflammatory letters or faxes or emails. There is never a need for foul language or threatening talk. If something needs to be said, put it in a short, to-the-point letter or fax or email, and always keep a copy of every communication. You should run your file as if you were a lawyer. Keep copies of all documents and, in particular, make copies of important evidence.

- On the issue of being polite and respectful—many court staff, lawyers and judges have seen frightening outbursts at the courthouse. The emotional strain of being involved in a court case can be compounded by the stress of representing yourself. Most court buildings have metal detectors and security screening devices, but this does not stop some self-represented people from engaging in screaming matches or even pushing and shoving and fighting, right at the courthouse. These outbursts can seriously harm a self-represented person's case. I saw one incident where the court security staff had to get involved, and a note was put on the court file. Every time the self-represented person appeared before a judge, two uniformed police officers slipped into the courtroom and sat near the self-represented person. You can imagine the impression that this gave the judge. Fairly or not, I think it hurt that self represented person's case.

- Be patient. The justice system, as you can probably tell by now, does not work quickly. There is a lot of waiting and standing around. If something is scheduled to start at ten, you should be there ten minutes early, but do not expect your case to actually be reached until perhaps an hour or more later.

- If you are in court, remember the judge knows very little

about you. Judges have hundreds of cases to deal with and may or may not have read your file. Their first reaction is going to be one of caution in dealing with a self-represented person, and they are not going to look forward to having to spend time explaining the procedures to you. You can also bet that the lawyer on the other side of the case (if there is one) is going to resent the judge spending a lot of time explaining the case, when that lawyer's client is paying good money for them to be there.

- Regardless of which court you are in, always refer to the judge as "Your Honour," and refer to the other lawyers in the case as "Mr." or "Ms." and use their full surname.

- At some point, you will be given an opportunity to speak. Just remember that this is not an invitation to tell your life story to the judge. Try to make short, effective points. Tell the judge what you would like to have happen in your particular case. I have seen many people arrive in court and start rambling on in a long narrative. Simply tell the judge who you are, what you want and what evidence you have to present.

- You many find that you accomplish one or two steps quite effectively in a proceeding. Do not let this go to your head. I have seen self-represented people get quite full of themselves in court, tossing around references to rules and evidence. When the judge saw this, he cut them right down to size.

- Be prepared to be physically and emotionally drained. It is stressful. The courthouse is never a stimulating environment. People who represent themselves often find that the strain makes them ill. Be aware of the old saying that lawyers are taught in their first year of law school, "A lawyer who represents himself has a fool for a client."

- Always consider consulting with a lawyer from time to time during the course of your self-representation. It never hurts to buy an hour of advice about how your case is proceeding and how to go forward with it.

Self-representation is not for everyone, but, with the right attitude and in certain kinds of disputes, there is absolutely no reason why you cannot represent yourself in the Canadian justice system. I wish you good luck.

Part 4 — Paralegals

As we have seen above, there is no rule that says you must use a lawyer when trying to deal with some legal issue. In other words, you can do it yourself. But, what if your brother-in-law is particularly helpful and he wants to assist you with the case and, perhaps, even speak on your behalf when the matter goes to court? Again, there is no problem with someone helping you represent yourself. What if your brother-in-law wants to charge you for the work that he does helping you? Then we move into a different area: non-lawyers or "paralegals" representing the public for a fee. It is an issue that has troubled the Canadian justice system for more than a decade now.

Paralegal specialists have popped up in the justice system, helping people with everything from Small Claims Court appearances to Traffic Court cases, to landlord-tenant problems and even, in some cases, separation and divorce and drafting of wills. Paralegals have emerged for a few reasons: people cannot afford lawyers; they are afraid of lawyers or, in some cases, there is a language barrier that the paralegal can solve that a lawyer cannot. Sometimes, it is simply a matter of convenience or (dare I say it?) the paralegal is better at this particular work than a qualified lawyer.

Retired police officers often work in Traffic Court helping people charged with provincial offences, and there is little doubt that most of those police officers know far more about that process than lawyers. Their fee arrangement—if you are convicted, no charge (in some cases)—is certainly better than a lawyer's arrangement, where the hourly rate for the advice probably exceeds the potential fine. In a situation like that, the paralegal probably knows more about that corner of the justice system "maze" than an ordinary lawyer and offers a much more affordable service than a lawyer. So, what's the problem? Why aren't paralegals everywhere?

Until recently, there were limits on paralegals' work because lawyers had one of the last remaining monopolies on the delivery of a professional service. Provincial laws prohibited anyone but lawyers from delivering legal services. At one time, doctors had a monopoly on the delivery of medical services. Their monopoly ended when governments decided that x-ray technicians and other sub-specialists could start to do things that only doctors had been able to do. The same thing happened with architects when architectural technologists were allowed to offer certain kinds of services. Over the years, cracks began to emerge in the monopoly that lawyers had on the delivery of legal services. I think lawyers were able to hang on to our monopoly longer because no one could ever define what a "legal service" was. There are so many nuances to some of the things that lawyers do that we simply said that everything is a legal service and only we can deliver it! Not everyone agreed: people began to appear as "agents" in Small Claims Court or in Traffic Court; "immigration consultants" began to help people with their immigration applications; and some people got help with simple divorces from paralegals. Lawyers screamed loud and clear and insisted that the law societies prosecute these paralegals for the "unauthorized practice of law." Sometimes, there were convictions; sometimes, there were not. For example, the courts said that it was okay for people to hire an "agent" to represent them in Small Claims or Traffic Court. Slowly but surely, the monopoly started to dissolve, and more and more paralegals arrived on the scene.

There are advantages and disadvantages to this development. One advantage is that some experienced paralegals are able to help consumers with smaller legal problems that lawyers cannot afford to work on. However, in some cases, the individuals providing the paralegal service have no experience and know little, if anything, about the legal problem with which the client is confronted. They are simply charging a fee to try to figure out a solution. Sometimes, they solve the problem, but sometimes, they make it worse. Paralegals are able to charge lower fees than lawyers, in large part because they do not have to pay for insurance, and they do not have any educational investment to recover. The advantages and disadvantages really depend on the kind of service that a consumer is looking for from a paralegal.

Once paralegals became more common, horror stories began to circulate. In one situation, a paralegal arranged for a woman to get an immediate divorce. Unfortunately, getting the divorce terminated her rights to claim an interest in a valuable matrimonial home. Lawyers had to get involved to fix the matter, and it was very expensive. In another case, a paralegal helped a woman with a claim for compensation after a car accident. She had lost her hand in the accident, and the paralegal settled the case for a very low sum and took a very large fee. Lawyers, again, had to get involved to set aside the settlement and get the woman the proper amount of compensation. Many wills and estates lawyers live in fear of wills that have been done by paralegals. The problems will surface only once the person who made the will passes away, and then, of course, it is too late to do anything. A person who is upset about a poorly drafted will is likely to find that the paralegal had no insurance, and there will be no compensation.

But, enough about the problems caused by paralegals. Many paralegals are experienced and do have a legitimate, affordable service to offer to the public. Ontario recently passed the Access to Justice Act, meaning paralegals in the province will now be regulated by the Law Society of Upper Canada. There will be a method of certifying their services for the public, a method of ensuring that they are trained and a method of ensuring that there is some form of compensation for a consumer if things go wrong. The entire regulatory system for paralegals in Ontario is being created as I write, and I expect that the first wave of certified paralegals will emerge over the next couple of years. Other provinces will likely follow suit and law societies across Canada will begin to regulate paralegals. In the meantime, be very careful using paralegals, especially for serious claims for compensation, family law matters and wills and estates.

The lawyers' monopoly on the delivery of legal services is dead. Long live *qualified* paralegals.

Part 5 — Judges and Juries

Judges and juries are two of the more mysterious elements of our justice system. In this section, I would like to demystify their roles.

Judges—and there are thousands of them in Canada—are former lawyers. Both the federal government and the provinces and territories have the authority to appoint judges to courts. Judges that have been appointed by the federal government deal with cases involving offences under the Canadian Criminal Code and, when dealing with civil disputes, hear cases involving large claims for negligence, breach of contract, labour disputes and other serious matters.

Provincially appointed judges, on the other hand, do not deal with matters that are any less serious than the federally appointed judges, but the cases that come before them are usually related to provincial or territorial law. There is a great deal of overlap in the duties of judges. For example, in the area of family law, provincially appointed judges can consider family law cases under provincial family laws, but federally appointed judges also consider family law matters as they relate to the Divorce Act.

Thrown into the mix we have justices of the peace. They are not necessarily lawyers but are judicial officers appointed by the province or the territory, and they deal with thousands of issues related to such things as provincial offences, municipal bylaw problems, parking issues and so on. While many of the disputes that arrive before a justice of the peace may seem small in comparison to disputes considered by provincially appointed and federally appointed judges, we should not forget that it is justices of the peace who look after such things as making sure that people accused of crimes are able to arrange for bail and be released from jail. In some cases, they also deal with mental health issues, and they can issue arrest warrants and summonses to require that people attend court. They have considerable authority, and they operate in the true "trenches" of our justice system.

Federally and provincially appointed judges, as I mentioned above, have spent time practicing law. Typically, lawyers cannot be appointed as judges until they have practiced for at least ten years. In order to be considered for appointment, lawyers must submit their names to a committee composed of lawyers, judges and others. The committee considers the application and usually passes it on to the provincial attorney general for consideration for "appointment to the bench." Appointment to the bench means becoming a judge. Once appointed, a judge cannot practice law and must stop working on cases immediately.

It is a considerable honour to be appointed a judge in Canada and, despite what some judges may tell you, the remuneration is quite good. Lawyers often say that they earn more money if they continue to practice law, but judges earn more than $150,000 per year, plus very good benefits, ensuring their financial independence and therefore impartiality. Judges appointed by the federal government earn more than $240,000 per annum, plus benefits, and judges appointed to the Supreme Court of Canada earn even more than that. It is a job for life, with most judges retiring at age seventy-five. It is a good job, with a lot of prestige.

The judge's role in the justice system is to act as an impartial decision-maker for disputes. Those disputes can include criminal cases, where citizens are being prosecuted by the government, and private disputes between individuals and/or companies. Because judges are often asked to rule on cases involving the government (for example criminal cases), it is critical that they be impartial in their decision-making. For this reason, the law says that a judge cannot be removed from the bench unless there have been extraordinary circumstances. The Canadian Judicial Council deals with complaints against judges appointed by the federal government. Judges have been removed from the bench for misconduct, but it is very rare.

Some judges describe their work as being "lonely." It is difficult, for example, to continue to socialize with lawyer friends because judges need to be seen as impartial, which means that they cannot be seen socializing with some lawyers and not others. One very good judge told me that he did not feel comfortable having a drink in public because he thought it would reflect poorly on him as a judge. For the most part in Canada, our judges are excellent. They work long hours, and they struggle with very important decisions virtually every day. The matters before them mean a lot to the parties, in terms of money, families and their future. There is tremendous pressure to get it right.

As judges hear the evidence and testimony, they sift through and make decisions about validity of evidence and credibility of witnesses and then render a decision. That decision is subject to appeal and reconsideration by other judges further up the ladder, but appeals are really confined to a minority of cases. In the vast majority of situations, once a judge rules, that is the end of the matter.

Juries are used in both the civil justice system and in the criminal justice system, although they are used far more often in the latter.

In the civil justice system, a jury is made up of six people, and it is sufficient if five of the jurors agree on the verdict or the answer to any questions submitted to them. Their decisions do not have to be unanimous. The Jury Acts (each province and territory has one) ban certain categories of people from serving on juries, including Members of Parliament, Senators, judges, justices of the peace, lawyers, law students, doctors, coroners, people involved in law enforcement, jail guards, police officers and (interestingly) the spouses of people in those categories. In addition, people cannot serve on a jury if they have a physical or mental disability that would seriously impair their ability to discharge their duties as a juror. Finally, if you have been convicted of an indictable offence and have not been granted a pardon, you can be denied the opportunity to serve on a jury.

In criminal trials, juries are much more common, and the situation is a little different. First of all, there are twelve jurors, selected by both the Crown Attorney and the lawyers representing the accused. If a juror gets sick or dies during the course of a criminal trial, it is possible for the jury to complete its work with fewer than twelve jurors. Also, unlike in civil proceedings, for a jury to convict an accused person of a criminal offence, the decision must be unanimous.

Sometimes, we hear the expression "a hung jury." This means simply that the jury could not come to a conclusion. One or more people on the jury could not agree with the rest on some aspect of the case, but, in particular, on whether the individual should be convicted. In a situation where the jury cannot agree on its verdict, and where a judge thinks that it would be a waste of time to ask the jury to continue working, the judge can either discharge the jury and ask that a new one be selected to start the trial over again, or the judge may simply adjourn the whole trial and let the Crown Attorney think about what they want to do next.

The requirement for unanimity in a criminal verdict leads, in some cases, to an interesting moment in a courtroom. If the defence lawyers watch the jurors closely when they come back with a unanimous verdict of guilty, they may see little flinches or hints in the jurors' body language that suggest that maybe they are not as unanimous as they say. Maybe one of the jurors was pushed into concluding that the accused was guilty when they really, in their heart of hearts, think the person is not guilty. If that situation arises, the defence lawyers may ask the judge to "poll the jury." This means that each juror is asked individually to stand up and state that they consider the accused person to be guilty.

The members of a jury are prohibited by the Criminal Code from divulging any information about the discussions that happen in the jury room. Those conversations are intended to be kept in the strictest confidence so that jurors are free to speak their minds and debate the evidence that they have heard during the trial. It is not uncommon in the United States to see jurors interviewed on television after the conclusion of a trial, but it is virtually unheard of in Canada.

There was an exception to this rule of confidentiality in British Columbia a few years ago when a woman juror in a murder trial began an affair with the accused. The affair continued during the course of the trial, and the woman managed to keep it a secret from the judge, the prosecutor and the defence lawyers. Her lover was acquitted—of course. When the affair was finally discovered, the juror was charged with obstructing justice. During the course of her trial, other jurors who had served with her, gave evidence about what went on in the jury room. The other jurors reported that she virtually demanded the acquittal of her lover. The woman was convicted of obstruction of justice and sentenced to eighteen months in jail. That case had at least two remarkable aspects. First, the fact that the jurors gave evidence about what happened in the jury room was extraordinary and, second, the juror who was convicted of obstructing justice maintained, even as she was taken off to jail, that she had done nothing wrong and that she was "the victim."

If called for jury duty, you can expect to spend some time cooling your heels at the local courthouse. The process for jury selection in a criminal case can be quite involved. The juror's name, number and address are written on a card, and the card is deposited in a box. Cards are selected from the box and the individual's name or number is called out. Each juror steps forward and the Crown Attorney and the lawyers for the accused person are given an opportunity to either select that juror as acceptable or to challenge them. If a juror is acceptable, they are given the oath and asked to take a seat in the jury box. The science of selecting a jury for a criminal trial is quite involved and can be something to watch when the prosecutor and the lawyers for the accused person exercise between them dozens of challenges to jurors who come forward. In some cases, it may be a matter of race. It may be a matter of gender, economic level and so on. Each side is hoping to select a complete jury of twelve men and women who will give the accused person a fair hearing but will also be sympathetic to their side of the case.

Judges and juries are the decision-makers in civil and criminal proceedings. Their job is to listen to the evidence, weigh credibility and make profoundly important decisions with respect to money, family and, in some cases, liberty.

Part 6 — Suing and Being Sued

I wish I could say that either of these experiences is exciting or even remotely satisfying, but anyone who has to sue another person or ends up being sued themselves is in for a draining—financially and emotionally—experience.

If you are suing or being sued, then you are not in the criminal system. The criminal system is reserved for allegations by the Crown that an individual has broken a specific law. The onus is on the Crown to prove beyond a reasonable doubt that the crime was committed. In rare situations, the criminal process may allow a private citizen to lay a charge against another person, but that is unusual.

In the civil justice system, private citizens and corporations (and, in some cases, governments) sue each other and ask the courts to provide them with a judgment. The judgment can be for damages related to some wrong that was committed, such as a negligent act, or damages related to breach of contract. Civil courts, in some cases, grant injunctions, or they may order a person to follow through on a contract that they signed (this is known as specific performance), but the bottom line is that when people sue or are sued in the civil justice system, they are asking for the court to order the other party to do something or to pay some sum of money to them. It is not a case of seeking a finding of innocence or guilt.

The process of suing and being sued is governed by hundreds of rules and has evolved over hundreds of years of litigation. Regardless of which level of court, lawsuits are always started by someone issuing a claim. The claim is then delivered to the other side, and the person who receives the claim then has an opportunity to respond. Each province sets a specific number of days within which the response must be given. The times can change a little, depending on what level of court is being used. In Small Claims Court, the response time may be different than if the claim was launched in the Superior Court of the province. In either case, though, the person who starts the case, generally known as the "plaintiff," sends the claim to the "defendant" and the defendant then has an opportunity to go and speak with a lawyer and prepare a defence. The defence may also include a counterclaim, where the defendant counter sues the plaintiff for some type of judgment from the court as well. The plaintiff and defendant send various documents back and forth to each other (known as the "pleadings"), and through those pleadings the issues in dispute become clearer. The pleadings are designed to provide the court with a summary of what is actually in dispute between the plaintiff and the defendant.

Once the pleadings have been exchanged, there may be

some preliminary matters that need to be sorted out with the court. This is sometimes done by way of motions, whereby one of the parties to the lawsuit can ask the court to make orders related to how the lawsuit moves forward through the courts. These motions can be very time-consuming and expensive and can involve a lot of sniping back and forth between lawyers and clients.

In some cases, it is possible to ask the other party in the lawsuit questions about the case under oath in advance of the trial. When this questioning occurs, a court reporter is present, and a transcript of the questioning and answers is made. This process is known as "questioning" or "examinations for discovery." The point of the exercise is to "discover" what the other side's case is about and to determine what evidence they have to prove their case. In civil proceedings, there is no such thing as "trial by ambush," whereby one side waits until the last moment, and then at trial whips out a piece of paper with some important evidence, thereby winning the case. The whole process of discovery is designed to avoid exactly that type of situation. Any piece of evidence that a person intends to rely upon in a civil lawsuit must be provided to the other side well in advance of any trial. This approach is designed to encourage people to settle cases without having a trial. The examinations for discovery and the disclosure of evidence can be very time-consuming and, if there are many documents involved, it can be expensive just coming to grips with the paperwork.

Anyone can start a civil lawsuit, provided they are over the age of majority for the province in which they live. If you are not over the age of majority, it is possible to have a guardian appointed to look after the case on your behalf. I was involved in a case many years ago where an uncle had taken his nieces and nephews to a drive-in movie. Unfortunately, they arrived too late and could not get into the drive-in. The children were disappointed and, I think, in a way, the uncle was trying to appease them by taking them on a "special ride" home. He decided to take a little-used road and drive quickly over an old wooden bridge. The objective of this special ride was to get the car airborne as it went over the old wooden bridge, à la *Dukes of Hazzard*. You can imagine what happened. On that particular evening, there was one other vehicle coming in the opposite direction at exactly the moment they crossed the bridge. The cars collided head-on and the children were injured. One child was pushed under the front seats of the car, and another one was pushed up under the dashboard. Those children, obviously, had the right to sue their uncle and his insurance company, but it was necessary to have litigation guardians appointed to look after their rights. The litigation guardians are usually the minor child's parents—unless children are suing their parents. The court must approve any settlement involving children.

The goal of the process of being sued or suing is to resolve the issue somehow. Certainly, everyone encourages people to settle, but if the case is not settled, then it is put before a judge (and, in some cases, a judge and jury) and a decision is made. Once the decision is made, it is recorded in a judgment, and it is then left to the person who was successful to recover not only the judgment but also their legal costs.

Suing and being sued is not a pleasant experience. Anyone contemplating a lawsuit, other than perhaps something in Small Claims Court, should certainly speak with a lawyer in advance to make sure you not only have a claim and have evidence to support the claim, but also that you have a reasonable prospect of collecting any judgment that you obtain against the other person.

Part 7 — Evidence and Proving a Case

One of the most interesting, but also one of the trickiest, areas of law concerns evidence. There are different standards in the ways that the civil justice system and the criminal justice system handle evidence. Since a person's liberty is at stake in the criminal justice system and because the impact of being convicted of a crime can be so serious, with at least a criminal record involved, the criminal justice system has a very high standard for accepting evidence. This does not mean that the civil justice system has low standards for accepting evidence, but the ways in which the courts look at various issues of proof and the evidence related to those issues is slightly different in the two systems. The difference in these courts' treatment of evidence is seen in the way in which they come to a conclusion. In the criminal justice system, a person will not be convicted of a crime unless the court is satisfied *"beyond a reasonable doubt"* that this person committed the crime in question. It is not a question of the court thinking that the evidence is fairly good, and the person probably committed the crime. The court must be convinced beyond a reasonable doubt that the person committed the crime in order to have a finding of guilt. It is different in the civil justice system, where the standard is based on *"a balance of probabilities."* If the plaintiff or the defendant has slightly better evidence and is able to convince the judge that their version of events is probably right, then that person may get a judgment. In other words, 51% versus 49% may just win the case.

Related to this difference in approach is a difference in the way that the courts handle evidence, and when I say "evidence," I mean information that can be documents, electronic data, oral testimony, experts' opinions or, in some cases, even circumstantial evidence.

Before we go any further, I want to add one small note about evidence in family law proceedings. If any court has "different" standards for the receipt of evidence, I think most lawyers would agree that it is the family law courts. Evidence that would never be accepted in a criminal proceeding or in a serious civil lawsuit (such as emails, recordings or hearsay) may very well be accepted in a family law case if judges think it is relevant and may assist them in coming to a conclusion. This is just something that family law lawyers have come to accept about the way in which family law cases are decided in Canada. The hard and fast rules of evidence applied in serious civil cases and in criminal law cases are just not used in the family law system.

I met with a client recently to review his case. It was related to a civil claim that would be proceeding through Superior Court. As we worked on this person's pleadings (those documents that are exchanged between plaintiffs and defendants), he looked at me and said confidently, "I have a great case, don't I?" I said that I thought the facts were strong, but we now needed to concentrate on the evidence. He looked a little puzzled and repeated to me step-by-step what had happened and said, "There, you see, the evidence is quite strong. I have a good case, don't I?" I then spent a few minutes explaining to the client the difference between "a fact" and "evidence of a fact." If I take a trip on a train, that is a fact. If I produce a copy of the train ticket that I purchased, that is evidence. The evidence proves the fact. If my client is being sued for damages caused by a fire that occurred in the lockers in his apartment building, that may be a fact. If the person suing him proves that he was a smoker who regularly carried matches, was seen going into the locker area after having an argument with the landlord and then ten minutes later a fire started, that may be circumstantial evidence. The evidentiary circumstances suggest a conclusion of fact. When proving a case, in civil court or in criminal court, it is not only important to understand all of the facts of a case, but also to have specific pieces of evidence to prove each fact. Oral testimony in a court can be extremely important. Unfortunately, we have learned from scientific studies that eyewitness testimony about certain events can also be notoriously unreliable. We do not often see as much as we think we see, and for this reason courts are often in search of hard evidence that backs up someone's version of events.

A confusing, but very common, form of evidence is "hearsay evidence." TV lawyers are regularly seen objecting to a particular individual's evidence on the basis that it is "clearly hearsay." A court is not interested in hearsay evidence because it is considered essentially unreliable. By hearsay, I mean a person coming to the court and saying, "I heard Mr. Brown say the following to Mr. White." In other words, a witness tells the court what a third person said. The court will not consider that evidence for the purpose of establishing the truth of what the third person said. The person who actually said it cannot be cross-examined in the court, so the evidence cannot be tested to see if it is true. This is why the court does not want to hear hearsay evidence. If oral testimony is being given, it must be a first-hand account.

Most of the evidence considered by courts is oral testimony. A witness is sworn in or asked to affirm that they are telling the truth, and then they tell their story, usually with some guidance from their lawyer. When they give their oral testimony, the lawyer asking them the questions is not allowed to ask leading questions. The only time a lawyer is allowed to lead a witness is during a cross-examination. By "lead," I mean suggesting the answer to the question in the question itself. So, for example, a leading question would be, "Mr. Brown, you arrived at the scene of the collision by taking Highway 401 westbound from the City of Toronto?" A proper question would be to ask, "Mr. Brown, how did you come to be at the scene of the collision?" Lawyers are allowed to ask leading questions on cross-examination because they wish to test the evidence of the person. They wish to probe it and poke holes in it. The court allows the lawyers to suggest answers to the witnesses. In fact, it is a rule among experienced trial lawyers that they should never ask a question to which they do not already know the answer during cross-examination.

Although it can be difficult for them to restrain themselves, judges are not supposed to ask witnesses questions, other than to obtain a clarification on some piece of evidence. It is the lawyer's job to ask a witness important questions during the course of a trial. In fact, there have been some cases that have been successfully appealed because the judge became too involved in the questioning of witnesses and lost the appearance of impartiality.

One last comment concerns evidence from experts. By its very nature, the evidence of an expert is hearsay and is often about something of which the expert may not have first-hand knowledge. Medical experts, engineering experts and scientific experts all give evidence to the court that typically begins with the statement, "Based upon my experience, training and expertise in the area, I suggest that certain conclusions be drawn..." The experts have a special insight into an area. In order to receive their evidence, the court must first be convinced that the person is indeed an expert and that it can ignore the rule against hearsay evidence and listen to what is, essentially, an opinion rather than a statement of facts. In some cases, the court insists on some introductory questioning of an expert witness to determine whether the court will accept this individual as an expert witness or not. In this process, the party wishing to rely on the expert offers the individual to the court as an expert witness. The lawyers then spend a few minutes zeroing in on the expert's credentials. They cross-examine the expert to satisfy themselves that the person is indeed knowledgeable enough about the particular issue in question.

The law of evidence bedevils law students and lawyers throughout their careers. It is not uncommon to see experienced trial lawyers poring over their cases from the outset, ensuring that every single fact has a piece of evidence supporting it.

In an earlier section, we discussed self-representation, and if ever there were an area that would trip up people trying to represent themselves, it would be a situation involving rules of evidence.

Part 8 — Costs

At the end of any legal proceeding, the court has an opportunity to deal with what is known as "costs." Each party to the dispute will have a few minutes to express to the judge their view about division of responsibility for the legal fees incurred in bringing the case to the court. It is difficult, although not unheard of, for people who have lost in court to ask the judge that their legal fees be paid. Usually, parties who have been successful ask the judge to order the unsuccessful party to reimburse them for all or a portion of their legal fees and any disbursements that have been incurred bringing the case to court. Legal fees include the charges that the lawyers make to the client for their time. Disbursements include such things as photocopying, long-distance telephone charges, courier expenses and, if it was a part of the case, transcripts of questioning that may have been ordered, if one or both of the parties were examined under oath in front of a court reporter. Transcripts can be very, very expensive and their cost is a disbursement for which any successful party will want to be reimbursed. Other disbursements that form a part of the ordinary expenses in a case that has gone to court can be the cost of subpoenas to witnesses, the cost of medical reports or experts' reports and even

mileage claims. It is not unusual for disbursements on a particular case to reach into the thousands of dollars. At the end of the
case, the lawyer for the successful party will present what is
known as a "Bill of Costs." The Bill of Costs summarizes all of
the hours that the lawyer spent working on the case and all of
the disbursements that were incurred. The Bill of Costs is hand-
ed to the judge, and the judge makes a decision about how much
of that total expense should be reimbursed. It is unusual to see
a successful party recover all of their costs. Somewhere in the
vicinity of half to three-quarters would be considered a good
recovery. This means that *even if you are successful* in a claim
before the court, you will still likely be out of pocket for some
of the legal fees and disbursements that you incurred pursuing
the case. If you do not use a lawyer, then you will not be able
to recover any fees for your own time. You will, however, be
able to recover your disbursements.

If a person's conduct has been abusive or uncooperative, the
judge has the discretion to order more costs. It is in such situations that a court will be tempted to order a full reimbursement
for legal fees and disbursements incurred. One of the things that
a judge will consider when awarding the costs is whether the
parties were reasonable in their attempts to settle. After the case
is complete (and only after the case has been completed), a
judge will ask the parties to show any written offers that they
made to settle. (Remember those "without prejudice" offers you
made?) At that time, lawyers will stand up and show to the judge
letters that were written or formal documents offering to settle
the case. The lawyers will be telling the judge that they should
receive the maximum amount for reimbursement of legal fees
and disbursements because, prior to trial, they offered to settle
the case for less than what the judge has just ordered. This
means that making offers to settle a case is not only a good idea
in order to try and get the matter resolved but it can be strategically very helpful at the end of the case when speaking to costs.
Remember, judges will not look at an offer to settle before
deciding the case. They will only consider the offer to settle in
the context of setting costs that need to be reimbursed to a successful party.

Let's consider the situation of a party who has lost the case in front of the judge at the trial, but made an offer to settle the case prior to coming to court. If the judge finds that the person who was ultimately successful could have got the same thing or better from the losing person without having to come to court, then the judge has the discretion to deny the successful party recovery of any of their costs and disbursements or reduce the amount, perhaps, to a nominal one. Making an offer to settle is very important in improving your chances of receiving your costs. All offers to settle should always be in writing and you should keep a copy for your own records. These offers are always marked "Without Prejudice" and are kept confidential until the end.

There is an unusual provision in the rules of most courts in Canada that allows a judge to order *the lawyers* to take responsibility for some of the legal fees and expenses incurred. This can happen if the judge thinks that it is the lawyer's fault that the case dragged on or that the lawyer did not do a very good job. The rules of court sometimes authorize a judge to order that a lawyer not charge the client for work that was done or to reimburse a client for legal fees that were paid. In very unusual cases, the judge can also order a lawyer to pay costs, if the judge thinks that the lawyer was responsible for trouble in the case. If a judge is going to order that the lawyer be personally responsible for the costs, the judge will give the lawyer some advance notice so that they can speak to a lawyer of their own and make presentations to the judge about why they should not be ordered to pay the client's costs. It is a rare thing to see a judge order the lawyer to pay the costs, but it does happen. It is a way of keeping difficult lawyers under control. In a recent Ontario case, a lawyer was ordered to personally pay $25,000 in costs to the client on the other side. Ouch!

Costs are a very important consideration when going to court. There can be little joy if a client goes all the way through a process, is successful, but does not recover the cost of hiring a lawyer. That is why it is important to make offers to settle and to keep an eye on the costs of litigating. The important goal is to *net* money, not to spend more money on the process than you actually recover.

Part 9 — Alternatives to Court

When people face a legal problem, they usually assume that they will end up in a courtroom in front of a judge. Traditionally, this has been true. People hire lawyers. The lawyers battle it out. If it settles, it settles, but if it does not, we are off to court. This approach, which we call the "adversarial approach" (where each party is an adversary to the other), is the way our court system evolved. The judge is above the dispute and impartial. The clients, with their lawyers (if they can afford them), try to convince a judge to accept their version of events. This approach applied whether they were arguing over a defective automobile, a breach of contract, a car accident or a divorce. I think, in large part, many people lost confidence in lawyers and the justice system because of this one-dimensional approach to legal problem solving.

Over time, some alternatives emerged that gave people a different way to tackle their problems without necessarily going to court. The two main alternatives to the court system are "mediation" and "arbitration." A third method of problem solving related primarily to family law cases has also developed recently. It is known as "collaborative law." In this section, I would like to set out the meaning of these alternative approaches and some of the advantages and disadvantages.

Mediation is a process in which two (or more) parties to a dispute, any kind of dispute, use a skilled third party to assist them in discussing the legal issue they face. The mediator helps the parties reach a mutually satisfactory solution. Instead of having a judge impose a solution, the parties to the dispute design their own. Mediation is different from the adversarial courtroom approach because the mediator, who has very specific training, encourages the parties to look at the problem from different angles and to develop an understanding of each side's needs and interests. The goal is not to develop two competing positions and then slug it out. The goal is to determine whether everyone's interests can be met through some creative solution that might not otherwise be available in a courtroom. After all, who is in a better position to develop a solution than the people who are involved in the dispute? This is particularly so in family law cases where mediation is very, very popular. For the most part, mediation is voluntary and non-adversarial, and it works best when you have a skilled, impartial mediator leading the discussion. One of the advantages of using mediation is that people who go through it report that they actually develop better negotiating skills and are then able to resolve subsequent disagreements without the use of a mediator. In other words, mediation seems to empower people. The other advantages are that mediation seems to be faster, less expensive and it tends to produce happier people, if a settlement is reached. It can also be much less stressful than participating in an adversarial courtroom process.

In some court systems, such as Ontario's, mediation is mandatory for certain types of cases such as fights over estates. Judges will not let a case come into a courtroom unless there has been an effort to resolve it through mediation. The vast majority of mediations, however, are voluntary. This is probably the best way to conduct mediation because a settlement is really only achievable if both parties to the dispute want to be there and negotiate in good faith.

In the family law area, all provincial family laws and the federal Divorce Act encourage families to use mediation to resolve their disputes, however, the process is not mandatory. In other words, for family law, if you accept mediation, it is because you have agreed to mediate, not because you are being forced to.

There are national and provincial organizations that train, certify and organize mediators in Canada. Participation in these organizations is voluntary. This means that anyone can hang out their shingle and say that they are a mediator. You should only use mediators who are trained and who are members of provincial or national professional associations. It is important that you be cautious and select a mediator who is experienced and qualified.

A mediator will usually meet with both sides at the same time at the outset, listen to the respective problems and then help the people explore some options. In some cases, the mediator may separate the parties to the dispute in different rooms and shuttle back and forth trying to find a solution that meets everyone's interests.

Do mediators help avoid the need for lawyers? In some situations, such as Small Claims Court cases or disputes between neighbours and so on, it is not necessary to obtain independent legal advice if a mediator has helped you reach a satisfactory solution and provided you used an experienced and qualified mediator. However, in cases involving substantial sums of money or family law problems, it is important that people obtain independent legal advice to ensure that the mediator has heard the full story and developed options that are acceptable to both sides. Lawyers will look over a settlement and, in some cases, strengthen it to make sure that it holds up in the long term.

At the outset of mediation, the mediator will ask the parties to the dispute whether they want the mediation to be *open* or *closed*. If the mediation is open, then statements made in mediation may be admissible later in court if the mediation fails to achieve an agreement. A closed mediation is the opposite. It is confidential. Nothing said in the sessions can be used in a court. For most mediations, it is better to err on the side of caution and only participate on the understanding that it is a closed mediation.

Another advantage of mediation, aside from its being faster and possibly less expensive, includes the privacy that is given to the people involved. There is no need to thrash things out in a public courtroom. It is also more creative because the parties to the dispute can come up with a solution that might not be available to a judge, who is often required to see things in black and white. I think the overriding advantage of mediation is that most people just feel better having gone through it. It is rare to meet someone who has a warm and fuzzy feeling after spending a day or a week or months in a courtroom.

Mediators charge an hourly rate and it can range from $50 per hour to $500 per hour, depending on how complicated the dispute is and how senior the mediator is in terms of training and experience. Remember, though, that the two parties (or more than two if it is a multi-party dispute) will share the mediator's fees So, spreading the cost of the mediator around actually can be quite effective.

If the dispute is over something that is significant and important to you, you will want to speak with a lawyer prior to going into mediation. Lawyers can find experienced mediators in the community, or by contacting a provincial or national mediation association.

Arbitration is different from mediation. Arbitration is the same as hiring a "private judge." It is a process that has been used for hundreds of years in commercial matters and in construction matters. When using arbitration, the parties to a dispute select a private individual, often an experienced lawyer, a retired judge or some other expert in a particular field, to hear their dispute in private. After the hearing, the arbitrator renders a decision. It can be a fast, effective and less expensive way of resolving a problem.

One of the reasons I like arbitration is that you are able to select the person who will resolve the dispute. In the justice system, judges are often randomly assigned to the cases on which they work day-to-day. This can mean that the judge assigned to your case may or may not have an interest or expertise in whatever issue your case concerns—motor vehicle accidents or family law cases, for example. In arbitration, the parties hire the absolute best and most effective person to decide that case.

One of the disadvantages, however, of arbitration is the added cost. Now the parties are paying for two lawyers and "a judge." At least in the public courts, the judges are "free," since our tax dollars pay their salaries. A private judge, however, can cost between $2,000 and $3,000 per day, for each day of a hearing. True, that cost is shared by the parties, but it is still an added expense that must be dealt with.

Like mediators, arbitrators are certified by provincial and national associations, and you should only ever use an arbitrator who is certified. A lawyer can direct you to a recommended list of arbitrators in your community.

I want to add a caution about mediation and arbitration, particularly mediation. If you go into this type of process, make sure that everyone is there in good faith. The last thing you want to do is waste your time and money in a mediation only to find out that the reason the other party is there is to find out what your "real" bottom line is before they drag the matter back into court. The point of mediation or of arbitration is to do things quickly, effectively and inexpensively. Make sure that the process does not simply add to your costs. Lawyers and clients have used mediation and arbitration for many years in the family law area, and there is no doubt that it works. In fact, the justice system is often so slow and ineffective that many people cannot afford to stay in it, and they opt out to use mediation/arbitration simply to get the case over with. This is a sad comment on the state of our justice system for families.

Collaborative law is a new way of trying to solve problems in the area of family law. It developed because some people who are going through separation and divorce do not necessarily want to follow the exact letter of family law in their province or territory. In collaborative law, the lawyers and clients work in a process of principled negotiation to try and meet each client's interests through creative solutions. What distinguishes collaborative law from mediation is that there is no mediator present. It is just a simple negotiation involving parties and lawyers. The clients and lawyers sign an agreement stating that if the collaborative process does not produce a settlement, neither lawyer can be hired to take the matter to court. In other words, the clients must drop the lawyer they used for the collaborative process and hire a new lawyer to take the matter to court. That added expense can be a strong disincentive to wasting time in a collaborative law process. This approach is relatively new and requires special training for the lawyers involved. People using collaborative law for a family law dispute will only enter into such a process if the lawyers are qualified to do so. If you are interested in this kind of process, speak to your lawyer about it to see if they are qualified to handle it. If not, perhaps they can recommend you to a qualified lawyer in your community.

So, when it comes to resolving any kind of dispute, whether it's a fight with your neighbour, a breach of contract or a separation and divorce, consider being creative and using mediation or arbitration or—in family law cases—a collaborative law process. It may just save you—not only time and money—but your sanity as well.

Part 10 — Lawyers' Fees

I left the scariest section for last because, let's face it, the most frightening thing about speaking with a lawyer is the potential cost. Lawyers charge their fees in a number of ways. The most common is an hourly rate. The lawyer will charge $200, $300, $400, $500 (or even more) per hour for their advice. A client is, essentially, paying the lawyer for their time, and when I say "time," I mean every second that a lawyer spends working on a case is recorded and billed. Telephone calls, reading emails, sending letters, doing research, thinking about strategies, talking to other lawyers, and so on. Obviously, the lawyer working on a case does not work in blocks of one hour at a time. Sometimes it is a ten-minute telephone call or forty-eight minutes of research or one minute arranging for a meeting. In order to capture all of that time for an account, lawyers divide their work hours into tenths or units of six minutes. Ten units of six minutes make up each hour. The lawyer will, regardless of how much time was actually spent, never record less than one-tenth of an hour being spent on a matter because that is the smallest unit of time that a lawyer records. I have met some lawyers who will only record two-tenths as the smallest unit of time. This means that if the lawyer works on something for one minute, the client will be billed *as if the lawyer spent twelve minutes working on the case.*

Throughout the day, lawyers keep track of their time, sometimes by way of written dockets, sometimes on the computer. Every single step taken is recorded and the time is accumulated in the office computer. At the end of the case, or at periodic points throughout the matter, the lawyer will produce a "statement of services." This statement will list every single step taken on behalf of the client. The total time will be multiplied by the lawyer's hourly rate, and the fee is calculated. Added to the fee are any disbursements that have been made on behalf of the client for such things as photocopying, couriers or service of documents. GST is added to that amount and once it is all tallied up, the lawyer has an account to render to the client. If the client has given the lawyer some money in advance, as a part of the initial retainer, that amount will likely be deducted from the account, and any balance owing will be due at that time.

In some cases, lawyers charge "block fees." In other words, they quote a fee for delivering a particular service. Perhaps, a real estate transaction can be done for $900, including disbursements. Perhaps, a will can be drafted, along with Powers of Attorney, for $1,000 plus disbursements.

Clients who cannot afford to pay a lawyer must apply for "Legal Aid." Legal Aid is delivered individually in each province and territory, and it is a matter of near-unanimous agreement among lawyers that Legal Aid plans are woefully underfunded. Legal Aid is now reserved primarily for serious criminal cases, family law cases and refugee or immigration cases. In order to see if you qualify for Legal Aid in your province, contact the provincial Legal Aid plan. There will be a "means test," which means the Legal Aid plan will want to know how much you earn, how much you owe, how much you own and how much, if any, you are likely to recover in the litigation that you are pursuing. There are people who own their own homes and still qualify for Legal Aid. However, in a case like that, Legal Aid will often take a lien against the individual's home. The lien is repaid at a later date, if the home is sold or if the litigation is successful and funds are available to pay the Legal Aid back.

Contingency fees are available in Canada. A true "contingency fee" means that the lawyer is agreeing to take the case on the understanding that a fee will be charged only if the lawyer is successful in recovering money for the client. No recovery means no fees. In other words, the fee is *contingent* on success. Contingency fees are also often tied to a percentage of the recovery. A lawyer will take the case contingent on success but also state that in the event of success, the lawyer's fee will be a percentage of the sum recovered. The lawyer will not be calculating their time on an hourly basis and then simply charging for the work that was done. Instead, they are saying to the client, "I will take your case, and I will work on it. If I am successful, I expect to receive, for example, thirty per cent of what is recovered, regardless of the amount of time I spend working on the case." I heard recently of a lawyer who represents people in the financial services sector when they are negotiating termination packages. This lawyer does not record his time on an hourly basis. Instead, his fee is 15% of any improvement that he secures in the termination package for the employee—regardless of the amount of time that he has spent working on the case.

It is important to have any fee arrangement with a lawyer in writing. This writing can be in the form of a retainer or contract that a client has with a lawyer. The retainer should set out the work that is being done on behalf of the client, the hourly rate that is being charged, how fees and disbursements are calculated and charged to the client and so on. If the fee is to be a block fee, that should be in writing. If the fee is a contingency arrangement, that, most assuredly, must be in writing.

Of course, lawyers and clients will sometimes end up in conflict over fees charged. Many clients are shocked when they see how much time was spent on a case, and they object to paying the fee that the lawyer wants to charge. If the agreement between the lawyer and the client is in writing, this type of difficulty is less likely to arise. However, if a client is unhappy about a lawyer's bill, it is possible to have that bill reconsidered by a judicial officer. Every province in Canada has a way for clients to have their lawyers' bills reviewed by an assessment officer. This person will consider the details of the retainer, the details of the work that was done and the details of the account that was rendered by the lawyer. The assessment officer not only looks at what was done and how much was charged, but whether the work was of value to the client. On any given day in Canada, thousands of lawyers' accounts are being assessed. In some cases, the assessment officer explains to the client that the bill is fair and that it should be paid, but, in many cases, the assessment officer tells the lawyer that his or her retainer was not clear enough, that services should not be charged for and that the account must be reduced.

The answer to the disputes that arise between lawyers and clients over fees lies in the retainer. Personally, it is my view that lawyers should be required to enter into written retainers with clients and that those retainers should be standardized, province by province. The retainer should set out, in detail, what the client expects the lawyer to do, what the lawyer promises to do, what the hourly rate is to be charged by the lawyer and how the fee is to be calculated and how that bill is to be paid. This improvement would go a long way towards assuring Canadians that the work done on their behalf by lawyers and the fees charged are appropriate, if not fair.

Conclusion

The system can be a confusing maze. It is slow and it can be very expensive. Lawyers and, in some cases, qualified paralegals are best equipped to help you through the maze but you have to be a smart consumer; you have to cut through the legal mumbo-jumbo. Pick your guide carefully and the journey will be a lot easier—not painless, but easier.

Chapter 2

10 Things You Absolutely Need To Know About
Family Law

There is no denying the fact that separation and divorce is one of the most painful experiences for adults and children alike. The end of personal relationships brings out the absolute worst in some people. It is a rare thing to see someone suddenly become more compassionate, more generous or more tolerant in the middle of their divorce than they were when they were actually married. In this chapter, I will provide an overview of ten key areas, including some strategic advice about how to minimize the pain.

Part 1 — Lawyers, "The System" and Divorce

The justice system is flooded with family law cases in which one or both estranged spouses are forced to represent themselves. In some cases, the individuals cannot afford a lawyer. In many cases, they simply do not trust lawyers to look after their case adequately. Some people turn to paralegals in order to save money, and many people are forced into self-representation due to lack of money. They have all my sympathy and support. However, obtaining some advice from an experienced family law lawyer in cases involving your children, your home, savings and so on, is absolutely critical. As we saw in the previous chapter's discussion of paralegals, little things can have profound consequences, and that is why I recommend getting some legal advice. Even if you are choosing to represent yourself, check in with a lawyer from time to time.

In terms of the actual process, you would be hard-pressed to find someone who would defend the current system for family law in Canada. It is slow, expensive and not particularly sensitive to the needs of families. Judges are often sick and tired of family law cases; for many, a family law case ranks right at the bottom of the list of things that they would prefer to work on. That is not to say that there are not good judges, but not many enjoy hearing a family law case. I have always marvelled at the fact that we expect people to resolve their divorces with the same kind of process that we use to resolve breach of contract cases, car accidents and negligence claims. Our court system is based on an adversarial approach that encourages two combatants to fight it out. When we base our family law system on the same adversarial approach, I wonder if we are really trying to help families or destroy them. In any event, that is the system you will be stuck with when you get involved in a family law or divorce action.

You can obtain a divorce in Canada for one of three reasons:

- Your marriage has broken down and there is no chance of a reconciliation. Showing one year of continuous separation can prove this.
- You can prove that your spouse committed adultery. This will get a divorce almost immediately, whether you have been separated for one month or sixteen months.
- You can prove mental or physical cruelty. In this case, the court will grant a divorce immediately.

In Canada, the vast majority of divorces are granted on the basis of one-year separation because, more often than not, by the time you are able to prove adultery or cruelty, a year has gone by. It is unusual to see someone seek a divorce on the basis of adultery or cruelty.

The courts allow spouses to work at trying to reconcile. As long as your attempts at reconciliation do not add up to more than ninety days of continuous cohabitation, they will not generally interrupt your one-year period of separation, if the reconciliation is ultimately unsuccessful and you want to go ahead with the divorce.

Part 2 — Custody and Access

This is the hottest issue in family law cases and it will seem simplistic to tell you this, but the only rule of thumb that a court uses in making decisions for children in divorce is to do what is in "their best interest." This essentially gives judges the discretion to do whatever they think is appropriate for the children. Often, in reaching conclusions, they will have not only the opinions of the parents, but also experts—psychologists, social workers, teachers and others who are willing to express their opinion on what is best for these children. Most of the orders for custody or access fall into a limited range of options. Sometimes, parents will agree that one will have custody and the other will have access. If a parent has custody, this means that the child is primarily in their care and control. The child will have their day-to-day residence with that parent, and the custodial parent will make all decisions concerning health, education, general welfare and religious upbringing. That custodial parent may consult with the access parent, but they are under no obligation to take their views into consideration. The access parent, on the other hand, has essentially the right to visit with the child from time to time. In many cases, particularly for modern Canadian families, a simple custody and access arrangement is not acceptable. The parents have more often than not raised the children together, dividing certain responsibilities in the household, and now that the family is separated, artificial schedules for visitation seem, frankly, ridiculous.

Many parents express the view that they cannot go from seeing their children every day to only seeing them every second weekend. As a result, there are some new options: joint custody, shared parenting, co-parenting, parallel parenting and so on. The idea with these options is to divide responsibilities for the child in such a way that they are shared. The parents may work out a more generous schedule of time for each to spend with the child and work cooperatively. They may divide up a specific list of responsibilities. If the mother has always taken the children to their dance and music lessons, she may continue to do so while the father continues to coach the children's sports teams. In these kinds of arrangements, parents also share decision-making concerning the children's important needs such as health, education, religion and general welfare. For these kinds of arrangements, where responsibility is shared, it is necessary for the parents to cooperate. Our courts have been clear in saying that if parents cannot do this, then joint custody or shared parenting will not be an option for them.

One of the common complaints in custody cases is the problem caused when a parent needs to move. Parents will inevitably meet new partners or take new jobs, and they might want to relocate, but this can upset existing custody and access arrangements, especially if one parent wants to move a considerable distance. In such circumstances, the court will revisit the arrangement and try to determine what is in the best interest of the child. In a sole custody arrangement, the courts tend to err on the side of what the custodial parent needs, provided there is a good reason for the move. In joint custodial arrangements, the courts are more reluctant to encourage change and have even reversed custody or told a parent that if they wish to move, they will only be able to do so on their own. In some cases, where the move has been permitted, the other parent may be able to offset their increased travel expenses to see the child against their child support obligation.

Part 3 — Child Support

The issue of child support has become much more understandable in Canada as a result of the introduction of the Child Support Guidelines in May 1997 (updated in May 2006). Essentially, these guidelines work by taking the gross annual income of the parent paying support and factoring it by the number of children to generate a base monthly amount of child support. Each province has its own set of child support guidelines. So, for example, in Ontario if a parent earns $117,400 per year and has two children, the monthly child support sum will be $1,614. If the parent earned $76,000 and had three children, the monthly payment would be $1,448. The tables include a wide range of income brackets and calculate the exact amount of the monthly child support payment for as many as six children. Child support payments are tax free, in other words, the recipient does not include them in their income and the payer does not deduct them. This information is accessible on the federal government website (*www.canada.gc.ca*). In addition to the base monthly amount, parents share special expenses related to the child's upbringing in proportion to their annual incomes. If a child goes to university or has orthodontic expenses, or if the child needs special equipment for pursuing sports or music or some other activity, then the parents will typically share that expense provided it is reasonable and they agree that it should be incurred.

Child support obligations continue until age eighteen if the child is no longer in school. If the child continues in university then the child support obligations may continue until the child is twenty-three or twenty-four and has completed their first university degree or certificate. Another reason to continue child support might be that the child, while not in school, has some physical or mental incapacity that prevents them from being financially independent.

Part 4 — Property Division

Each province and territory in Canada has its own system for dividing property when a marriage breaks down. All of the systems operate approximately the same way and that is to take the value of property acquired between the date of marriage and the date of separation and divide the value of that property fairly between the two spouses. This will also include offsetting debt that has been incurred during the course of the marriage. The date of separation is very important as this is the date upon which many of the calculations are done. Property acquired after the date of separation will generally not be included in the pot for property division. Arguments can arise over the value of assets that must be put into the pot. In such cases, experts are hired to tell the family the value of their home, their businesses, their farms, their cottages, their art collections and so on. Everything can be valued from a farmer's milk quotas to toy train collections. In most provincial property division systems, spouses are given a credit for the value of the property they brought into the relationship. They are given exemptions for such things as inheritances or gifts from third parties, which means that not everything is automatically included in the division of property. It is important to consult with a lawyer in your province or territory to ensure that you're including the right pieces of property and liabilities and excluding the right pieces of property and liabilities. The objective is to make sure that each spouse leaves the marriage with a fair nest egg so that they can start over again.

Part 5 — Spousal Support

Unlike the child support area, spousal support is not calculated in accordance with any guidelines (although some draft ones are under discussion). It is done on a case by case basis looking at the needs of the person asking for spousal support and the ability to pay of the person who is being asked to pay. There are many factors that are considered including the lifestyle that the couple was accustomed to while they were married. Child support payments are not deducted by the payer or included in the income of the recipient. It's different with spousal support. The recipient of spousal support that is set out in an order or a separation agreement must include that as income on their tax return and pay taxes on it. The paying spouse, on the other hand, deducts the amount that is paid and receives a credit on their tax return.

Most individuals involved with spousal support have only two questions: how much do I pay, and how do long do I have to pay? The "how much" part is only answered by looking at the circumstances of their relationship and the needs that each of them has after the separation. I have compared the making of a spousal support order to the building of a bridge over a river. Once the individual is across the river they can be considered economically self-sufficient. The size of the bridge is determined by the size of the river. If the person looking for economic self-sufficiency is older, has medical issues, has no specific job experience, has no educational background, has been out of the workforce for some time, has low self-esteem, then the river may be very wide and the bridge very long. Spousal support might be required indefinitely. However, if the marriage was short and the person exiting the marriage has job skills and was in the workforce recently, spousal support may only be required for a short period of time until they re-establish themselves.

When couples separate, I suggest that whoever is being asked to pay spousal support consider investing a reasonable amount of money in retraining their former spouse to re-enter the workforce. Perhaps he or she needs an occupational assessment. Perhaps they need to return to school to upgrade their education. That investment will pay dividends in the long run—for both of you.

Part 6 — Common-Law Spouses

For all intents and purposes, common-law spouses are treated exactly the same as legally married spouses when it comes to spousal support. However, it is very different in terms of property division. To make matters even more complicated, each province and territory has its own system of dealing with property division for common-law spouses. In Ontario, for example, common-law spouses who are separating have no statutory right to property division. They leave the relationship with what they brought in or what they acquired in their own name. If their name is on the car, they keep it. If their name is on RRSPs, they keep them. If the house is in their name, they keep it, and so on. In other provinces such as Manitoba and Nova Scotia, systems have been put in place to allow common-law couples to opt into a process whereby they're able to share their property as if they were legally married. These are relatively new developments, and if you are a common-law couple anticipating separation then a consultation with an experienced family law lawyer in your province or territory is absolutely essential. I say this not only so that you will understand your rights in that province but also because you can well imagine the disappointment of a common-law couple that moves from Manitoba or Nova Scotia to Ontario and then separates. In the process, they lose the rights that they might have had as common-law spouses in their former province of residence. It is mandatory now that common-law couples understand first of all, how they qualify to become a common-law couple in their particular province, and what rights they have or do not have if they separate. Qualifying as common-law spouses differs from province to province as well. Some provinces and territories only require two years of contin-

uous cohabitation in order to be considered a common-law couple, other provinces require three years, and yet a couple quali-
fies for federal marital benefits, such as pension, health and
medical benefits, after only a year of cohabitation. Common-
law couples are definitely at risk when it comes to property division and should seriously consider obtaining an opinion about
their rights. If you are living common-law and are not satisfied
about the way in which your property would be divided in the
event of a breakup, you should consider a cohabitation agreement, which is discussed below in Section 9 — Domestic
Contracts.

Part 7 — Same-Sex Couples

For all intents and purposes, same-sex couples that marry
are treated exactly the same way as heterosexual legally married
couples in Canada. If they do not marry and live common-law,
same-sex couples are treated exactly the same way as straight
common-law couples in their jurisdiction. Same-sex couples
should reread Section 4 and Section 6 to determine areas that
may require more investigation.

One issue that has caused me some concern is fast becoming a regular occurrence—same-sex "tourist marriages" in
Canada. Lesbian and gay couples come to Canada from other
jurisdictions and marry pursuant to our laws. They apply for a
marriage licence, marry, vacation and then head home to their
own jurisdiction, which in all likelihood does not recognize
same-sex marriages. That couple may then live in that jurisdiction, married and acquiring property and responsibilities to each
other, and then, like many other relationships, the marriage may
come to an end and the couple separates. As the jurisdiction in
which they reside may not recognize their marriage, it may not
entertain granting a divorce. The couple might consider returning to the Canadian province in which they married, but in order
to file for divorce (for example) in Ontario, one must be a resi-
dent of the province for at least a year prior to the application
for divorce. Foreign residents will not qualify. As a result,
same-sex couples that marry in Canada should be careful about
the long-term significance of relying on that marriage to create

any rights vis-à-vis property or support. In other words, the marriage may be purely symbolic and will not create automatic legal rights in the jurisdiction in which you actually reside. Bottom line: See a lawyer first.

Part 8 — Paternity

The question of a child's paternity can arise from time to time in family law cases, often in the context of child support. The mother of a child may ask a man for child support. He, in turn, may challenge paternity, and the court must consider evidence of whether this man is the father of this child. Recently, there have been a number of cases involving the concept of paternity fraud. In that situation, a man learns, sometimes long after the child has been born, that he has been paying child support for a child that is not biologically his. In such cases, men have returned to court seeking not only a refund of child support that was paid but also damages and costs against the mother of the child.

The law of paternity varies a little from province to province in Canada, but the general approach is similar. The law allows a person to apply to the court for a declaration that another person be recognized in law as the father of a child. Similarly, a person can ask for a declaration that a female person is the mother of a child. In such applications, once the court has made a declaration of parentage it is good for all purposes and binding on third parties. For example, if a man was accused of adultery by his wife and she proved that he was the father of someone else's child while still married to her that would be conclusive grounds of adultery for her divorce.

Paternity is now most often resolved through the use of blood or DNA testing, and the results are absolutely conclusive. In the absence of such evidence though, provincial laws establish presumptions designed to assist a court in reaching a conclusion about someone's paternity. So, for example, if a man was married to the mother of a child at the time of the child's birth, he will be presumed to be the father, unless he proves otherwise. If a man has certified the child's birth as the child's father, then under the provincial birth registration laws, he will be presumed to be the biological father, unless he proves otherwise. These presumptions are important because under provincial law individuals cannot be forced to submit to blood or DNA testing. If someone refuses to submit to testing, the court will exercise these presumptions against them and possibly presume paternity simply by drawing an inference based on facts. For more information about paternity and DNA testing, see Chapter 10, Part 1—DNA and Its Impact on Canadian Law.

Assuming that paternity is admitted or established, the mother and the father of the child involved may enter into a paternity agreement. In this agreement, they may set out responsibility for payment of expenses for the child's prenatal care and birth. They may set out an agreement related to support for the child and so on. A paternity agreement need only be in writing, signed by the parties and witnessed to be a valid agreement, but independent legal advice is still a very good idea before signing.

Part 9 — Domestic Agreements

In the previous section, we considered briefly a paternity agreement whereby a mother and a father acknowledge, in writing, that they are the parents of a child and set out some provisions with respect to the child's expenses and even child support. A paternity agreement is a form of a domestic agreement. Other much more common domestic agreements are: marriage contracts (for people who are married or intend to marry), cohabitation agreements (for people who are living together or intend to live together) and separation agreements (for people who have been married or were living common-law and have decided to separate). All forms of these domestic contracts are valid, according to Canadian law, and will be enforceable if prepared properly and fairly.

There is no legal requirement that a person obtain independent legal advice prior to signing a domestic contract, but it is certainly a good idea. In order to be valid, a domestic contract must meet some very simple guidelines. It must be in writing, it must be signed by the parties to it and it must be witnessed. Let's take a moment to look separately at each of these types of domestic contracts.

A marriage contract (or what is referred to as a pre-nuptial agreement if it is signed before the wedding) allows a couple to set out rules and agreements that they have to govern their marriage while it exists, at the time of separation and in the event that one of them should die. Marriage contracts allow a couple to create a tailor-made set of rules for their marriage. A common reason for a marriage contract is to protect a significant asset that one partner is bringing into the relationship. So, for example, if it is a second marriage and the woman entering it has a home that she managed to retain after her first marriage and divorce, then she may wish to provide that the home will be exempt from division in the event the second marriage breaks down. Some couples will provide rules for payment of spousal support if the marriage ends. There are very few limitations on what can be dealt with in a marriage contract, but the court disapproves of a couple trying to predetermine who will have custody of the children or predetermining child support obligations in the event the marriage ends. The court never considers itself bound by such agreements and will simply throw them out if it does not like what the couple included in their marriage contract. This does not mean that a couple cannot agree about things related to children. So, for example, if a couple wants to agree that the children will be raised in a particular religious faith, or that they will attend a particular religious-based educational institution, or that the children will be raised in a particular environment that is, for example, free of corporal punishment, this is permissible.

Unfortunately, sometimes the circumstances under which marriage contracts are negotiated create unseemly pressure. Many lawyers receive telephone calls asking for marriage contracts the week before a wedding. Lawyers have even seen marriage contracts signed at the wedding rehearsal, and in one well-known case in Canada, the marriage contract was signed between the wedding ceremony and the reception.

Cohabitation agreements are virtually identical to marriage contracts except they are for common-law couples. The same rules for preparation and contents apply to cohabitation agreements as to marriage contracts. Again, a couple is given an opportunity to make their own rules to govern their relationship while it exists, in the unhappy event of separation or even for the situation of one of them dying.

By far, the most common form of domestic contract is the separation agreement. This is a contract signed at the end of a marriage or a common-law relationship. In it, the parties agree to such things as a division of property, custody of their children, payment of spousal support, payment of child support and so on. There may be releases with respect to property, with respect to estates and a promise to live separate from each other from that point forward. There may be terms in a separation agreement concerning the payment of costs for the negotiation of the separation agreement and subsequent divorce. Again, the same rules apply for a separation agreement as other domestic contracts. It must be in writing, signed by the parties and witnessed. There is no requirement for independent legal advice, but it is certainly recommended.

In the case of any domestic contract, there is always a concern about enforceability. A domestic contract will be much more likely to be enforced by a court if it was prepared in accordance with the above rules. If it is fair, if there was full disclosure of assets and liabilities at the time the contract was negotiated and, most important, if there was independent legal advice, it will be enforced. It is difficult for a person to say, "I didn't know what I was signing" if they have consulted with a lawyer and the lawyer has certified, as a part of the agreement, that he or she explained the contents of the agreement to the person and they understood it and that they were signing it voluntarily. So, again, while there is no requirement for independent legal advice, it will certainly help you sleep a lot more comfortably at night knowing that the agreement itself will be more likely to be enforced by a court because lawyers looked it over and certified it.

For more information about family law, see my recent publication, *Surviving Your Divorce: A Guide to Canadian Family Law* (4th edition).

Part 10 — Strategic Advice

Family law problems call for people to be level-headed.

There are some very distinct emotional stages that couples move through as they separate and divorce. In *Surviving Your Divorce*, I have compared these to the stages that Elizabeth Kübler-Ross says people move through when dealing with death and dying. They may begin in a period of denial, move on to a phase of intense anger, fall into depression, engage in what is known false bargaining (an unrealistic attempt to resolve matters) and, finally, with patience, they move on to a period of acceptance, when they are ready to end the relationship and settle their legal issues. Lawyers, more often than not, meet their family law clients when the client is in the angry phase. People show up at a lawyer's office with instructions to seek revenge on the other spouse or to punish them for perceived wrongs. This is entirely the wrong attitude to have and, in this section, I want to provide you with the following ten simple tips:

- If you are planning to separate, do not be impulsive but, instead, go to see an experienced family law lawyer and get a pre-separation legal opinion about what will happen if you separate. This is a time to be level-headed and strategic. Understand what is going to happen to you prior to "pulling the plug."
- If your marriage or relationship has collapsed, and you know that you are separating, consider changing your life insurance beneficiary designations from your spouse to another individual. If there are children involved, you may wish to make a third party the beneficiary in trust for the benefit of your children. This means that if you should pass away suddenly during the course of your separation and prior to concluding the legal documents involved, any life insurance proceeds will flow to the designated trustee for the benefit of your children.
- Change your RRSP and pension or death benefit beneficiary designations. The same reasoning applies here as with respect to your life insurance beneficiary designations. All family law lawyers have seen situations in which there was an acrimonious separation, but one

spouse passed away prior to concluding all of the legal documents, and the surviving spouse benefited, even though that would be the last thing the deceased person would have wanted to happen.

- If you are separating and divorcing and have a will leaving everything to your current partner, you should consult with a lawyer immediately about making a new will that revokes that previous one. Try to anticipate what your estate plan will look like after your separation and divorce. Of course, if you have not made a will to begin with, now is a perfect time to do this. You are in the lawyer's office anyway.

- Make new Powers of Attorney for Personal Care and Property. If you have existing Powers of Attorney designating your spouse as the one who can make decisions on your behalf, you may not wish to continue to have that person in that capacity. Do you really want to have your estranged spouse making decisions about whether you should be resuscitated at the hospital? Now is the time to make sure that your old Powers of Attorney are revoked and replaced with new ones designating a new trusted individual as your Power of Attorney for Personal Care or for Property.

- I said at the beginning of this chapter that many people are representing themselves in the family law system because they have no choice. At the very least, make sure that you obtain advice from an experienced family law lawyer from time to time during your divorce, or use your best efforts to find an experienced family law lawyer who can assist you at a reasonable rate. There is too much at stake to take chances. Remember, this is not just about getting a divorce; it is about dividing the care and responsibility for your children, your property and future financial situation.

- The court system, in my view, is not particularly useful in resolving family law disputes. It is expensive, time-consuming, insensitive and slow. Consider opting out of the justice system into mediation or arbitration, which may allow you to create a much saner resolution of your family law issues.

- As you prepare to separate or divorce, and as you consider the use of a family law lawyer, make a budget for possible legal fees. Canadian lawyers typically charge between $200 and $500 per hour. If you hire a lawyer charging $375 per hour, and that individual works on your case for forty hours, you will be charged $15,000 plus GST, plus any disbursements that are incurred. Forty hours of work on a hotly contested separation and divorce is not a lot of time, but $15,000, in my view, is a lot of money. Think carefully before you act using such expensive advice.

- Marriage contracts or cohabitation agreements that incorporate independent legal advice can save a lot of misery later on, especially in second and subsequent marriages. I know that everyone thinks that it is unromantic to talk about a marriage contract, but let's be realistic: about 40% of Canadian marriages end in divorce. This means that there is a very good chance there could be trouble.

   A domestic agreement done fairly, negotiated and signed in advance could certainly make life a lot easier for those people who end up separating and divorcing.

- Many people are marrying for a second and a third time, and they need to think strategically about what that will mean, not just for themselves personally, their first spouse (to whom they may still have financial obligation) and their new spouse, but also for their children from previous relationships. Consult with an experienced family law lawyer and estate-planning lawyer to work on understanding the potential relationship between a marriage contract governing your second or subsequent marriage and your previous family or spouse. All of these documents should be seen as a part of an estate plan. You are now making decisions that will affect not just you and your spouse, but also your children and grandchildren. In this regard, I will give one small example, and that is the situation of a man who is marrying for a second time but has children from a previous relationship. These children will be justifiably nervous that their father is remarrying and may divorce this new spouse at some time, or may die and leave his entire estate to his second spouse. This can create tension between the children from the first marriage and the second spouse. This tension is completely unnecessary because there are solutions that can be incorporated in wills and marriage contracts to address the situation. For example, it may be possible for the husband and his second wife to enter into a marriage contract and make a will that allows his second spouse the use of various assets during her lifetime but, upon her death, those assets are passed on to the children of the first marriage. This can be done by way of an *inter vivos* or testamentary trust. So, the husband could say to his second wife, "You may continue to live in this home if I pass away, and you may live here until you die, at which time the property will then pass on to my children." The second spouse is cared for properly, and the children are able to relax. Relatively simple solution, isn't it?

Conclusion

As I said at the outset, family law can be a painful experience for the people involved. In my view, maintaining a level head, understanding the law and being strategic goes a long way to obtaining a good result for yourself, a fair result for your spouse and a peaceful result for your children.

Chapter 3

10 Things You Absolutely Need To Know About
Wills, Estates and Powers of Attorney

This area is by far one of the most popular topics on *Strictly Legal*. Every week I receive telephone calls and emails with very sensible, practical questions about how to make wills, the need for powers of attorney and other related matters. In this chapter, I will be reviewing the ten most common areas of concern and the most important things that Canadians need to know about wills, estates, powers of attorney—and telling you a few other interesting things as well.

Part 1 — Power of Attorney for Personal Care

There are lots of different names for this document. In some provinces it is called a mandate or a Representative Agreement, in some a Living Will, but the purpose is always the same: to give someone (or more than one person) the power to make decisions about your personal care should you become unable to make these decisions for yourself. The goal in making a Power of Attorney for Personal Care is to create some peace of mind should something happen and you cannot make decisions for yourself. Personal care can include many important things, such as your privacy, your safety, medical and health treatment, your hygiene, diet and nutrition, clothing and, of course, where you will live.

To make a Power of Attorney for Personal Care, you and the person you are appointing have to be over the age of majority and mentally competent. The person that you are appointing as your Attorney (not always a lawyer) must be willing to take on the responsibility. The document is easy to make. It only needs to be written, signed and witnessed by two people, both of whom are over the age of majority and who are present at the same time when it is being signed by the person making the

Power of Attorney. There are some limits on who can be a witness, for example, the person being appointed as Attorney cannot witness, nor can their spouse. Children of the person being appointed as Attorney cannot be witnesses either. The person making the Power of Attorney can revoke it the same way, that is, in writing and with two witnesses. I recommend that if you do revoke a Power of Attorney, make sure to tell someone. If you are revoking it, replace it with a new one. Don't leave a gap in such an important area of decision-making. A Power of Attorney takes effect the minute someone, in most cases the person appointed as Attorney (or your doctor, if that is what you stipulated), determines you are incapable of making decisions about your own personal care.

Unless the person acting as Attorney is your spouse (whether common-law or legally married), child or other relative, they cannot be paid for their work. So, you cannot pay the nurse who is looking after you to be your Attorney. Your Attorney can resign, but they have to notify the subject of the Power of Attorney and must do so in writing. In addition, if the person who has been given the Power of Attorney dies or becomes mentally incompetent themselves, their authority is terminated.

Why is the Power of Attorney for Personal Care like a Living Will, or what some people describe as "an advanced health directive?" When making a Power of Attorney for Personal Care, I recommend that you attach a schedule to the document setting out some limits for the kind of care you would like to receive if things are getting serious. By serious, I mean, if you don't want to have doctors and family members take heroic measures to keep you alive, if you don't want to be fed by tubes or have your breathing maintained by a machine, let the person who has the Power of Attorney know that. This way, even though you are incapable of making any decisions at the time, you will have provided some guidelines for the person you have authorized to make decisions on your behalf.

The person who has your Power of Attorney should be someone you trust implicitly. They have an obligation to act in your interest and to keep financial records with respect to any decisions they take concerning your care. If they are not acting in your best interest, it's possible for the court to remove them.

Given that a Power of Attorney for Personal Care is a "must have" document, and since you only need to be able to answer two questions in order to make one—who is going to have the Power of Attorney, and what kind of guidance you want to give them for managing your care—it is hard to believe that many people have not made one. This, of course, begs the question, what if you have not made a Power of Attorney for Personal Care? In most cases, the caregivers, doctors, hospital workers and (we hope) your family will do their best to work together. This does not always happen, however. It is hard to know who will rise to the occasion if someone becomes mentally incompetent. Some people may not be willing to get involved and take the time to look after your interests. If no one is available or no one can agree on what should happen for your personal care, then an application to the court will be made to appoint a guardian. This will likely be a family friend, someone who is over eighteen and who is willing to act. All provinces and territories have laws allowing the appointment of what are known as "substitute decision makers." They are given the authority to make decisions, such as whether you should go into a long-term care facility and what kind of care you should receive once you are in there. If there is no friend or relative to be appointed as a substitute decision maker for you, the court will appoint a government official. While it is nice to know that someone will be appointed, that person may be a complete stranger. All the more reason to take a few minutes and make a Power of Attorney for Personal Care, appointing someone you know and trust to look after your interests if you can't do it yourself.

Part 2 — Power of Attorney for Property

The Power of Attorney for Property will give someone, or more than one person, the power to make decisions about your property. Property can include real estate or financial matters, such as bank deposits and bill payments. The only thing related to your property that someone with your Power of Attorney cannot do is to make or change your will. The Power of

Attorney can be very general, giving a trusted person the power to do things on your behalf, whether you are mentally competent or not, or it can be very specific. For example, you can give someone the power to complete a specific real estate transaction while you are away on vacation. It can be for a limited time, or it can continue indefinitely. Many people want it to continue in the event of mental incompetence, but to do so, it has to say so expressly in the Power of Attorney for Property itself. In some cases, the Power of Attorney for Property can be set up in such a way that it takes effect immediately or upon the occurrence of a specific event.

The same rules for making and revoking the Power of Attorney for Personal Care apply for a Power of Attorney for Property. It must be written; two people who are over the age of eighteen and who are present at the same time when it is signed by the person making the Power of Attorney must witness it. The person being given the authority cannot be a witness, nor can their spouse or children be witnesses. When appointing a trusted person—preferably someone who understands financial matters—you need to be clear in stating what you have in terms of property, and you must be clear in demonstrating that you understand that giving this authority is the equivalent of giving the person a blank cheque over your property and finances. There is always the risk that the Power of Attorney can be misused. That is why it so important to select someone that you can trust absolutely. This is not to say that there is no accountability if someone misuses a Power of Attorney. There is accountability, and a court will review their decisions if asked, but just remember that a Power of Attorney, whether for personal care or for property, is a powerful document.

If you don't have one (unlike the situation with a Power of Attorney for Personal Care) family members, spouses and close friends cannot just go to the bank or to other financial institutions and say that they are helping while you are in a coma. If there is no Power of Attorney for Property, then only a person appointed by the court can make decisions concerning your financial situation or property. The court will only grant the authority to someone else if a medical professional has declared you incapable of making decisions yourself. This can involve a full medical assessment and delay. If no one has been appointed as Power of Attorney, and if no one is available or willing to act on your behalf, then a government representative, sometimes called the Public Trustee, may be appointed.

It is not uncommon for people who have been given a Power of Attorney for Property to be challenged about some of the decisions they are making. Sometimes people allege that the authority shouldn't be used because the person is not totally incapacitated. In some cases, the Attorney is accused of not keeping good records, referred to as "accounts." Sometimes they are accused of spending too much on the person who has been rendered incapable, or not spending enough. You can imagine the situation where an elderly person has been rendered incapable and the person with Power of Attorney for Property is looking after their bank accounts and other assets. All of those family members who are waiting for their "inheritances" may quibble with the person given the Power of Attorney about the way they are spending the money. In a case like that, the person who has been given the Power of Attorney can look at the incapacitated person's will and gain an understanding of the incapacitated person's intentions, however, they are not supposed to disclose to the beneficiaries who is getting what—if anything.

Remember, the bottom line when making a Power of Attorney for Property: you are selecting a trusted person to look after your assets and property in the event that you are rendered incapable of doing so for yourself. That person will manage your property until your death. At that time, the executor of your will, assuming you have one, will take over and then administer your property, look after any outstanding debts and then distribute the balance to your beneficiaries.

In terms of costs, if you give a professional person authority, by way of a Power of Attorney for Property, expect to pay a fee of 5% - 6% on the assets that are administered.

Part 3 — Making a Will

This topic probably ranks as one of the most common that I discuss on *Strictly Legal*, but making a will could not be easier.

If you are over the age of eighteen and mentally competent, you can make a will. If you can make a list of all of your property, sign it and get it witnessed by two people, you have made a will. It is one of the easiest documents to prepare but, even so, you should still have a lawyer prepare it for you.

In an emergency, it is possible to make a valid will by simply writing it out entirely in your own handwriting, dating and signing the document, creating what is known as a "holograph will." In the old days, these used to be referred to as "seaman's wills," because sailors facing shipwreck would scribble out their last will and testament by hand, sign it and leave it behind. This was a valid will. In order to be valid, however, this kind of will must be in your own handwriting; it cannot be partially typed and partially handwritten. So, if you are stuck at the airport and you suddenly realize that you probably should have left a will behind, take a clean sheet of paper, write out on it that it is your last will and testament, appoint someone as executor, set out what property you have and who you want to receive it, date it, sign it, put it in an envelope and mail it to yourself. If anything happens to you, you will have mailed yourself a valid holograph will, which can be used to distribute your estate.

Assuming you are not going to be making a holograph will, but instead are going to do it in a more formal way, your will must set out your name and some identifying information, such as your occupation. It should state that you revoke all previous wills. It must name an executor (or two, if you have more than one person in mind). In order to select an appropriate executor, keep three things in mind: the person must be over the age of eighteen; they must be mentally competent and they should be somebody that you trust absolutely to do a good job with your estate. This individual is going to gather up your assets and then determine your debts and distribute the property after payment of your debts. You are going to help them out by listing all of your assets and liabilities and setting out who should get what— maybe it will be easy and everything will go to one person.

When making a formal will, it is also a good idea to put in a "basket clause," or what is known as a "residue clause," stating that anything that has not been dealt with specifically in the will should go into the basket and be given to some specified person. Don't forget to sign your will. Don't forget to date it, and don't forget to have two people witness it *at the same time*. That's right, both witnesses must watch you sign at the same time. I know that seems like a formality, but there have been cases where wills have been thrown out because the witnesses did not watch at the same time.

Your wishes, as set out in the will, are going to come into effect when you die, no sooner. If you have made a Power of Attorney for Personal Care or for Property, whoever has that authority is going to look after everything until you die. Once you die, the executor takes over. That person's jobs are not only going to include finding out what assets and debts are involved, but also making your funeral arrangements, filing your income tax returns and then, after all the paperwork is done, distributing property to the beneficiaries.

Depending on how complicated your estate is, the executor may seek "probate" from the court. Probate is simply court approval of the will and the role of the executor. Most banks will not accept anything but a probated will, particularly where there are significant assets or if there is real estate that needs to be dealt with.

For all this work the executor can charge a fee, which varies, but 5% to 8% is a good estimate. Don't forget the other things, such as probate fees and taxes, that will need to be paid out of the estate. The more property in the estate, the higher the fees. Check with a lawyer in your province or territory to see what types of fees are applicable.

If you need to make changes to your will or you want to revoke it, do not simply write the changes that you want to make on the will. Changes or revocation must occur in the same way in which the will was made. In the case of changes, what is known as a "codicil" can be made. A codicil is just an amendment to a will that is made in writing. The person making the will signs it and, again, it is witnessed by two people witnessing the signing at the same time.

Many people don't realize that once they have gone to all the trouble of making a will, a marriage will revoke it. Divorce, on the other hand, does not automatically revoke a will, and we have seen cases in which a husband and wife separate, one dies, and the other inherits everything, leaving the deceased person spinning in their grave. In order to make sure that your marriage doesn't revoke your will, state in the will that it is made in contemplation of your upcoming marriage, or remember to make a new will immediately after your wedding. In the case of divorce, it is best to enter into a complete separation agreement in which your estranged spouse releases any interest in your estate. In some cases, if it cannot be settled and it goes to court, those kinds of things are dealt with within the divorce judgment, so that once the full divorce is granted, any interest in the respective estates is terminated.

The bottom line is one that you have heard a thousand times before—you absolutely have to make a will. It could not be easier. It is one of the least expensive things that a lawyer will do. Rarely does a lawyer charge the full rate for preparing a will, but dollar for dollar, it is the most valuable service that you can obtain from a lawyer.

I am often asked whether will kits are a good idea. I think that they can be a great help in planning to provide instructions to a lawyer. In my experience, sometimes people do not fill the wills out properly when using these kits, and it is better to be safe than sorry. By all means, buy a kit and then use it as a way of preparing everything for a lawyer who will then do a full version of a will for you. By arriving with all the information organized, you will be keeping your costs to an absolute minimum, but you have the peace of mind that it has been done properly and will be stored safely with the lawyer.

Part 4 — Death, Guardianship of Children and Other Dependents

It is one thing to look after distributing your property when you die, but many people are also worried about who will care for their children and other dependents. Parents of younger children often worry about making sure there is a guardian in place to care for their children, in case they have not reached the age of majority when the parents die. There are two kinds of guardian that can be appointed, one for the children and one for the children's property. One guardian can do both jobs, but this has to be set out specifically if the parents want one person to have both guardianship of the child's personal interests and guardianship of the child's property. The guardian is being given authority to step into the parents' shoes. This means that medical decisions, education decisions, religious upbringing and other important matters can be decided by the guardian.

Trouble arises, typically, after a divorce, when one parent wants to appoint someone other than the other biological parent as the guardian in the event of their death. This can happen, for example, if the divorce has been bitter and one parent does not want the other to have custody in the event of their own death. The custodial parent will often ask whether they can designate someone other than the access parent as the custodial parent for the child in the event of their death. If there is a joint custodial arrangement, neither parent can designate anyone other than the surviving parent as guardian. If you are a custodial parent and you want to appoint someone other than your child's other parent to be the guardian of the child in the event of your death, you can do so by stipulating in your will who you want to have the role of guardian. Make sure the person that you have identified accepts the responsibility. That designation of guardianship will be valid for at least ninety days after your death, even if someone else decides to challenge the decision. However, even if there is a challenge, the guardian should still apply to the court for full custody, as it will boil down to one thing and one thing only—what is best for the children. The same thing will apply for guardianship of the children's property.

Spouses should make their wills together and share them so that each knows what the other has provided. This is not always possible, particularly if the couple has separated. Some couples share all their information and make, for example, mutual wills, whereby they leave everything to each other, but in the event of a mutual disaster they leave it to the children or to some other beneficiary. If the children are too young to receive the estate, then the parents appoint a trustee to act on their behalf.

Other couples, who are either very private or hostile, make

their wills individually and say nothing to each other about what provision they have made. You should be aware that provincial laws allow surviving spouses to choose to take what they are given in the will of the deceased spouse or to elect to take the amount they would have received if the couple had separated instead of one of them passing away. This means that the treatment of a surviving spouse is the same as the treatment of a divorcing spouse. You can well imagine the scenario where the spouses are not separated but have made wills that do not leave everything completely to each other. If the surviving spouse does not like what they have received by way of the deceased spouse's will, they can reject the will by electing not to take what is left to them. This can, in turn, trigger a problem in the deceased spouse's estate. This can be particularly troublesome in situations of second marriages, where the deceased spouse intended to give away their property to children of a first marriage, only to find out that the second spouse has turned the estate plan on its ear. The message here is that spouses should try to make their wills work together in order to benefit the children.

Part 5 — Dying without A Will

Now, why would you want to die without a will when I have just told you how easy it is to make one? To die without a will means that you have died "intestate." It even sounds awful. I can almost imagine someone at a memorial service whispering to grieving friends, "He died *intestate*." (Maybe I feel that way because it rhymes with "reprobate.") In any event, let's assume the worst: for some inexplicable reason you could not get to a lawyer's office to make a will, or you died on the way to the lawyer's office, intending to make a will. The law of every province and territory provides a system for dividing an intestate's property. It is going to be slower than using a will (and it is probably going to be more expensive), but at least there is a framework for dividing the property. The way it works depends on whether you have a surviving spouse and/or children. If you are married but do not have any children, then your legally married spouse will inherit everything. The entitlement of a common-law spouse in a case of intestacy is far from guaranteed. I was involved with a case about two years ago where a husband and wife had separated, but they had not signed a separation agreement or completed their divorce. The husband started a new and very good common-law relationship, but he could not marry that common-law spouse because he was not yet divorced from his first wife. You can imagine what happened. He died and the legally married spouse (from whom he had been long and acrimoniously separated) inherited everything.

If you are married and have children, the framework for dividing the property of an intestate varies from province to province. A surviving spouse receives what is known as a "preferential share," right off the top of the estate. This preferential share varies from province to province.

After the preferential share has been paid, the surviving children and the surviving legally married spouse split the balance equally. Again, this rule is different from province to province and you need to check with an experienced wills and estates lawyer to see how this intestate property is allocated in the case of a surviving spouse and children.

Another scenario is that, perhaps, only your children survive you. In other words, your spouse has predeceased you. If that is the case, then most laws of intestacy allocate the estate to the children in equal parts. After that, the provincial law allocates property to surviving parents, surviving brothers and sisters, surviving nieces and nephews, and so on. If you have absolutely no one surviving you, the government gets it. So, you can see that not having a will creates trouble and expense for your family members and probably results in your property being divided in a way you might not approve. If you have no surviving family members, the very least you should consider doing is leaving your property to a deserving charity. Having a valid will beats intestacy hands down.

Part 6 — Organ Donation

Even though all provinces provide the opportunity to donate organs as a part of driver's licensing, and even though some private insurance companies provide cards that can be carried in your wallet indicating that you agree to organ donation, and even though we all seem to agree that organ donation is a good thing, for some reason, organ donation just does not happen at the optimum level. Why? I used to think I did not want to consent because doctors might be tempted to pull the plug on me if they needed my organs! This is, of course, "dead wrong" because two independent doctors have to decide that an individual's condition allows organs to be removed.

It seems we Canadians are not very good at donating our organs when we die. Our seat belt and helmet laws have actually reduced the number of organs available for transplanting, although traffic accident victims are still the majority of organ donors. There is a desperate and growing need for organs. Put yourself in the shoes of someone whose child or spouse is waiting for a transplant, and sign an organ donor card.

How can you let people know you want your organs donated? You can put it in your Power of Attorney for Personal Care. You can put it in your will. You can fill out the portion of your driver's licence. You can fill out that wallet card. No witnesses are needed for those latter methods. You can tell two people and ask them to pass that on to your personal representative if you die, and you can generally let your family know that you want to have your organs donated. I recommend that you do all of these things if it is important to you to have your organs donated because, even if you want it, your doctors may find that a family member opposes it. The doctor will not remove organs if your family opposes their donation. So, make sure they know that you want them to consent to organ donation. If nobody has any information about your wishes, generally, the doctors will ask your spouse first, then they will ask your parents, then your brothers and sisters and then any adult next of kin. The bottom line? If you want to donate your organs, let people know.

Part 7 — Funeral Arrangements

Funeral arrangements can be one of the toughest responsibilities we will ever undertake. What a relief it would be to learn that our loved one made a will and all the funeral arrangements in advance. A few Canadians—a minority—have the foresight to set out simple instructions in their will or even just in a letter. Do you want to be buried or do you want to be cremated? Do you want to be embalmed? (There is no legal obligation to be embalmed, and you can set out your opposition to being embalmed, perhaps for environmental reasons.) Do you want your organs donated to science? Do you want your organs donated to help someone? Do you want a memorial service or a funeral service? Do you want a funeral home to do all of the work, for example, transferring your body from hospital to funeral home, or do you want to use a transfer service? This is a service that will transfer you directly from the hospital (or the place of your death) to a crematorium or a cemetery. All of these questions can be answered in advance and make life a lot easier for people who survive you.

Prepaid packages are becoming more popular and are subject to provincial consumer protection law, so you can shop with a little bit more confidence that you will not be exploited. Provincial funeral associations also offer assistance, and either your provincial consumer ministry or the funeral association can help you get out of a funeral package if you feel that you were subjected to undue pressure to buy something that you did not need.

Now, here is the kicker: regardless of all of that effort, the final decision-making falls to the executor or estate trustee of your will (if there is one). These decisions do not fall to your wife or husband, to your lover, your children, your parents and especially not to your common-law spouse, unless they are your executor. It is the executor of your will who makes these decisions. The executor is the one who decides whether the estate can or will pay for your funeral wishes to be implemented. They will not follow every single instruction without question, especially if it turns out that your wishes for the funeral or cremation were unduly expensive. Most executors will work with the family and survivors, but if your now deceased loved one wanted a civic parade and a gold coffin, it might not happen.

If there is no will, a court appointed administrator or trustee will be faced with all the same decisions and more, since there will be no guidance at all on the deceased's wishes. Again, the administrator will try to work with the family, but there is no legal obligation to do so.

A cemetery plot is an expensive option, unless it has been bought by a family with the expectation that more than one person will be buried there. The owner of the plot has to give permission to the executor. Competition for space is growing, particularly in large cities. Oh, and by the way, you cannot simply bury somebody on private property or in your back-yard. Provincial law prohibits that.

If you have selected cremation (this means being burned at 1,000 degrees centigrade in a chamber, one body at a time, after removal of any medical devices or prostheses) it cannot occur any earlier than forty-eight hours after death. Many families choose cremation but wonder what to do with the ashes. Can you simply scatter the ashes on your property or at other locations? You may scatter ashes on property that you own, and you are also free to scatter ashes on federal or provincial property, lakes, rivers or at sea, unless it is an environmentally protected area. You cannot sprinkle ashes on someone else's property, even if that property is a cemetery. If you ask them in advance, you will find out that they may even charge you to scatter ashes at the cemetery, and you will definitely need their permission to do so.

Executors have the final say on funeral arrangements, because the estate pays for all of this—not the executor or the family personally. It all comes off the top as a debt that must be paid out of the estate. There are many possible sources of funds for paying funeral expenses. In some cases, money can be taken directly from a bank account or from the proceeds of a life insur-ance policy. Perhaps, the deceased belonged to a union or frater-nal club and funeral expenses are covered that way. Many other sources provide funeral benefits such as Worker's Compensation, welfare, motor vehicle policies and last, but certainly not least, veterans can sometimes get assistance from the Department of Veterans Affairs in covering their funeral expenses.

What if your loved one has died while away from Canada? It is possible to use a funeral home located in Canada or in the country in which the death occurred, or both, and they will coor-dinate having the remains returned to Canada. It is possible, also, for the local Canadian embassy to help with arrangements, but they will be the first ones to tell you that bringing a body home from abroad can be quite expensive, costing anywhere from $2,000 to $25,000. Insurance may cover that and a check of employee benefits or other funding methods should be made upon learning of a death occurring outside of Canada. If the expense of returning the body to Canada is prohibitive, you have the choice of either burying the person where they died, or cremating their remains in that country and having the ashes returned. That can be a much more cost-effective way of handling the matter. Once again, the executor looks after this work.

Funeral arrangements can be very trying and any assistance that can be provided in advance, as a part of a will or by simply writing a letter communicating your wishes, can be a big help to your family.

Part 8 — Stepchildren — Some Interesting Twists

The high rate of separation and divorce is combining with the high rate of remarriage to create thousands of blended families. When individuals have children from their first marriage and then remarry to someone who does not have children, this can create a little tension in the family as the children from the first marriage watch their parent marry, live with and blend their assets with a second partner. It is common knowledge that second spouses can get a pretty rough ride from the children of the first marriage. One of the concerns is that the second spouse will inherit everything from the parent, and the children of the first marriage will see their inheritance transferred into the hands of the infamous "gold digging" second spouse.

In this section, I would like to examine a couple of situations involving stepchildren. The first situation concerns what are known as "mutual wills." A husband and a wife will often agree to make mutual wills. This means that they enter into an arrangement (that is, essentially, a contract) to pass on their property through their wills in an agreed-upon way and they undertake not to change their wills after the first spouse passes away. So, imagine this as a contract to make specific wills, leaving everything to each other and then to an agreed-upon list of beneficiaries. Imagine a situation where a couple marries and both have children from a previous marriage. They may wish to make wills leaving everything to each other, but then, upon their deaths, ensuring that a will leaves the estate to children from *both marriages*, not just to the children of the last surviving spouse.

In a recent case, a woman we'll call Emily died after having signed mutual wills with her second husband, John, who died about eleven months after his wife. In her will, Emily left everything to John and nothing to her daughters. She did so on the understanding that when John, in turn, passed away, he would leave some of the estate to his children and some of the estate to Emily's children.

As the reader will have guessed, John didn't follow through on the agreement and, after his wife had been diagnosed with Alzheimer's, he made two further wills, leaving everything to his natural children and nothing to Emily's children. The question arose as to whether John's disappointed stepchildren could sue him to enforce the mutual wills that their mother told them she and John had made. The court reviewed the situation and concluded that Emily and John had expressed a clear intention to enter into an agreement for mutual wills. In fact, they had actually made identical wills at one point. Their first wills were mirror images. There was also evidence given to the court that they had told all of the children that they would be taken care of equally. That was enough for the court to conclude that a surviving spouse had to honour the terms of an agreement for mutual wills. Emily's children got a share of John's estate.

In another case involving a stepchild, the court had to consider the meaning of "child" in a will. If someone says, "I leave my property to my children," who will be included in that expression? According to most provincial laws in Canada, the word "children" includes a naturally born child of the person making the will, an adopted child of the person making the will, a child born outside of marriage (meaning an illegitimate child), and a child conceived before the testator dies but born after the testator dies. Interestingly, the definition of "children" or "child" does not include a stepchild. In the past, the courts have concluded that if a testator wanted to include a stepchild, then they would have named the child specifically as a beneficiary.

A woman, who had no children of her own, left her entire

estate to the nieces and nephews of her husband who had predeceased her. She said that the nieces and nephews should receive
the remaining estate in equal shares. Her will also said that if
any of the nieces or nephews had already passed away, then that
person's share should be passed on *to their children* in equal
shares. Now, as it turns out, one of the nephews had, in fact,
predeceased the woman who was making this will and that
nephew had no natural children, *but he did have two stepchildren* who were the natural children of his wife. He had never
adopted these children, but had treated them as his own and
raised them in the marriage. The question arose as to whether
the two stepchildren of the nephew could share in the estate that
was being divided among nieces and nephews. In this Ontario
case, the court felt that, since the nephew had treated these
stepchildren as his own and as those children were very close
with the entire family, they should be treated as children and
should inherit under the will.

The lesson to be learned, of course, from such a case is that
when working with a lawyer to draft a will, the language is very
important and it can be necessary to tell the lawyer, not just the
names of children that have been born inside the marriage (or
inside the relationship, if common-law), but also the names of
children, if any, born outside the marriage, or the names of
stepchildren that the testator wishes to benefit in the will. A
good wills and estates lawyer will ask the right questions to
ensure that these kinds of problems do not occur when your will
is read by your beneficiaries.

Part 9 — Jointly Held Property

The will or intestate administration will deal with property
owned by the deceased at the time of death. Property that is owned
or held jointly with another person will not flow through the estate.
This can be a very positive development if it keeps costs of the
estate down and thereby reduces the cost of probate. It also means
that property will flow directly to the other co-owner and it will,
therefore, not be eligible for satisfying debts of the estate. In addition, it can be less expensive, since title, for example, of real estate
will change automatically. The property that is held jointly with

someone else flows automatically to the other joint owner by virtue of what is known as the "rule of survivorship."

The downside of joint tenancy is that, if this was done as a form of estate planning, it really is an immediate gift because the joint tenant or co-owner owns their share of your property now. They do not have to wait for you to die in order to benefit. This means that if that co-owner gets divorced or is sued, then the asset that you have given to them may be available for division in their divorce, or it may be available to their creditors. It also means that if you want to sell your property, you will need to get the consent of the joint tenant in order to dispose of it, or even to mortgage it or refinance. There may also be tax consequences at the time of a later disposition, if the property has not been used as a principal residence by one of the co-owners. If you change your mind at a later date and do not want to give that property to the co-owner, it is too late. You cannot revoke the gift. It may be possible to sever the joint tenancy by arranging to transfer your interest as a joint owner to yourself alone. This will have the effect of severing the joint tenancy and prevent the rule of survivorship from applying. The other joint tenant does not need to consent and in some cases may not even know until after the first joint tenant has died. If this is something you may need, consult a lawyer about how to do it.

Other assets can also flow outside of and around the estate. For example, life insurance proceeds do not go through an estate if there is a specific beneficiary. Registered Retirement Savings Plans (RRSPs) also offer the opportunity to designate someone as a beneficiary so that the funds will not flow through your estate. Pensions have death benefits and there is no need for the executor to be involved in the flow of these assets around the estate. Creditors cannot get at the assets so it can be quite advantageous to do a little estate planning in advance.

Part 10 — Trusts

Trust me, trusts are not for everyone, but, for some people, they offer great advantages, including estate planning opportunities, lower taxes, the deferring of taxes, the opportunity to look after children and spouses, and other benefits as well.

Typically, trusts are for people who are dealing with assets of over $100,000 or $200,000. It is a simple concept, whereby a person known as a "settlor" transfers ownership of assets to a trustee, along with some rules on how the trustee must manage the assets for the benefit of the beneficiaries. The trustee (who can be a professional who manages it for a fee, or someone who does it simply on a friendly basis) has legal ownership of the assets. The beneficiaries of the trusts, themselves, have no legal ownership, so the trustee has full control and, depending on the rules that you have created for the trust, may have considerable discretion. Even with that discretion, the trustee has to manage the assets responsibly, honestly, without a conflict of interest and with skill. It is their responsibility to maintain the trust at optimal performance for the benefit of the beneficiaries, without having to follow any advice from the beneficiaries themselves.

Trusts can either be *inter vivos* (which means a trust that operates while the settlor of the trust is alive)—this type of trust can be revocable or irrevocable—or the trust can be created by a will. Whether designed to operate during a settlor's lifetime or after their death, the trust can be:

- for the benefit of a spouse. In this case, the trustee manages the assets for the benefit of that spouse until they die. This can be terrific in the case of a second spouse and where there are children from a previous marriage;
- for the benefit of a whole family, including spouses, children and grandchildren. This would allow, for example, a family cottage to be maintained for generations;
- for the protection and benefit of a child who has some special needs, or for children who have not reached the age of majority;
- to address concerns about a child who, while not having special needs, has trouble managing money. The trustee parcels it out;
- to provide incentives for beneficiaries of a trust to meet certain expectations of the settlor. For instance, the settlor may require that the trustee not pay out funds to beneficiaries, unless the beneficiaries have finished

university or have invested on their own and generated some wealth that the trustee can then match by following the rules of the trust; and

• the trust can also be used to protect assets from creditors.

Trusts can be used to reduce probate fees and can even be used in conjunction with, or to replace completely, Powers of Attorney for Personal Care and for Property. They are also great privacy providers, since all the terms are confidential.

The trust agreement sets out the purpose, assets, beneficiaries, names of trustees, the intended benefits of the trust and, of course, how the assets are ultimately to be distributed.

A person creating a trust cannot avoid taxes on those assets forever, so after twenty-one years all trusts are required to report what is known as "a deemed disposition" of all the assets held by the trust. This deemed disposition is stated to have occurred at fair market value and is then taxed at that point.

A trust may be a good way to deal with a family cottage. A person could state in their will that the cottage is held in trust for all their children and grandchildren. The trustee owns it and the others benefit. The testamentary trust or *inter vivos* trust would set out rules related to the cottage property and rules for sharing of its use.

If considering a trust, it is mandatory that you consult with an experienced wills and estates lawyer to find out how this type of device can be used for effective estate planning.

Conclusion

The law of wills and estates is a fascinating area, and the cases and situations always provide an insight into the amazing realities of Canadians lives. It is my hope that if you take only one thing away from reading this book, it is that you will go home and make a will and draw up Powers of Attorney for Personal Care and for Property. If you do that much, it has been worth the price of this book, and a lot more.

Chapter 4

10 Things You Absolutely Need To Know About
Criminal Law

An encounter with the criminal justice system can be one of the scariest moments in a person's life. Criminal problems can arise in a number of areas. Maybe you have been stopped for impaired driving. Maybe one of your children has run into trouble or maybe it is a much more serious thing, like violence, drugs or damage to your property. In this chapter, I would like to demystify the top ten things that most Canadians need to know about the criminal law in Canada.

Part 1 — Criminal Law Courts and the Criminal Law Process

Everyone knows the basic starting point for criminal law—you're innocent until proven guilty! But, ignorance of the law is no excuse! To be convicted of a criminal offence, the judge or jury (depending on the charge), must be convinced of your guilt beyond a reasonable doubt. This is a higher standard than is used in the civil courts. In the civil courts, the judge or jury is simply trying to decide which party should be successful based on a balance of probabilities. Determining that someone is guilty beyond a reasonable doubt is a much higher standard to reach.

Canadian law defines a crime very specifically. The Canadian Criminal Code, the Narcotics Act and other federal laws set out every offence considered to be a crime. In order for a judge or jury to convict a person of a crime, they must be satisfied two things exist: an *actus reus* (a guilty act); and *mens rea* (a guilty mind). Criminal offences are divided into three categories: summary conviction offences, which are considered less serious: indictable offences, which are more serious; and hybrid offences, which are offences where the Crown Attorney who is prosecuting the offence chooses whether to proceed with the charge by way of a summary process or an indictment.

Assuming a person has been charged with a crime, they can expect to attend court a number of times. First, they may attend for a bail hearing, where a court will be trying to decide whether the person charged needs to be detained pending the trial or if they can be released subject to certain conditions. The second time a person will need to attend court if they are charged with a crime is to set a date for trial. This is the event that really starts the process rolling. The third court appearance in the criminal process may be for a preliminary hearing. At this hearing, the court determines if there is enough evidence of a crime to justify having a full trial. In advance of a trial, there may a fourth reason to go to court. This will be for pre-trial hearings. At pre-trial hearings, the court hears arguments about whether certain evidence will be admissible at the full trial. And then, after all those appearances, an accused person may finally get to have a trial, perhaps in front of a judge (or perhaps, in front of a judge and a jury).

After all of the court appearances, the accused person may never even have an opportunity to tell their story because the onus is on the Crown Attorney to prove all the necessary elements of the crime with which the accused has been charged. No Canadian charged with a criminal offence is obliged to give evidence that might help convict them. The Crown has to prove everything on its own.

The evidence that the Crown Attorney intends to rely upon must be shared with the accused person and their lawyer in advance of the hearings. This disclosure of evidence allows the person charged with the crime to know exactly what kind of evidence the Crown Attorney is going to present to the court. It also allows the lawyers representing the accused person to know whether certain pieces of evidence should be challenged in those pre-trial hearings that I mentioned above. The rules for evidence can be very strict: the evidence must be gathered correctly; it must be handled correctly; it must be proved to the court correctly. The justice system has always been based on the premise that is it is better to set a high standard and allow a few guilty people to go free, than to run the risk of convicting one innocent person.

This is as good a time as any to get one of the most common questions asked of lawyers out of the way: "How can you represent someone you know is guilty?" As you can see from the previous discussion, the defence lawyer is, more often than not, simply making sure that a Crown Attorney does their job. Defence attorneys not only ensure that the court process is followed correctly, but they also make sure that evidence gathering and evidence proof in court is done properly. It is not up to the defence lawyer to determine whether the court will or will not find the accused person innocent or guilty. That is for the judge or jury. In terms of representing a person that the lawyer knows is guilty, there are some limitations on the defences that can be presented. So, for example, if defence lawyers know that their client was present at the scene of the alleged crime, they will not attempt to present alibi evidence that the client was at some other location. This would clearly be misleading the court. However, in all other respects, a defence lawyer is not simply "trying to get the client off." The lawyer is trying to make sure that the Crown Attorney and the justice system work hard to meet the high standard of proving guilt and in doing so ensure that innocent people are not convicted.

Part 2 — Contact with the Police

The police have a tough job and nobody would look forward to having to deal with the work that they must do. It is 99% trouble. There are a few different ways we may encounter police in the course of our lives:

• the police may need to question you and no charges are laid;
• you may be charged with a criminal offence;
• you may be driving a vehicle and be stopped by the police;
• the police are searching for someone or for evidence.

Let's look at your rights and obligations in these situations. In the first situation, if the police are questioning you, you have the right to remain silent. However, most lawyers recommend cooperating by at least identifying yourself. Refusing to do so could result in a charge of obstructing justice. Giving a false name will guarantee that the police will lay a charge against you.

If the police questioning goes on to a point where you feel you cannot leave if you want to, then it may be that the police are detaining you. At this point, you have a right to know why they are detaining you and whether you are being charged. At this stage, you also have a right to talk to a lawyer.

In the second situation, which involves being charged with a criminal offence, the police have a right to stop you if they suspect you have committed a crime or see you committing a crime. Once they stop you in such circumstances, they have the right to search you: if you let them; if they believe you have or are committing an offence involving weapons or drugs; if they arrest you. You have the right to consult a lawyer in this situation.

Anything they find while searching you that is illegal— whether it is what they were searching for in the first place or not—can be used to lay charges against you. The bottom line? If you are stopped, identify yourself, cooperate, say nothing, ask why you are being stopped and if you are charged, and ask to see a lawyer.

In the third situation, if you are in a vehicle, there is an increased police entitlement to stop you and to talk to you. If you are driving a motor vehicle, the police can stop you at any time to determine if you have consumed alcohol or drugs, to see if you are licensed and insured or to see if your car is mechanically fit. This last case is why the police will sometimes stop someone who has a burned-out headlight or tail light on their car. They may be using it as an excuse to see who is operating the car and to determine whether alcohol or drugs have been consumed. If you are stopped while operating a vehicle, you are entitled to know why you have been stopped and you are entitled to speak to a lawyer within a reasonable time. The above applies to someone *operating* a motor vehicle. It does not apply to passengers. So, for example, the police have no right to pull over someone who is operating a motor vehicle because they wish to talk to a passenger in that vehicle (unless they want to arrest the passenger).

Assuming you encounter the police somewhere other than in your car, the question arises from time to time whether the police can search your home or office. The police can always search your home or office if they have your permission, or if they have a search warrant. Permission to search an office or home has to be given by an adult, and it can be withdrawn at any time. If a police officer arrives at your door and asks to search your home or office, don't be shy about asking for the officer's name and badge number. If the police arrive with a search warrant, ask to see it, get the officer's name and badge number and ask why they are searching. The search warrant should set out exactly what they are looking for. If they find what the search warrant specifies, then the search is over and they must leave the premises. Unnecessary damage is not permitted just because the police have a warrant.

If the police have an arrest warrant (as opposed to a search warrant), they are allowed access to your home and can do a limited search of the surroundings. If they find other illegal material while using the arrest warrant, that information can lead to more charges. Last, but not least, if there is an emergency, or if someone will be harmed if the police officers don't assist, then the police can enter your home. And guess what? If, while assisting in an emergency, they find anything illegal in your home or office, they may lay charges against you.

If you have been arrested, the police do not need a search warrant to search you. You have the following nine rights:

- the right to remain silent, and the police must tell you that you have this right;
- you have the right to be told why you have been arrested or detained;
- you have the right to hire a lawyer (although this assumes that you can afford to hire one or will qualify for Legal Aid);
- you have the right to speak with duty counsel (a lawyer) and to determine whether there's Legal Aid available to assist you in hiring a lawyer;

- you have the right to speak with a lawyer in private as soon as possible;
- you have the right to a trial within a reasonable period of time;
- you have the right to be presumed innocent;
- you have the right to bail, unless there is good reason to keep you in custody; and
- you have the right not to be forced to testify against yourself at your own trial.

Part 3 — Young Offenders

When it comes to the commission of criminal offences—as opposed to, for example, a simple driving offence, which is a provincial law matter—young Canadians, that is, people between the ages twelve and seventeen are treated differently than people over the age of seventeen. If someone is under the age of twelve, they cannot be charged with a criminal offence. But people over twelve and under seventeen have a special set of rules that govern their offences. Any violation of the Canadian Criminal Code or other federal criminal laws is governed by a special law—the Youth Criminal Justice Act.

Unless it is a serious crime, such as murder or some other violent act, adult sentences are not imposed on youth offenders. Instead, their penalties focus more on rehabilitation, community service, apologies to victims and treatment for disorders. Placing a young offender in custody is intended to be used as a last resort.

In addition, young offenders' identities are protected. They have a right to a lawyer and they have the right to speak with their parents.

Part 4 — Theft

Shoplifting is probably the most common form of theft, but lately there are growing concerns about theft of such things as intellectual property—this includes DVD copying, music downloading and computer program theft. Whether you steal a movie from the local video outlet or a hammer from the local hardware store, it may still be considered theft under the Canadian

Criminal Code. These charges are determined by the value of that which has been stolen and in particular, whether the value of that stolen property is more or less then $5,000. Earlier I mentioned the hybrid offences where the Crown Attorney can choose either the less serious summary conviction process, or the more serious indictable offence. A theft under $5,000 is a good example of a situation where the Crown Attorney has a choice. Penalties for theft upon conviction range from an absolute discharge to ten years in prison. So, if a person copies one movie and is convicted, it may mean a penalty of community service. But if they copied ten thousand CDs and sold them for profit, it could be a penalty of a big fine and/or jail.

This is also a good opportunity to reiterate two aspects of criminal law: the need for a guilty mind (*mens rea*); and a guilty act (*actus reas*). If you did not intend to steal the hammer, simply forgot it was under a newspaper in your shopping cart, then you are not guilty. However, not knowing that copying a DVD is a crime is no defence as ignorance of the law is not a defence.

Part 5 — Violence

This section could have included a lot, but I'd like to focus on five things:
i) Simple assault;
ii) Domestic violence;
iii) Sexual assault;
iv) Stalking; and
v) Offences involving weapons.

i) Simple assault

Simple assault is easy enough to understand. Threatening to harm a person, or actually doing it, may be an assault. If you tell someone that you are going to punch them in the nose, it is as much of an assault as actually doing it. Any forceful contact that is unwanted is technically an assault on a person whether there's actual physical harm caused or not. Penalties for simple assault can range, again, from a discharge and posting of a peace bond (which means you promise to keep the peace and post, say, $500) to jail, depending on how serious the threat or the harm.

ii) Domestic violence

Domestic violence is a variation on assault. It is an assault within a spousal relationship. The spousal relationship includes heterosexual and same-sex couples, whether married or living common-law. The vast majority of domestic violence is committed by men against women, but lawyers also see violence by women against men. Regardless of gender, it's violence and will—if reported—attract the possibility of a criminal assault charge. There's a difference, though, between assaulting your neighbour and assaulting your spouse. There's always a chance that the charge of assaulting your neighbour may be withdrawn if you and your neighbour can come to terms about what happened. This is not the case with domestic violence committed against a spouse. Once a charge is laid, it cannot be withdrawn except in the most unusual circumstances. Why? This is to protect victims from being pressured by spouses to have the charge withdrawn. Domestic violence charges figure more and more in family law cases and custody disputes.

iii) Sexual assault

This variation on violent assault involves some sexual aspect and often concerns whether the person assaulted gave consent. Were they perhaps under the influence of alcohol or drugs? Were they capable of giving consent? For example, were they too young to consent to the sexual activity? Or were they mentally able to appreciate what was happening? For example, were they mentally handicapped or unconscious when the sexual contact occurred?

An amendment to the Criminal Code is pending as of this writing raising the age at which consent to sexual activity can be given from fourteen to sixteen. Several years ago, the concept of rape was replaced with graduated levels of sexual assault, sexual assault with a weapon, sexual assault that results in bodily harm and aggravated sexual assault. Penalties range from discharge to jail.

iv) Stalking

The word "stalking" does not appear in the Criminal Code

of Canada. It is captured, however, by the offence of criminal harassment and applies to the person who follows around a celebrity or the neighbour who threatens to harm you or your family (or even your pets). Stalking, or the crime of criminal harassment, includes following someone, repeated unwanted communication, monitoring them, watching them at home or at work, threatening harm to their family. Courts take this crime seriously, especially if it is repeated. The maximum sentence is ten years in jail.

A related offence is loitering (which seems to boil down to wandering around without any particular purpose), or prowling (sneaking around at night between nine p.m. and six a.m. on someone's property or near someone's house). If someone is following you around and they are found on your property, they will likely be charged with both offences.

v) Weapons

Thankfully, Canadian law sets out a much longer list of restricted weapons than most countries. We are not allowed to carry a large number of dangerous things. That may be hard to believe based on what we read in the papers, as it seems every day the papers are filled with stories of people being attacked with guns, knives, swords or machetes. It sure seems that there are a lot of weapons out there, but they're all restricted!

The following are examples of prohibited weapons in Canada:

- any automatic firearm;
- shotguns;
- sawed-off rifles;
- silencers;
- switchblade knives;
- tasers, or similar electronic stun guns;
- mace/tear gas (but pepper spray is fine);
- martial arts-type sticks joined by chains; and
- whips and replicas of weapons.

Part 6 — Drugs

There's a gap between what Canadian law says is illegal and what the police and the courts in Canada can deal with when it comes to illegal drugs. This gap has a lot to do with police discretion. Police are overburdened in the war on drugs and they must pick and choose where they can enforce the law.

The basics? Federal law lists as illegal drugs marijuana, heroin, cocaine, amphetamines, and on and on. New designer drugs are developed almost daily. It is a crime to knowingly possess any of these drugs at any time. If you have it in your possession and you know it is a drug, then technically, you're guilty. I say technically because we all know of situations where the police have not charged, or a Crown Attorney has not prosecuted some teenager for "simple possession" of marijuana that they were using and not selling. That decision is called "discretion" and cannot be guaranteed. It depends upon the police officer, the Crown Attorney and the accused. Even if the Crown Attorney decides to proceed with the charge, the possession of marijuana is one of those offences where the Crown Attorney has a choice to proceed with it as a hybrid offence, a summary offence (if it's not serious), or an indictable offence (if it is serious). If the Crown elects summary procedure, the accused person, once convicted, can expect a small fine of between $250 to $500 and probation (which means don't get caught committing any other crimes again, or this will be reactivated). Oh, and if the Crown says "indictable" because you had a lot of the marijuana and it was your third offence, you can get up to seven years in jail.

Police and prosecutors are more interested in trafficking and "grow ops" (houses or apartments where marijuana is grown) (see Chapter 7 — Real Estate—Part 8 Marijuana Grow Houses). Trafficking goes beyond possession. It means that a person has sold the drug or distributed illegal drugs. The penalties demonstrate how serious it can be—life in prison is the maximum and a conviction always includes jail time and of course, a serious criminal record.

Usually a marijuana grow house operation will also involve theft of electrical power and related charges.

Part 7 — Art Thieves

Have you been stealing valuable art lately? Me neither. But others are apparently turning Canada into an art thieves' haven. Internationally, art theft seems to be a regular news item with a Leonardo da Vinci painting called the *Madonna of the Yarnwinder* worth $65 million being stolen, and who can forget the much-publicized theft of *The Scream* painted by Edvard Munch. These priceless works of art have joined the other hundreds of thousands of missing and stolen works of art. So art theft is occurring all over the world, but it is not nearly as glamorous as portrayed in movies like *The Thomas Crown Affair*. Experts and in particular, curators of museums refer to the "Lost Museum," an imaginary museum that contains all of the art missing and stolen from around the world. This crime is second only to drug trafficking with about $6 billion worth of art stolen every year, sometimes to launder money or to finance terrorism.

In January 2004, five ivory statues (valued at approximately $1.5 million) were stolen right from under the noses of staff at the Art Gallery of Ontario. The thieves apparently only had to lift the lid of a glass case to be able to reach the eighteenth century statues carved by Huguenot craftsman, David Le Marchand. After a $150,000 reward was posted, a Toronto lawyer was approached by someone who wanted to return the statues in exchange for the reward. The $150,000 was paid and the stolen property was returned. Did the reward, in fact, go to the thief? No one knows for sure.

In 2006, a huge bronze statue of a famous Ukrainian poet was stolen from a park in Oakville (just west of Toronto). All that was recovered was the statue's head. The rest? Apparently, melted down for the value of the bronze. Perhaps, the two bronze Rosenthal statues stolen in October 2002 from downtown Toronto met the same fate.

After the US invasion of Iraq in 2003, thieves emptied Iraq's National Museum in Baghdad and their priceless antiquities have flowed into the market for stolen art, including one incident where Toronto's Royal Ontario Museum was approached to buy and display artefacts from Iraq. The ROM declined.

They say that art thieves love Canada because there are no dedicated police officers or detectives working in the area and, even if they are caught, our prisons are considered quite comfortable. In the United States, the FBI has a designated "art crime team," and American courts have been a little more enthusiastic in punishing criminals. At least a part of the solution for this crime, which admittedly has almost no impact on the average Canadian's life, is for galleries and purchasers of art to insist on a full history of the piece. This is what art experts refer to as provenance—the history of the artwork. Unless there is some dramatic change in investigative techniques or dedication of resources to this crime, my guess is that Canadians will continue to see art stolen and disposed of for great financial gain that flows into the hands of criminals.

Part 8 — Gambling

The law concerning gambling in Canada, in my view, can be summarized in one word—hypocrisy. Now don't get me wrong: although I buy the occasional lottery ticket, I am not a gambler. But anyone who spent ten minutes looking at what is going on in Canada (and the US for that matter) would be scratching their head trying to figure out why some forms of gambling are legal and others are not. I think the hypocrisy of it became clear when I watched the media frenzy that broke over Wayne Gretzky's wife and sports betting back in February 2006. The New Jersey state police had launched Operation Slap Shot and discovered—Oh, My God—people are betting on sports! Yes, it's true, the police themselves may have been involved in the illegal sports bookmaking and yes, it's true that players and coaches and the like should not be involved in betting on their own sports. But it's almost impossible to determine what it was that they were doing illegally that is different from most sports-betting opportunities that are operated by government. The bookmaking ring was highly organized and allegedly could process one thousand wagers totalling in excess of $1.7 million in a forty-day period. Athletes and celebrities participated in the bets, and their betting involved professional and collegiate sports events. The key difference between illegal bookmaking and legal bookmaking on sporting events seems to be that organized crime, instead of the government, gets the profits.

To understand gambling in Canada, we really need to go back to the beginning of the Canadian Criminal Code, which, as of 1892, had a complete ban on any and all gambling activities. Since then, the idea of a ban of gambling in Canada has, slowly but surely, been wiped out. Some of that can be traced to the Montreal Olympics, which were preceded by some amendments to the Criminal Code that allowed federal and provincial governments to use lotteries to fund worthwhile activities. The Montreal Olympics were among the first such "worthwhile activities" to benefit.

Provincial and territorial governments have virtually taken over the gambling and lottery scheme business in Canada with the federal government being left to enforce the Criminal Code to block gambling unless it is approved by government. And that is pretty much the way gambling operates in Canada. The Canadian Criminal Code says it is against the law, *except as it is approved and delivered by government*.

Most observers would say that Canadian governments are addicted to revenues from gambling. And we now see not only ticket lotteries but also horse racing and extensive charitable gaming, in the form of bingo usually. Every province has legal opportunities to gamble in these areas, as do the territories. There are only three provinces that do not have casino-style gambling (New Brunswick, PEI, and Newfoundland and Labrador). Slot machines are widespread in many provinces as are VLTs (video lottery terminals which are considered to be the crack cocaine of gambling) and the latest addition, Internet gambling. In this last respect, there is no doubt that, for Canadians, Internet gambling is, and will likely continue to be, illegal. Go figure that one out.

Canada's approach to the regulation of gambling is different from that of other countries. Under the control of provincial and territorial governments, gambling options are available through charities, through private operators licensed by government and now through First Nations.

It's not possible to reproduce in this book, but most

Canadians would find it amusing to read Part VII of the
Canadian Criminal Code, which deals with "Disorderly Houses,
Gaming and Betting." I think most Canadians would find it
hard to believe that Section 206 of the our Criminal Code states
that "Everyone is guilty of an indictable offence and liable to
imprisonment for a term not exceeding two years who... i)
receives bets of any kind on the outcome of a game of 3-card
Monte." I could go on and list the dozens of similar bizarre prohibitions. The key, however, to understanding lotteries and
other forms of gambling in Canada is located in Section 207 of
the Canadian Criminal Code which states that *notwithstanding
any of the provisions of the Criminal Code related to gaming
and betting*, it is lawful for the government of a province to conduct and manage a lottery scheme in that province and for charitable and religious organizations to be licensed to run lottery
schemes and so on. With all the legal gambling opportunities
available in Canada, it's a wonder that any hardworking criminals can make a living at offering illegal gambling.

However, the aspect in which it takes the strangest turn is in
online gaming. There's no doubt that this is an active area, and
it is well known, for example, that the biggest servers for
Internet gambling are located on reserves. However, to date, the
presence of these gaming companies on Canadian soil has
attracted little interest. The reserves rent space on huge Internet
servers located on their territory. It is rumoured that there have
been negotiations between the federal government and the
natives on the reserve, but to date, no police force has attempt-
ed to take steps to shutdown this potentially illegal—at least by
Canadian standards—online gaming.

It is an open question in law about whether First Nations
have the right to license and regulate gambling activities.
Certainly, the federal government has not acknowledged any
such gambling entitlement.

So there you have it. The Criminal Code is filled with laws
that prohibit gambling—unless, of course, the gambling is made
available by government. Forms of online gambling are clearly
illegal, but no government has taken steps to enforce the law.

Part 9 — Driving Problems

I had a case once where a young man was charged under provincial law with failing to remain at the scene of an accident. He had lost control of his car in a snowstorm, crashed into a snowbank on a quiet side road and then decided to leave the car and walk home. The police tracked him down and charged him with an offence. He came to see me and we set a date for trial. But before we could convince the court that he should not be convicted, he killed himself, his depression caused in part by the charges. That case has always stuck with me, and I think about him when I hear about some of the predicaments Canadians get into when driving their cars.

The Canadian Criminal Code and provincial laws contain numerous crimes and offences related to the operation of a motor vehicle (and boats and other things as well), but in this section, I'm just going to deal with motor vehicles. The typical difficulties that Canadians encounter in their vehicles fall into the following categories:

i) Dangerous or careless driving;
ii) Driving while impaired;
iii) Driving without insurance;
iv) Driving while suspended.

Before looking at each of these offences, anyone operating a motor vehicle in Canada should understand that the police have a greater entitlement to stop people operating vehicles to check on things than in other situations, such as, say, just walking down the street. They can stop a vehicle to determine whether the driver has consumed alcohol or drugs, has valid car insurance and to determine whether the car is mechanically fit. Once the police do pull you over, they're entitled to ask you questions including whether you've consumed any alcohol or drugs. Not answering such a question amounts to an invitation for the police to ask that you take a breath test to determine if you've been drinking. They can also ask you to "walk a straight line," or to ask you to perform some other tasks that might allow them to assess whether you have the ability to operate a vehicle. Again, there's no legal

102 — Michael G. Cochrane

requirement that you perform the tasks that they set for you, but not doing so may again be interpreted as an invitation to have them administer a breath test to you, which, of course, will only determine if you've consumed alcohol.

i) Dangerous driving

Dangerous driving is a Criminal Code offence. Section 249 of the Criminal Code states that "everyone commits an offence who operates (a) a motor vehicle in a manner which is dangerous to the public, having regard to all the circumstances, including the nature, condition and use of the place at which the motor vehicle is being operated and the amount of traffic that, at the time, is or might be reasonably expected to be at that place." The penalty, if you are convicted, can be as high as five years in jail. Note that there does not actually have to be some other person or vehicle endangered by the dangerous operation or dangerous driving by the accused person. In other words, a person can be driving dangerously even though they're the only person on the highway. To be convicted, there has to be an element of reckless disregard. The individual laws of each province also provide an offence of careless driving. It is considered to be a less serious offence than dangerous driving. Careless driving does not have that reckless component. It could simply be driving without due care and attention. Depending on the province, the penalty upon conviction is a fine and, possibly, demerit points.

ii) Driving while impaired

Despite all the advertising campaigns directed at discouraging impaired driving, the police continue to pull over record numbers of people who drink and drive. The applicable provision in the Criminal Code is Section 253 and it states "Everyone commits an offence who operates a motor vehicle whether it is in motion or not (a) while the person's ability to operate the vehicle is impaired by alcohol or drugs, or (b) having consumed alcohol in such a quantity that the concentration in the person's blood exceeds 80 milligrams of alcohol in 100 millilitres of blood. You will note that under subparagraph (a), it is not necessary to have exceeded the 80 mg. of alcohol. A person can be convicted of being impaired having less than 80 mg. of alcohol in 100 ml. of blood. The breath tests that are administered (there are two kinds—the roadside breath screening test and the Breathalyzer test, which is administered back at the station) are used to determine whether there is impairment. For the police to obtain a conviction, it is much easier for them to prove after a Breathalyzer test that the concentration of alcohol in your blood exceeds the acceptable limit than to give evidence that, for example, your speech was slurred and you could not walk a straight line. While a conviction is not guaranteed simply because of the Breathalyzer test results, it is best to avoid the consequences of failing that test.

And, of course, if you do fail the test—the price is considerable. One estimate of the potential cost of a conviction for driving while impaired is $18,000. This figure is arrived at as follows:

- the legal costs incurred in defending the charge can range from $2,000 to $10,000;
- the Criminal Code fine for a first offence is $600;
- the "back on track" program (which a court may order the person to participate in) is $475;
- there will be a $150 fee to reinstate a driver's licence;
- there will be an estimated increase in the premium for automobile insurance of $13,500 (being $4,500 extra per year for three years); and
- there is also the possibility of an ignition interlock being ordered at a cost of $1,300.

The total cost can therefore run to *more than* $18,000. This does not include other expenses, such as property damage (if there was an accident involved) and loss of employment income if you're off work or—horror of horrors—fired because you needed your licence in order to perform your job.

iii) Driving without insurance

Of course, everyone needs to have insurance on their motor

vehicle in order to be able to drive in Canada, and the police are entitled to ask for proof that you have insurance, so carry that card with you. Many people may have experienced what has happened to me on a couple of occasions. The police have pulled me over and asked for proof of insurance, and I have not had it in my wallet. The police in both situations generously gave me an opportunity to go home and get it and come to a police station within forty-eight hours to show that I did indeed have insurance on the vehicle. If you don't have the insurance, the fine can be steep depending on the circumstances of the offence and the number of convictions. I met a fellow a couple of years ago who was convicted of driving without insurance and the penalty was $5,000 for his first offence. The court also has the option of suspending your driver's licence if you have been driving without insurance. This is considered a serious offence because if the uninsured person has an accident, the compensation of an injured person is much more complicated. A fast way to bankrupt yourself is to drive without insurance and then have an accident. All of your personal assets may go up in smoke to pay for the damage you have caused.

A young woman consulted me recently about a serious accident in which she was involved. She gave some drunk friends a lift home in an uninsured vehicle, which was actually registered in her mother's name. The accident was serious, with multiple injuries. The drunks sued her for more than $2 million. With no insurance on the vehicle, she faced tens of thousands of dollars in legal fees and possible bankruptcy for her and her mother.

The reason why people drive without insurance, of course, is that many of them have been convicted of impaired driving, or some other driving offence, and have lost their licence, which, in turn, costs them their insurance. This means that if they are pulled over for any particular reason, let's say even an illegal left-hand turn, then the police are going to have a busy day filling out reports and tickets for the following: the illegal left-hand turn; then the driving without a licence; then the driving without insurance and so on. The fines can end up in the tens of thousands of dollars.

iv) Driving while suspended

I don't think there's much more I can add to the depressing news on these types of convictions. Someone who drives while their licence is suspended, which means that they are probably driving without insurance as well, is playing Russian roulette.

Another offence related to the above is the "failure to stop at the scene of an accident." Section 252 of the Criminal Code states that "Every person commits an offence who has the care, charge or control of a vehicle, that is involved in an accident with a) another person or, b) a vehicle and with the intent to escape civil or criminal liability, fails to stop the vehicle, give his name and address and where any person has been injured, or appears to require assistance, offer assistance. The penalty under the Criminal Code can be five years in jail and even as high as ten years, if the person who left the scene did so knowing that bodily harm had been caused to another person. This provision is designed to deal with the "hit and run" problem which plagues many Canadian cities.

Insiders state frankly that the reason, more often than not, that someone leaves the scene of an accident is that they do not have insurance, or they are driving while suspended, or they are driving while impaired, or all three. The consequences are brutal when they are caught—and they are always caught.

Part 10 — Criminal Records

Criminal records come in a number of varieties:

- after a criminal conviction;
- an Incident Report, which may or may not have led to criminal charges or a conviction; and
- fingerprints taken of an individual who has been arrested, whether that person goes on to be convicted of the crime or not.

Incident Reports are generated when there is a criminal investigation and a person is a suspect. Whether the case goes forward and results in charges or conviction or not, the police keep that Incident Report in their files in case there is more reason to be involved with the accused person, the crime that may have been committed or the need for ongoing investigation. These Incident Report records are typically destroyed after five years.

Fingerprints and the photos that are sometimes taken at the same time stay on file with the police whether the accused person was convicted or not, and all police forces have access to them. This includes the RCMP and local police. This record of fingerprints and the photo will stay there unless you do something to have them destroyed. This can take up to a year and is not guaranteed, especially if you have other convictions.

Obtaining a pardon for a criminal conviction is quite a bit more involved. First, the person applying for a pardon must wait for three to five years after they have completed their sentence or paid their fine. The length of time that a person must wait depends on whether their conviction was for a summary offence or an indictable offence. The more serious the crime, the longer the person must wait. In order to apply for a pardon, a person must collect any and all information related to the conviction as soon as possible. All of this information will be needed in order to apply for the pardon. Once a person begins the process, it can take up to two years to complete, and a person applying for a pardon may want to obtain help to do this. So, consider calling Pardons Canada or visit their website at *www.pardons.canada.ca* or try their toll-free number 1-877-929-6011.

If a person has been convicted, but received an absolute or a conditional discharge, the clearing by way of pardon can be a little faster, but still can take from one to three years.

Why should you care about getting a pardon and clearing the criminal records from your name? Having a criminal record can affect employment opportunities, especially if you need to be bonded (that is, insured against theft or fraud), or if you need to hold a particular type of licence, or work with children. If you are applying for a sensitive position, you may be asked to give your employer permission to search for criminal records.

Immigration is much more difficult if you have a criminal record. Travelling with a criminal record can be more than a nuisance—it can be an absolute barrier, as sometimes you will need to get special permission to enter countries. The United States, in particular, takes a very dim view of criminals crossing its borders, and US immigration will often require that people with criminal records wishing to enter the U.S. obtain an entry waiver (check out the website *www.DHS.gov*) from US immigration. Once US immigration has your record downloaded from the RCMP, it is with them for good. You may be denied access to the United States. Trying to sneak over and getting caught only makes matters worse.

Whether you were simply interviewed by police and they have your fingerprints and photo on record, or whether you were convicted of a criminal offence, it is in your best interests to apply for and obtain a pardon at the earliest possible opportunity.

Conclusion

No one likes to have contact with the police or criminal law. Most of the time, a person in touch with the criminal law system is either an accused person or a victim. It can be a painful experience and advice from an experienced criminal law lawyer may not make it enjoyable but it will certainly make life a little easier.

Chapter 5

10 Things You Absolutely Need To Know About Business Law

In this chapter, I want to demystify some of the key legal aspects of carrying on business in Canada. Incorporation? Partnership? Sole proprietorship? Buying a franchise? These and many other questions need answers when Canadians become involved in the world of business.

Part 1 — Sole Proprietorship

I think most businesses start off in this way—one person begins a business on their own. The person *is* the business, owning all of the assets of the business and, of course, bearing all of the liabilities. Any earnings are theirs alone and income of the business is that person's personal income for income tax purposes.

With this form of business, there is no protection for the owner. If the business does not succeed, then the owner's personal assets may be available to creditors.

The business is required to register its name. This usually costs less than $100 and is mandatory by provincial law, but also recommended if you want to protect the name of your business. The registration accomplishes at least two things: it lets the public know where to find you, and it protects your business name from competitors. This ensures that two businesses do not operate under the same name. There are a number of ways of checking available names. The best is a system called NUANS (Newly Updated Automated Name Search), which allows a very thorough national search for a small fee. Once registered, the registration proof will be handy when you open a bank account to start depositing all of those profits!

Sole proprietorship involves minimal costs, protects and registers a name, but offers no real protection if things go wrong, as the owner continues to be personally responsible.

Part 2 — Partnerships

Partnerships are fairly easy to start. There can be a written Partnership Agreement, whereby two or more people agree to carry on a business together. This agreement sets out each partner's role, their expectations of each other, financial contributions, responsibilities in terms of running the company and profit and liability sharing (this could be 50-50, or 75-25, or any other percentage agreed upon).

Even if there is no written agreement, simply carrying on business "as partners" can create a partnership in law. Whether you have written it down or not, if you simply do all of the above "partnership-like" things, you will be treated as partners. Carrying on in this informal way is not recommended, especially because of what can happen if a disagreement arises. A Partnership Agreement in writing is an easy way to ensure a peaceful partnership and an organized dissolution if things do not work out.

There are two types of partnerships—a *general partnership* and a *limited partnership*. In a general partnership, all profits and losses are shared equally, or in accordance with the Partnership Agreement. In a limited partnership, some partners may limit their exposure to any financial losses of the partnership. Usually, such a partner will have a limited role in the operation of the company and be more of a "silent partner" or investor in the background.

Even though this form of business is more structured than a sole proprietorship, the partners are still personally liable for any financial responsibilities incurred. It is also an "all for one, one for all" arrangement because all partners are bound by any decision or commitments made by any one partner. In addition, if a partner dies, the whole partnership comes to an end, unless some specific provisions have been put in a written Partnership Agreement to say otherwise. While it may be nice to work with others—each partner contributing a different skill—partnerships are not particularly flexible, especially when it comes to selling the business as a going concern. Even having another person join the partnership can involve a rethink and, certainly, a rewrite of the Partnership Agreement.

Just like a sole proprietorship, a name to be used by the partnership must be selected and checked out through the NUANS system. The partnership name must be registered for all of the same reasons that you would register the name of a sole proprietorship. It is simply good business and required by law.

The best advice is to have a written Partnership Agreement. If the business is important to you, get a lawyer to draft the terms of the agreement for you. Partnership fights can be long and expensive and, of course, will tie up the business until they are resolved.

Part 3 — Incorporations

Ever wondered what the difference is between a business that has "Limited," "Ltd.", "Incorporated" or "Inc." at that end of its name? The answer is, there is no difference. They are all companies. Someone (perhaps a person who had a sole proprietorship) decided to take the next step and create a separate legal entity. It is the same as creating a new legal person, in that it can do things on its own, separate from the person who created it. A company, once incorporated, survives the person who created it.

Creating that new entity through incorporation is accomplished under federal or provincial law. There is a bit of paperwork, but the whole exercise can cost less than $500. Some of the things that need to be set out at the time of the incorporation include:

• Naming it. Many people use a combination of their names or the names of their children when thinking up the name of a company, or they try to find some combination of words that describes them and the business that they are carrying on. If there is no name, then a number will be given to the company at the time of the incorporation. That is why we often see companies that are, for example, "1234567 Ontario Limited." If a name is going to be selected, the same type of NUANS search is done to ensure that the name for the company is available and is not going to be confused with some other company that is already in business. There are some rules that govern the names that can be picked for corporations. For example, you cannot call your company "The Don Trump Real Estate Development Company," unless of course you get his permission first. Not likely.

• Where will the corporation carry on business? As a part of the incorporation, it is necessary to have a fixed address if only to receive mail and maybe ship product. If this is a federal incorporation, it will need to have a Canadian address. If it is a provincial incorporation, then it will need an address in that particular province. Some people just use the office of the lawyer who incorporated the company for them. That way, all the important corporate documents are kept at one location.

• All companies have shares. How a particular company structures its shares depends on the number of people who are involved and the plans for the corporation in the future. There may be a need for a couple of different kinds of shares. The two main kinds of shares are *common shares* and *preferential shares.* Common shares come with a vote, so that anyone who has a common share is able to vote on company business. Holders of common shares are entitled to share in the profit and can receive corporate dividends. Holders of preferential shares, or what are sometimes called *special shares,* may be allowed to vote, depending on how those shares are created in the first place, and they may have priority for receiving any dividends that are paid out by the company. That is what makes them preferential. It is even possible to have different classes of preferential shares, with different rights and entitlements attached to each. All of this needs to be reviewed with the lawyer who is helping you create the company. If it is a simple company, it may have only one or two people involved, carrying on business in a private way. All that may be needed are common shares.

• Who will be running this company? Key people in companies are generally in three categories: shareholders, directors and officers. Shareholders are the owners of the company and, as I mentioned earlier, they have the right to vote. Shareholders elect the directors of the company and they are not necessarily involved in the day-to-day operation of the company. In some cases, the shareholder is the director and is basically doing everything, but in other cases, the shareholders elect separate directors and officers.

- Directors are elected by the shareholders and every corporation must have at least one director. The directors are responsible for general oversight of the company and part of their job is to select officers who will be responsible for the day-to-day operation of the company. Officers include the president and the vice-president of the company. Of course, in many small businesses, the shareholder is the director and the director is the president, and they are doing everything to run the company. As the company grows, it may be necessary to expand to bring in more shareholders, more directors and more officers to look after different aspects of operating the company. That is a sign of success. At that stage, it may be advisable to have a Shareholder Agreement, which does the same thing as a Partnership Agreement but for a corporation.

People sometimes worry about taking on the responsibility of being a director for a company. It is true that they do have a special responsibility to the company. This responsibility is what is known as a "fiduciary" one, meaning that a director has the obligation to act honestly and always in the best interests of the company that they have been asked to oversee. It would make no sense if you were asked to be the director of a new fitness company and you then went out and, on your own, opened a competing fitness company across the street.

Directors may also be responsible for payment of debt that has been incurred by the company. Corporations provide protection for shareholders' personal assets, which are not available to satisfy debts of the corporation. This is one of the biggest advantages and best reasons for having a corporation—to shield your personal assets—but this shield does not apply to every possible debt that a corporation can incur. For example, if there are unpaid wages, unpaid income tax or GST, or unpaid CPP contributions for employees, then directors may be personally responsible for those debts. Also, if a director or a shareholder personally guaranteed a corporate debt, then they may find that their personal assets are available to creditors.

In addition, there are certain corporate offences for which directors may be personally responsible. For example, if a director authorized a company to do certain activities that result-ed in environmental damage, the corporation may not provide a shield if that company is eventually charged. So, becoming a director for a company is not simply being a figurehead. There are responsibilities and liabilities that go with it.

When setting up the corporation, some thought needs to be given to what work the company will actually be doing. For example, is it a fitness studio business alone or is it also going to be selling products, importing and exporting or manufactur-ing something? All of this will need to be considered at the beginning because the incorporating documents need to set out the purposes of the company. At the same time, some thought will need to be given to other things that the company may need to do, such as borrowing money and entering into contracts.

There is minimal paperwork involved in setting up a com-pany. There is a need for bylaws, minute books and resolutions to be passed, and all of these things should be kept up to date as the company grows. There are *supposed to be* regular meetings and there are *supposed to be* corporate records that are kept and, naturally, income tax returns should be filed every year and, nat-urally, there should be a Shareholder Agreement, but this is often not the case. People simply create their companies and go out and begin to work, collect their money, pay their taxes and carry on, without keeping the books up to date on an annual basis. Sometimes, it is only when there is a crisis for the com-pany that everyone realizes that these corporate records have not been kept up to date, and there is a scramble to do it all retroac-tively. If you are incorporating a company, be sure you keep the company up to date on an annual basis.

Just because you have created a corporation it does not mean that you can simply go out and start carrying on a business. There may be other licences and permits that you need to apply for. So, if you are going to be importing and exporting, apply to the federal government for the appropriate permits and licences. If you are going to be selling real estate or alcohol, or working, for example, as an electrician, check your province's rules about permits and licences. If you want to open a restaurant, café or butcher shop or a pet store and kennel, then you had better plan on asking your local municipality what permits and licences it requires. Imagine carrying on a business where you need to obtain permits and licences from all three levels of government. Importing food to sell at a bar that also has a kennel? Let's not forget about packaging either. If the company is going to be selling food, medical products or products for children, then there is likely going to be a requirement for labelling. Now you see why business owners complain about "red tape."

So, if you are planning to incorporate, there is quite a bit to think about, but certainly the advantages far outweigh the disadvantages and a corporation is a very highly recommended vehicle for carrying on business in Canada.

Part 4 — Franchises

Who has not stood in line at Tim Hortons thinking, "Oh man, if I had one of these franchises..." Franchises have become very popular ways of doing businesses in Canada. They come with many advantages and a few big disadvantages. No one should buy a franchise without first doing a lot of research. Essentially, a franchise is supposed to be a turnkey operation. Someone (the franchisor) has already had the brainwave, designed the business concept, made a business plan, registered the trademarks, designed the logos and paid to develop advertising, obtained licences and permits, lined up suppliers and so on. They have probably done quite a bit of work. The person who buys the franchise (the franchisee) buys a business operation that is, presumably, ready to go. Sounds great.

In addition to the advantage of all this work being done for the franchisee, the purchaser of the franchise has the advantage of the franchisor being available to help launch the franchise. The company will often provide training to ensure that the franchise gets up and running quickly and effectively. The franchise may come with name recognition, which will make it easier for the business person to get things going. As a franchise owner, you may find dealing with the bank to borrow money is a lot easier than when starting from scratch with your own business idea.

It all sounds so good. What could possibly go wrong? Well, several things. Consider the following—you pay for the franchisor's having done all that work in advance. You pay an upfront fee, annual fees, training fees and a percentage of profits. That entire pre-designed infrastructure comes at a price. It is a turnkey operation, but the key can be expensive. The franchisor will also have a lot of control over this business. You thought you would be working for yourself—think again. In addition, the franchisee must often buy their product from the franchisor. People in the franchise business have always heard the story of the franchisee who tried to save a bit of money by buying discount products someplace other than from the franchisor and ended up in trouble with their head office. Imagine each Tim Hortons trying to make its own donuts. This is exactly what franchisors want to avoid. They want to control the quality and image of their product in the marketplace. They do this by controlling where the franchisees obtain their product. In some cases, this can be good news because franchisors can use their clout in the marketplace to get the best possible price, but that is not always the case, and there are horror stories of franchisees being required to buy product directly from a franchisor at prices in excess of what they could buy it for at the corner store. Territory is key too. The franchisor wants to get as many franchises in the marketplace as possible. Each franchisee wants to have the maximum territory and the maximum number of clients available. That can create conflicts.

The best way to avoid such rude shocks is to do research in advance. Read the magazines that describe what is going on in the franchise industry. Do research on the web. Go to franchise conferences and, by all means, speak to existing franchisees. If you are going to buy, make sure that you get a Franchise Agreement in advance and have a lawyer review it. But brace yourself, there is not much room to negotiate the terms of these Franchise Agreements. Franchisors are required to give disclosure to potential purchasers. Make sure that you review that in detail.

There are lots of franchise opportunities out there. Some are, obviously, working extremely well, but there are other areas of the franchise market that are unproven and risky. Be one of the successful ones and do not end up like that sad fellow who bought the franchise thinking he was going to make a million dollars and wound up working 24/7 to net $30,000 per year. Be careful.

Part 5 — Buying and Selling a Business

Maybe buying a franchise is not for you. There are lots of other business opportunities out there, so let's consider just buying an existing business, whether it is a sole proprietorship, a partnership or a corporation.

Like a franchise, you may have to pay more to buy an existing business than just starting your own. After all, unless the business is in trouble, the vendor will want to recover their hard work in building up this business to the point of being able to sell it for a profit. Was the business incorporated? Did it build a good reputation? Did it acquire assets, such as machinery or land? Did it build up a customer list? These are the things that add value to a business.

When considering this decision, look at such things as the income the business is earning, money that it owes or money that is owed to it, its real assets, its employees and if it has existing inventory. These, among other things, are the items that will determine the price that you pay for a business.

If the business is a sole proprietorship, then you may simply be purchasing the assets of that business. After all, the business itself is not incorporated and the income that is being earned is the income of the sole proprietor personally. They are simply selling the assets, name (perhaps) and goodwill, if any, of the business that they have built up.

If it is a partnership, it is an asset purchase and a little bit more because the partnership will need to be dissolved or amended if someone intends to stay on and participate in the business with you. Although a partnership purchase may be a little more involved than the purchase of a sole proprietorship, it is still essentially an asset purchase and the purchase of any goodwill.

If the business is incorporated, then a person wanting to buy it has a choice. It can be a simple purchase of the corporation's assets, in other words, the corporation sells its inventory, its customer lists, its buildings and its machinery, but not its shares. However, simply buying the shares outright may be the best way to buy the entire company and all of its assets lock, stock and barrel, because the shares come with the assets and (don't forget) liabilities.

With a share purchase, there will be a need to double-check a number of things, such as: is the corporation validly incorporated? Are its books up to date? Have the taxes been paid? (If they haven't been paid, you will be stuck with them.) Is everything on the table? Have lawsuits been disclosed? It is possible that a company may be in the middle of a lawsuit. Sometimes suing can be just as dangerous as being sued because if the company loses, it may have to pay costs.

The value of a business is critical, but it all comes down to the same issue, whether it is a share purchase or an asset purchase—what are you getting? Inventory? Assets? Buildings? Goodwill? Territory? Customer lists? Employees? Or are you getting lawsuits, debts, liabilities and trouble?

It is advisable to involve a good business valuator, who can sort out the value of the above items as well as any tax consequences of each of the alternatives. The business valuator, along with a good lawyer, can give you advice about how to roll the purchase of a corporation into a solid Agreement of Purchase and Sale, signed, sealed and delivered to protect you.

Part 6 — Being an Employer

Let's face it; we cannot do big business alone. We need help. That can mean bringing in partners, or it can mean hiring contractors to help out, or it can mean becoming an employer, and these can be very different things with very different obligations.

Sometimes a business person will not want the responsibility of hiring employees. Contracting work out to an independent contractor may seem to be an easier way of dealing with the need for some assistance. Independent contractors usually work for a fixed term, that is, not indefinitely. They supply their own materials and tools for the job. They have their own place of work, and they are not supervised directly by the person who has contracted them to do the work. Independent contractors provide their own invoices. They are generally contracted to work for more than one person. They work for several others, so that they do not have only one source of income. In reality, independent contractors have their own business. They do not get benefits, they do not get vacation time and, importantly, they do not have any rights to notice if the person hiring them decides not to use them anymore.

It is quite a different kettle of fish with employees. There are extensive legal responsibilities for an employer to an employee. For this reason, business people often try to avoid hiring employees and keep most of the people who are assisting their business in the form of independent contractors, with minimal rights. However, sometimes it is just impossible to keep a person working for you as an independent contractor. Think about that list that I set out above. Maybe you have a person who is not working for a fixed term but indefinitely. Maybe they do not supply their own materials because you supply them. Maybe they always work at your place of business and are supervised. Maybe they do not invoice for the work that they do and they do not have any other clients—they work exclusively for you. This means that they look an awful lot like an employee, and this will mean that they have a right to benefits, such as vacation time, and other legal entitlements.

Both federal and provincial law provides rules for the treatment of employees and, in particular, provincial law sets minimum employment standards. These employment standards can include such things as the minimum hourly rate, the maximum number of hours that can be worked in a week, vacation rights, the right to not come to work on statutory holidays, protection from termination, occupational health and safety rights, worker's compensation rights, human rights, employment insurance rights, Canada Pension Plan rights, responsibilities for deduction of income tax and other payroll taxes and health tax deductions, depending on what province or territory your business is located in.

Expanding a business to include employees means additional work and many more obligations. This means that hiring the right employees is critical.

A source of great concern when hiring an employee is exactly what can and cannot be asked during that initial interview. Presumably, a resume of some kind has been delivered, and the employer wants to ask the potential employee some questions, but does not want to do anything that might fall foul of human rights legislation or employment standards. Unless the information is directly related to the ability of a person to actually do the job for which you have advertised, questions in the following categories are best avoided: race, colour, country of origin, ethnicity, citizenship, religion, sex, sexual orientation, age, marital status, common-law status, whether someone has children, whether a woman is pregnant, whether someone has physical or mental disabilities and, of course, politics.

Sometimes, however, it is unavoidable to ask a question in these areas because they are related to the ability to do the job. An employer is entitled to ask whether a potential employee is legally able to work in Canada. No employer is required to hire someone with a disability if the disability will prevent them from doing the very job that they are being hired to do. Businesses are expected to make reasonable accommodations for disabled people in the workplace, and what is reasonable depends on the size of the business. While it is not appropriate to ask someone their age with a view to keeping older people out of the office, it is appropriate to know whether someone is old enough to drive a car if operating a vehicle is one of the duties they will be expected to perform. So, as you can see, this area requires some caution. Just remember to ensure that questions should be related to a person's actual ability to do the job for which the employer has advertised.

One issue that comes up frequently is the entitlement to ask about criminal records. Generally, human rights legislation in Canada prohibits an employer from refusing to hire someone on the grounds that they have a criminal record *if the person has been pardoned.* Most people do not want to hire employees who have criminal records. However, when we scratch beneath the surface of that general rule, there may be a little more tolerance than we might first assume. If someone has a conviction for possessing marijuana when they were young, that may not affect an employer's willingness to hire them. However, if someone has had convictions in the past for fraud, trafficking in narcotics, weapons offences, and the like, that is probably not the kind of person you want to have in your workplace. How do you find out about that, and what if they have obtained a pardon? If a person has been convicted of a criminal offence and they have not obtained a pardon and, as a result, have a criminal record, then you are not obliged to hire them. So, while you cannot ask the question, "So, I really need to know, have you ever been convicted of a criminal offence?", you can ask (assuming it is related to the actual job) whether there is anything that would prevent that person from being bonded. In an application to be bonded the potential employee will need to disclose their criminal history, fingerprints will be taken and criminal records may surface. The bonding company will refuse to provide a bond for that employee, and you are then under no obligation to hire them.

Many employers are now insisting on background checks for potential employees in sensitive jobs. Financial institutions, daycare centres, and organizations that place people in contact with children and elderly people are now insisting that background checks be done. In that context, criminal records may surface and employment can be denied.

The next aspect of the employment relationship that causes anxiety is firing an employee. No one likes to terminate someone's employment but, in some circumstances, it is absolutely unavoidable. There are two general ways to fire an employee. The first is known as "for just cause." This means that the employee has done something that justifies their immediate termination. If just cause exists, there is no obligation to provide advance notice or to provide any lump sum payment in exchange for their leaving the workplace. The employer simply tells the employee that they are fired and they must leave the premises immediately. Typical things that would qualify as just cause include: theft or embezzlement, fraud (or some other kind of criminal activity), refusal to follow instructions, being rude and talking back to supervisors, sexual or racial harassment, drunkenness or abuse of drugs, not showing up for work without a good excuse, being incompetent or being discovered working for a competitor and, perhaps, sharing corporate secrets or other inside information. That type of conflict of interest and breach of trust by the employee would be just cause for an immediate termination.

As an employer, you may want to terminate someone's employment, but they have not done anything to justify being fired on the spot. In such a case, they must be given reasonable notice of the termination. The notice can mean that they are given an opportunity to work for, for example, four more weeks, at which time their employment will end and they are free to seek a new job. Alternatively, they may be paid the equivalent salary and asked to leave immediately. If the employee has just started and has worked for less than the minimum period of time required for notice (it depends on the province or territory), there is no obligation to give notice or to pay them a sum of money. However, if the person has worked for you or your company for an extended period of time, a reasonable period of notice up to, for example, a maximum of eight weeks is recommended. Check with your local Ministry of Labour to determine the minimum period of notice that should be given in your province. Most employers do not want a terminated employee on the premises, as there is a risk that they will do something to harm the business out of vindictiveness, or they will steal inventory, or they will simply be bad for morale. In cases like this, it is best to work out an agreeable period of notice and simply pay the individual to leave as soon as possible.

If an employee feels that they are being dismissed for the wrong reasons, in other words, if they do not think that you had just cause for firing them or they do not think that you have given them reasonable notice, it is possible for them to sue for what is called "wrongful dismissal." Here, they will be asking for not only the wages that they lost, but also damages for harm to them. While they have an obligation to go out and try to get a job as soon as possible, there may be some damages that have to be paid to such employees. This can apply even in situations known as "constructive dismissal," where the employer changes the employee's duties in such a way that it is obviously a demotion, designed to squeeze the employee out. This could be accomplished by changing their duties, reducing their pay, refusing to promote them and generally poisoning the work environment with the hope that the employee will simply quit. In such cases, the employee may be able to convince a court that they were fired without cause and were wrongfully dismissed, even though the employer never said, "You're fired."

Sometimes, the employee storms out. They, too, have an obligation to give notice that is reasonable, unless there is some good reason for them to simply walk off the job. So, for example, if you feel that your workplace is dangerous or that you are being asked to do something criminal or immoral, you can simply walk off without giving notice.

Any issues concerning employees are best recorded in writing and kept in the employee's file. All of this material will be required as evidence if lawsuits are started. If it looks like there is going to be trouble with an employee, it is best to speak with a qualified employment law lawyer to get some advice on how best to move an unwanted employee out of your workplace with minimal disruption to your business, minimal damage to your business and minimal likelihood of them suing you for damages for wrongful dismissal.

Part 7 — Corporate Crime

While I do not have the space to review every possible corporate criminal offence, I think it would be beneficial to at least review some of the criminal pitfalls and land mines that Canadian business people may encounter. It is easy to forget, in the heat of the moment, that some business practices go a little too far and can result in criminal charges.

As you go out there to carry on business, consider the following:

- There is heightened interest in environmental protection, and businesses must be careful to ensure that their products do not contaminate the environment. The release of harmful substances, whether by way of an accidental spill or deliberate dumping, can result in charges, not just against the company but against the directors personally.

- Fraud is a term that comes up often in the business community. Doing something as simple as writing a cheque that you know will bounce can result in criminal charges.

- Multi-level marketing and pyramid selling can attract the interest of the local police and officials in the federal government who enforce the Competition Act.

- A wide variety of selling practices are illegal, including advertising a product for sale at one price and then selling it at a higher price, putting two tickets on a product and trying to sell it for the higher price, price-fixing (whereby businesses enter into agreements to maintain a higher price level), misleading advertising, trademark violations, tricks, phony contests and other devices. These all can result in charges, again, not just against the corporation, but also against directors in some cases.

- Charging interest at a rate of more than 60% per annum on an overdue account is considered to be a criminal act and is against the Criminal Code (See Chapter 6, Contracts—Part 10, Payday Loans).

- Threatening to have someone charged with a criminal offence if they do not pay money that is owed to you is, in itself, an offence and is considered a form of extortion.

- Last, but not least, the practice of falsifying books, records and documents in order to defraud someone, such as Canada Revenue Agency, is a fast way to find yourself charged with a crime.

If you are convicted, sentences can range from absolute discharge (which is really no punishment at all) to fines and even imprisonment in some cases. As I said above, where it is a sole proprietorship or a partnership, the people running the business are going to end up being personally charged and may be convicted. In the case of corporations, the corporation itself, of course, will be charged, but if the directors were intimately involved in the commission of criminal offences, they may be charged as well. This is not a subject to take lightly, and if there is any hint that criminal charges will be laid either against your company, you or your partners, consult with an experienced criminal law lawyer immediately.

Part 8 — Bankruptcy

No one wants to go bankrupt, but sometimes things just do not work out. Maybe a customer of the business went bankrupt and could not pay a bill, thereby triggering a domino effect. A number of Canadian businesses were seriously damaged during the SARS crisis, and after the terrorist attacks in September 2001 cross-border business dried up and bankruptcies resulted.

Bankruptcy is never automatic. Someone has to do something to force the issue. Maybe a creditor will force it, although this is rare. Maybe the business itself will voluntarily decide to go bankrupt, or maybe the business has made a proposal to its creditors and the creditors have not accepted it and then a bankruptcy occurs. Bankruptcy is always caused when the business is "insolvent," or does not have enough assets or money to pay its debts as they come due.

To go bankrupt, a trustee in bankruptcy is required. This person, who is specially trained and licensed, will gather up and sell the assets of the business, if any, and distribute the proceeds to creditors. Will the creditors get ten cents on the dollar? Thirty cents on the dollar for the money that they are owed? Often, creditors get a fraction of what they are owed, if anything. Once the business is discharged from the bankruptcy, all debts are wiped out and everyone starts over.

To give you an idea of the scale of this problem, in 2005 the number of business bankruptcies was lower than previously, but still 7,519 Canadian businesses went bankrupt. By comparison, that same year in Canada, 84,638 individual consumers declared bankruptcy. That is a lot of bankruptcies.

Remember the advantages and disadvantages of incorporating as opposed to carrying on as a sole proprietorship or a partnership? Well, this is where it really is an advantage to be incorporated. If you have been in a sole proprietorship or a partnership and you are forced to go bankrupt, your personal assets are on the line. Your home, your RRSPs, your bank accounts, everything that you have will go to pay creditors. The trustee in bankruptcy will ensure that every available asset is used to pay the debts. However, if you were incorporated, that will shield those assets from your creditors, unless, of course, you personally guaranteed the corporate loans, in which case you can be sued on that personal guarantee and your assets are then made available to creditors. Similarly, if you did not pay some of those government bills that came due for such things as GST or employee source deductions, you personally may be responsible as a director to pay those amounts.

If you are facing financial problems in your business, talk to your creditors. Get advice from a lawyer and from your financial institution. No one wants a business to go bankrupt. Creditors will often work with a business to try and ensure it is successful over the long run. In some cases, I have seen creditors either buy or become a partner in a business that is in trouble, simply to ensure that it carries on its business until it gets through the rough period, thereby enabling it to pay its bills.

Sometimes the response of the creditors depends on whether they are *secured creditors* or *unsecured creditors*. A secured creditor is one who obtained a written promise from the business to get some property or collateral if the money is not repaid. An unsecured creditor does not have collateral and is, therefore, more exposed.

On the flip side, some creditors are suppliers who may have been delivering inventory to the business and are worried that they will lose the materials and not be paid for them when the business that has received them goes bankrupt. A business in such a position, that is having just supplied some goods to a business that appears to be going bankrupt, must act quickly and try to take repossession of those goods within ten days. For this reason, if you are a business person supplying products to other businesses and your bills are not being paid, your antennae should be vibrating. Do not end up supplying products to a business that then goes bankrupt. The material you supplied may become a part of their inventory that is sold to pay their debts, instead of returned to you.

If you need another wake-up call then take a look at those bankruptcy numbers again and see the number of consumer and business bankruptcies every year in Canada. Do not be caught in someone else's bankruptcy.

Part 9 — Insuring Against Risky Business

Lots can go wrong when you are in business. A business person, however, can have fewer sleepless nights if they have taken steps to guard against unforeseen disasters, which can always be lurking around the corner. Fires, storms, power failures and all kinds of other risks are a part of life. Without insurance such disasters can wipe a business out.

Property insurance can give you insurance coverage on your premises, equipment and inventory and even your business records. Make sure you read not only what is covered by the insurance policy, but also what is not covered. Obviously, no one expects to have coverage to protect them from the ordinary wear and tear on their business premises and equipment over time, but it can come as a shock to find out that your policy does not cover damage resulting from a mechanical or an electrical breakdown that ruins your inventory. Read the fine print— that's why they make it so small!

Business interruption insurance can reimburse you for lost earnings, lost profits and any extra expenses that result from an event that prevents you from carrying on business on your regular business premises.

Other forms of general insurance protect your business from lawsuits that may be launched over defective products that you have sold, situations where customers are injured on your premises, liability for negligence and even, in some cases, damage caused by accidental discharge of pollutants. Again, it is important to check to make sure that the coverage provided gives you the protection that you need.

A valuable form of insurance for a business is directors' and officers' liability insurance. This can give directors and officers of the corporation a little bit of peace of mind in the event that they end up being sued by shareholders of the company, creditors of the company, or even employees of the corporation who are dissatisfied with some action taken by the directors of the company.

Most business people try to have a disability insurance policy so that if something serious happens to them and they are unable to work for a period of time, the insurance policy covers their lost income until they are able to recover. Sometimes a business will want to insure the life of a key person in the corporation. If that key person dies and the company is unable to operate without their participation, the life insurance can replace the lost profits. It is easy to forget about this kind of insurance coverage early on when a business is just starting. Profits may be thin or non-existent, and the last thing on a business person's mind is paying extra money for insurance policies. That is an understandable attitude. However, once a business is on its way to success, some accident or disaster should not be allowed to derail your otherwise successful business plan. Insurance offers exactly the safety net that you may need. The minute you can afford it, get it.

Part 10 — Workplace Privacy

Running a business has some tough moments, and I do not just mean the financial risk of investing. In a business, the long hours and the stress of building something from the ground up can be really hard work. Starting a business certainly has its rewards, but let's face it, very little comes easy. Unfortunately, a new and growing challenge for some businesses is the need to monitor customers and employees in the place of business. Surveillance cameras are becoming very common and are almost taken for granted in many workplaces. No one is surprised to see a camera in a bank or even at the cash register at the corner store. As of the writing of this book, the City of Toronto is experimenting with cameras on the streets to monitor potential criminal activity.

The question that arises is: do businesses have the right to install cameras on their premises to monitor customers and employees? In dealing with this issue, I am only going to focus on the non-unionized workplace because issues of privacy in unionized workplaces are governed by collective agreements.

For the non-unionized workplace, the answer to the question is yes, business owners do have the right to put these cameras in their place of business, provided there is a good reason to do so and provided it is done in a reasonable way. When assessing the reasonableness of what a business owner is doing, the focus is on whether the customer or employee has a *reasonable expectation of privacy* in that particular location. For example, in the lobby area or at the customer service desk or at reception, customers and employees probably do not have a reasonable expectation of privacy. These are public areas. However, in a washroom or in the privacy of a locker room, employees probably do have a reasonable expectation of privacy, so it would not be reasonable to put cameras in those locations to monitor their activities.

This is why we see signs posted notifying the public and employees that an area is being monitored by cameras. The whole point of advising people of the cameras is to *remove* any reasonable expectation that they enjoy privacy in that particular area. If a business wants to reduce the likelihood of being challenged for the placement of cameras, the bigger the sign advising of the surveillance, the better.

Other methods of surveillance are also cropping up in the workplace. It is, of course, against the law to record private communications between two other people, unless the people involved have consented. It is not uncommon to have employees sign contracts waiving their entitlement to privacy in certain circumstances. We have all heard the warning given on some telephone service lines that "calls may be monitored for the purposes of ensuring customer satisfaction." In those situations, employees have been told that telephone calls are going to be recorded, and they will have consented to that in their employment contracts. Surreptitious recording of employees is simply not permitted.

Modern computer systems allow for the monitoring of activities on computers, right down to particular keystrokes. The employer owns the computers, and employees do not enjoy a special right of privacy in the use of the business' computers. This means that a business is entitled to monitor the use of the computer equipment without the employee's consent and an employee has no reasonable expectation of privacy in the use of that computer in the workplace.

Last and not least, it is sometimes necessary for businesses to search their employees' work desks, computers or even lockers. Again, these are all property that belongs to the employer who is entitled to access to it without the employee's permission. Searching the physical person of the employee, however, is another matter and should not be undertaken without the employee's consent. If an employer, for some reason, suspects that an employee is in possession of company property, the proper course is to ask the employee to voluntarily participate in a search of their person or, for example, purse. If the employee declines, the employer may have their answer.

Privacy in the workplace is evaporating before our eyes and the places within an office in which an employee has a reasonable expectation of privacy may soon be confined to the washroom cubicle. Sad, but true.

Conclusion

In the above ten sections, I have tried to answer some of the typical questions that arise concerning businesses in Canada. I have really just scratched the surface in answering questions ranging from the appropriate vehicle to carry on business through to the responsibilities of being an employer, corporate crime and some of the challenges facing business people. It is always a good idea to consult an experienced business lawyer when making some of these important decisions.

Chapter 6

10 Things You Absolutely Need To Know About Contracts

Canadians enter into contracts every day. Some are written and some are not. We may sign an elaborate Agreement of Purchase and Sale for our dream home or condo; we sign very detailed leases for vehicles, credit card applications, separation agreements, marriage contracts, employment contracts, and we enter into a contract every time we buy a product. In this chapter, I would like to demystify the basic elements of contracts and examine some of the situations in which Canadians may find themselves when they sign or verbally commit to a contract.

Part 1 — Making and Breaking Contracts

It is a bit of a popular misconception that if something is not in writing it is not enforceable. The Canadian justice system has long recognized that contracts can be in writing, or they can be verbal agreements. There are a couple of exceptions but, for the most part, whether something is in writing or not, if three basic elements of contract law are present (and can be proved to the satisfaction of a judge), then a contract will be enforceable.

The three basic elements are:

* Someone must make an offer;
* Someone must accept the offer;
* There must be what is known as "consideration" or "value" given for the agreement.

The "offer" and "acceptance" parts are easy to understand (eg. I want to buy this computer for $500). That is clearly an offer. A person who is selling a computer accepts that offer by communicating to the person who made the offer that they accept the $500. Offer plus acceptance and then some value flowing between the parties will seal the deal. In the case of buying a computer for $500, the payment is the consideration. Pretty easy, isn't it? Those are the basic components of enforceable contracts. Now, let's look at some of the additional interesting things that can go on around those basics.

There are limitations on who can enter into contracts, and some of them may seem more obvious than others. Our courts are prepared to enforce agreements that are entered into between people who are mentally competent. If a mentally ill person wandered into a showroom for luxury automobiles and managed to plunk down a $1,000 deposit for the purchase of an expensive car, the court would not enforce that agreement because the person did not know what they were getting into. The same thing applies if someone is intoxicated or under the influence of drugs. There was a time when the courts would not let convicts enter into contracts, but that has changed, and they are now free to enter into contracts—sometimes over the Internet! Infants have always presented a problem for the courts. The starting point is that a person under the age of majority cannot enter into a binding contract but, over time, the courts have been prepared to enforce contracts that are in the interests of the infant or young person. So, for example, where a person under the age of majority enters into a contract for employment on terms that are actually beneficial to the child, the court may enforce that. Similarly, if a child was forced to enter into a contract for necessities of life (food, shelter and so on) because the parent is not providing it, the court has been prepared to enforce those types of contracts. The bottom line seems to be that if a contract is bad for a young person, the court will treat it as being a void contract and unenforceable. On the other hand, if there is some merit to the contract for the young person, the court will often try to find a way to enforce it, or at least let the contract be voidable at the option of the young person.

It comes as a shock to most people in modern society that there was a time when a married woman was not allowed to enter into a contract, unless it was ratified or approved by her husband.

Corporations have the ability to enter into contracts. A representative or agent for a company, or any partners in a partnership, can make a binding agreement for the business. However, it is possible, in some circumstances, for corporations to place limitations on the ability to contract unless there is specific approval by one specific person. So, when dealing with a corporation, it is best to make sure that the person you are negotiating with actually has authority to bind the company to a contract.

Someone once asked me if it was possible for a person to enter into a contract with themselves and then breach the contract and sue themselves for damages. They would then consent to a judgment against themselves and try to claim on an insurance policy. This person has too much time on their hands and needs to understand that you cannot enter into a contract with yourself. The only time you can have a contract with yourself applies to land, because in some limited circumstances a person who owns land in joint tenancy with another person may "sell" the land to themselves, thereby severing the joint tenancy. This is a little known way for two people who own a property in joint tenancy to break it. For more information on joint tenancies and tenancy-in-common, see Chapter 7, Real Estate—Section 10, Forms of Ownership.

An expression heard from time to time in the area of contract law is "privity of contract." The people who enter into a contract are considered to be privy to the contract. Only they may enforce the agreement or complain about non-compliance with the agreement. Someone who was not a party to the contract does not have "privity of contract" with the other people and can do nothing to enforce it or complain about it. This could arise in a situation where two companies enter into a contract and one of the businessmen does not follow through and pay for goods that he has received. The person who was supposed to have been paid may have been relying on that money to pay his own creditors. Those creditors cannot sue to enforce the original agreement between the two businessmen to force that person (who did not pay) to cough up the money. Only the parties to the contract can enforce it.

An issue that comes up from time to time concerns "fine

print." Most people hate that expression because it usually means that they missed something in a contract that is now making their lives difficult. If a contract is in writing and it has fine print, and you sign that contract, then you have agreed to the fine print. Just because the font is smaller than the rest of the words, it does not mean that it is not binding on you. You are presumed to have read it. However, the courts have been prepared to relieve some people from the obligation created by fine print if the person who benefits from the fine print did not take time to draw the fine print to your attention. Car rental companies ask you to initial certain parts of the rental agreement. That is their way of drawing to your attention certain fine print and making it binding on you.

In certain circumstances, the court will be prepared to throw a contract out if it turns out that one of the parties was under a serious misapprehension about the meaning of the contract or the contents of the contract. This misapprehension usually comes about because of a misrepresentation made by somebody else. Similarly, if the contract was entered into because somebody was forced into it, or because they were under inappropriate influence, then the contract may not be enforceable. If a court concludes that it would be grossly unfair to a person to enforce a contract against them, they may let them out. All of these things suggest that it is probably a good idea to have a lawyer double-check everything someone tells you about the meaning of an important contract. Do not let people pressure you into signing things that you may later regret, and if a contract is grossly unfair to you, or grossly unfair to the other person signing the contract, it may not be enforceable at a later date.

If someone breaches a contract, there are a number of things that can be done about it. Obviously, we all know that a person can sue for damages if a contract has been breached, but you may not be aware that it is also possible to sue somebody and force them to comply with the agreement. That is known as suing for "specific performance." In that case, you do not care about getting damages. You want someone to perform the contract as originally agreed. Sometimes it is necessary to sue for an "injunction" to stop someone from doing a certain thing in a contractual relationship. It is also possible to sue for something known as "rescission." If the contract was entered into due to a misrepresentation or that undue influence that I discussed above, then the court may rescind the contract.

Those are the basic rules of contract law. In upcoming sections in this chapter, we will look at some of the special contracts and special rules that people may encounter, including employment contracts, domestic agreements, unlawful agreements and some special considerations concerning consumer agreements.

Part 2 — Contracts for the Purchase and Sale of Land

I touch on the importance of Agreements of Purchase and Sale in Chapter 7, which deals with real estate, but in this section I want to look at it from a contractual point of view. Buying or selling a home can be the biggest contract of our lives, and it is important to understand how these contracts work.

The importance of contracts for the purchase and sale of land reaches back as far as 1677 to a British law known as the Statute of Frauds. This ancient statute provides that an agreement to make or create an interest in land, or to make an agreement for the sale of land, must be in writing. This means that oral agreements concerning the purchase and sale of land are unenforceable.

In a recent case, a man and his wife got into financial trouble, and they were worried that they might lose their home to creditors. As a precaution, they transferred their home to a friend on the "understanding" that when their financial troubles blew over, the home would be transferred back to them. There was nothing in writing. You guessed it—when they asked for the home to be transferred back, their friend refused, and the court was unable to help them.

Transfers and title documents for property and in particular, mortgages and other forms of security registered against land, can be very, very detailed. Even the Agreements of Purchase and Sale now have pages of standard form clauses and conditions designed to cover every possible aspect of a purchase or sale of real estate.

Take a look at Chapter 7, Real Estate Law—and in particular, Section 1, Buying and Selling a Home, for a more detailed explanation of some of the terms required for contracts related to land.

Part 3 — Employment Contracts

Taking on an employee can be a great deal of responsibility for an employer. There is no law that states that employees must sign contracts, but it is certainly recommended for any position beyond the most basic job. A standard form contract would certainly be recommended for all employees. Whether a written contract is completed or not, however, there is a long list of rights and responsibilities between employers and employees that is provided by law. Employers have the obligation to pay the employee, to provide a safe workplace, to provide any tools that the employee might need to do the job, to provide supervision, to ensure that there is no harassment in the workplace and so on. Employees, on the other hand, are obliged to show up and do their job and to be competent while they are doing it. They have an obligation to not be insubordinate in the workplace and to take direction from their employer. Employment standards law provides most of the terms of importance to the employee, such as minimum hourly wages for their work, maximum hours to be worked, statutory holidays and benefits that must be paid. These are all stipulated by the laws of the various provinces and territories.

Sometimes, however, there is a need to go above and beyond what the law provides and include more extensive terms in an employment contract. Some employee positions involve a great deal of responsibility and are more involved and complicated than others. Sometimes the method of compensation is complicated or related to the employee's performance. Provincial laws do not contemplate that type of compensation, so it must be set out specifically in a contract. In other cases, the employer and the employee may want to include special provisions concerning when the employment begins and when it ends, and in particular, how much compensation (eg. the infamous "golden parachute") will be paid if the contract is terminated prematurely. There can be many reasons for a written employment contract, particularly in today's knowledge-based economy.

If an employment contract is needed, some recommended terms would include such things as:

• The parties to the contract—who is the employer and who is the employee. This may seem obvious, but, in some cases, the employer can be a division or a subdivision of a larger company, and the employee may wish to be described a certain way;

• The contract should provide a detailed job description;

• The contract should state when the position begins, how long it is expected to last and the circumstances under which it may come to an end;

• If the employment position is one for which the employer wants to "check out" the employee for a period of time in advance, it may be appropriate to include a probationary period. This would need to be set out specifically in the contract;

• Of course, remuneration and how it is calculated should be set out in a contract. If there are commissions or bonuses, it is advisable to not only set out what those commissions and bonuses are, but also to set out some examples of how they would be calculated.

There can be a long list of such details included in a written employment contract. Four, however, are of particular importance: non-solicitation provisions; confidentiality provisions; non-competition terms; and ownership of intellectual property.

The need for these types of provisions has arisen because some employees have access to sensitive business information. That information can encourage competitors to "hire away" those employees along with their information on business secrets and client contacts. Employers have begun to insist that written employment contracts include an agreement by the employee to non-solicitation in the event that they leave the company. This means that the employee is prohibited from either contacting or soliciting the employer's clients for a specific period of time after leaving the company.

Another term included in an employment contract is a confidentiality provision whereby the employee agrees not to disclose certain types of information that the employer wants to keep secret.

The third type of provision concerns non-competition and stipulates that a former employee will not be permitted to compete with an employer for a specific period of time. In some cases, this non-competition provision refers not only to a period of time, but also to a geographic area.

A good example of this type of problem is a case concerning two dentists. These dentists agreed to share an office, with the senior dentist referring patients to the junior dentist. The junior dentist, in exchange for this arrangement, agreed that if he ever left the shared practice, he would not open a dental office within a five-mile radius of the senior dentist for at least three years. You can imagine what happened. After a little over a year, the junior dentist moved out and opened up a practice right within the five-mile radius. The senior dentist sued the junior dentist for breach of the non-competition clause, but the court thought that the clause was too broad and refused to enforce it. The courts have been reluctant to inhibit employment opportunities too much by these clauses, but certainly if a clause is in writing, specific, justified and reasonable, the court will enforce it.

Another term that is now being used regularly in employment contracts concerns inventions and intellectual property created by employees during the course of their work. Employers are now including terms in employment contracts stating that the employer has exclusive ownership of the employee's inventions created using the employer's resources, even where the invention falls outside the normal scope of the employee's regular duties. In this way, the employer captures all of the benefits of employee brainwaves. Without this type of provision in an employment contract, the court may very well find that the employee gets to keep ownership of any inventions conceived during employment.

Part 4 — Domestic Contracts

Even our personal relationships can be governed by contracts. Whether we are marrying or separating, contracts can play a very important role. There are four types of contracts which can govern our personal situation:

i) Marriage contracts;
ii) Cohabitation agreements;
iii) Separation agreements; and
iv) Paternity agreements.

Under Canadian law, the requirements for such a contract are very straightforward. There is no requirement that a person have independent legal advice prior to signing such a contract. In order to be valid, a domestic agreement must be in writing, signed by the parties to it and witnessed. Let's look at each of these contracts separately.

i) Marriage contracts

A marriage contract is often referred to as a "pre-nuptial" or "pre-nup" agreement. The expression "pre-nuptial" is related to the fact that this kind of contract is often signed before the nuptials or wedding ceremony. However, many couples sign their contract after the marriage has taken place. A marriage contract is designed to provide a "tailor-made" description of rights and obligations during the marriage and in the event that the marriage comes to an end. Marriages can end through separation and divorce, but they are also terminated by the death of a spouse. This means that when lawyers are involved in the drafting of marriage contracts, they are not only helping the couple negotiate the terms of the marriage, but also what will happen in the event that one of them dies or they are divorced. Marriage contracts often work in conjunction with a couple's wills and estate plans.

The terms that people put in marriage contracts typically relate to property division. Someone has a particular asset, perhaps an inheritance or a valuable item that they wish to ensure is not divided in the event of separation and divorce. Spouses are also able to deal with the question of spousal support in the event that the marriage ends. From time to time, lawyers will see a couple include terms in a marriage contract related to sexual fidelity or recognition that the couple will have sexual partners outside of the marriage. If the marriage is going to involve one spouse bringing in children from a previous relationship, there can be terms about how those children will be treated, supported, educated and disciplined (or not disciplined) by the new step-parent. Just about anything can be included in a marriage contract, but there are a couple of exceptions. There are some things that a court will not allow a couple to put in a marriage contract. The court will not enforce an agreement whereby a couple tries to set out in advance who will have custody of the children in the event of separation and divorce. Similarly, the law does not allow a couple to agree to child support in advance of separation and divorce. If the couple eventually separates, the court will simply apply the law to the question of custody and child support as it sees fit at the time.

The same is not true for spousal support. A couple may include in a marriage contract an agreement to waive an entitlement to spousal support in the event the marriage ends in separation and divorce, or they may set out some predetermined formula for how spousal support will be calculated if the marriage does not last. This type of contract can be tricky to negotiate and lawyers recommend that the couple begin their discussions well in advance of the wedding ceremony.

ii) Cohabitation agreements

More and more Canadian couples are choosing to live in what are commonly referred to as common-law relationships. The definition of a common-law relationship differs from province to province but essentially it means that the couple are living together as spouses but have chosen not to marry. One estimate has suggested that by the year 2020, half of all unions in Canada will be common-law and half will be legal marriages. This is a very dramatic turnaround from just a few decades ago. Common-law couples are able to regulate their relationship in exactly the same way as legally married couples by way of a cohabitation agreement. All of the same rules apply as in a marriage contract and all of the same prohibitions apply. In other words, the couple can provide for such things as property division, spousal support and rules for how the relationship will operate. But they cannot provide for custody of children and child support. In all respects, cohabitation agreements are exactly the same as marriage contracts and, by the way, if you sign a cohabitation agreement while living common-law and then get married, it is automatically turned into a marriage contract.

iii) Separation agreements

It would appear that 30 to 40% of Canadian marriages will end in divorce. In addition, common-law relationships appear to be even more volatile than legal marriages and many end in separation. In either case, when the relationship ends, the parties to the relationship have a choice. They can either slug it out in court and get a court order deciding how they will manage custody and access of their children, child support, property division and spousal support, among many things, or they can negotiate a contract into which they place all of the terms upon which they agree for ending the relationship and resolving these issues. The majority of Canadian separations and divorces, for legally married couples and for common-law couples, are concluded by way of these domestic contracts—the separation agreements. In the agreement, the parties set out the history of the relationship, the names and birthdates of their children and their agreement with respect to the custody and access of their children, levels of child support, division of property, levels of spousal support (if any), releases of property and so on. Generally, these agreements are negotiated with the assistance of lawyers and are concluded with both parties obtaining independent legal advice. The independent legal advice helps ensure that the parties cannot back out of the agreement at a later date because they didn't understand some aspect of it. Again, there is no legal requirement for independent legal advice, but it helps to make the contract a little more "bulletproof" if someone changes their mind later on.

iv) Paternity agreements

These agreements are probably the least common of the domestic contracts. In a paternity agreement, a man and a woman, who are not spouses, agree upon paternity of the child in question and upon such things as the payment of expenses of a child's prenatal care and birth, ongoing support for the child or even funeral expenses of the child or mother if things take a very bad turn during birth.

There is one aspect of all domestic contracts that is different from all other contracts—their enforceability. Family law lawyers cannot provide a 100% guarantee that a domestic contract—even one signed with independent legal advice—will be enforced by a court. The courts reserve the right to set aside these agreements, and while they do not use that power lightly, they will do so in limited circumstances. For example, a court may set aside a valid domestic contract for the following reasons:

- one of the people involved in the negotiation of contract failed to disclose an important asset or liability;
- one of the people did not understand the nature of the contract; or
- any other reason that would be acceptable in the general law of contract.

This has generally meant that marriage contracts, separation agreements, or cohabitation agreements will be set aside if the couple signing it did not have all the important facts before them. Many lawyers will not allow clients to sign domestic contracts unless each person has provided a sworn financial statement setting out all their assets and liabilities. If, for some reason, whether deliberate or accidental, an asset or a liability has not been disclosed, the couple risks the agreement being thrown out.

Similarly, if the couple did not understand some aspect of the separation agreement, or if they signed it not understanding exactly what was intended, then the court may throw it out. For example, in one case, a man prepared a handwritten summary of how he thought their marriage contract should be prepared. He had his wife sign that summary and a friend witnessed the signatures. The wife thought she was signing *instructions to a lawyer* to prepare a draft contract. When the husband went to see a lawyer, he was told that technically what they had already was a marriage contract! The court would not enforce it though, as she did not understand that it was actually a contract.

As discussed earlier, there are many reasons for contracts to be set aside by the court. If the parties were under a misapprehension, if there was a fraud or if there is some sort of public policy reason that a contract should not be enforced, then the courts will set aside the agreement.

There's one last reason for throwing out a domestic contract and it is one that is unique to family law. It involves religious divorces. The Divorce Act and some provincial laws have unique provisions concerning Jewish divorces. In order for Jews to divorce, the husband must give and the wife must receive what is known as a "get." The "get" is a contractual release from the religious marriage. Without it, Jews cannot remarry within their faith. For particular religious reasons in Judaism, the husband is under no obligation to provide the "get." In some cases, when the family separated, the "get" was used to unfairly pressure a woman into an inappropriate settlement. The laws were changed to state that if the negotiation of a separation agreement had been affected in any way by improper reference to the husband giving a "get," then the court would reserve the right to throw out the agreement. The Divorce Act refers to one of the spouses "refusing to remove barriers that would prevent the other spouse's remarriage." But what it is referring to is the "get." One more curious twist for domestic contracts in the family law area.

Part 5 — Lawyer Contracts

Of course, lawyers could not call the contract that you sign to hire a lawyer a "contract." We call them "retainers." The vast majority of lawyers will have their clients sign a contract at the time they are hired to do work. This contract can come in a number of forms. Many law firms use a standard form contract/retainer agreement. This agreement will identify the lawyer who is doing the work, the client who is hiring the law firm, the work that the law firm is agreeing to do on behalf of the client, the hourly rate that is being charged (or block fee, if that is the case) and expectations for when the work will be completed. It may also go on to identify other lawyers, articling students or law clerks who will work on the case and their respective hourly rates. It will also, likely, set out the law firm's fees and disbursements policy. This will include a statement that law firms often disburse money on behalf of a client and these disbursements are billed directly to the client to be covered as they are incurred.

In most litigation (that is, cases that are going to court), lawyers will ask clients to provide an advance on account of fees and disbursements. To make matters confusing, lawyers refer to that amount also as a "retainer." The retainer is deposited into the law firm's trust account and held there to be applied against bills or other expenses that are incurred during the course of the work that is being done on behalf of the client. This retainer amount can range anywhere from $500 to $50,000, depending on the complexity of the work that is involved.

Some lawyers are prepared to do their work on behalf of a client on a "contingency fee basis." Contingency can mean a number of things, depending on where in Canada you are retaining a lawyer. The contingency relates to not only a percentage of the money recovered, but also the success of the work being done. A true contingency fee, therefore, is a statement by the lawyer that they will only charge a fee to the client if the lawyer is successful with the case. If successful, the fee that will be charged is a percentage of the money recovered on behalf of the client. Contingency fee arrangements are notorious across the United States, and I have even heard of one situation where a law firm in Florida charged a 66% contingency fee to recover damages for a motor vehicle accident victim. In Canada, we do not see that type of high contingency fee arrangement. It is not uncommon for a lawyer to stipulate that 30% of the recovery will be applied to fees and disbursements incurred—if the lawyer is successful.

It is this part of the contingency retainer that is important to understand, because many people think that contingency fee arrangements increase the likelihood of lawyers suing other people. Most lawyers or law firms are not prepared to undertake long, expensive cases on behalf of clients, unless there is a very reasonable prospect of success. Lawyers, generally, are not prepared to "tilt at windmills," hoping that they will recover millions of dollars in speculative or experimental litigation. If anything, Canadian lawyers tend to be quite conservative in their use of contingency fees. In my experience, most of the contingency fees have been used to allow a lawyer to proceed with a case that, in all likelihood, will be successful, but where the clients cannot afford to provide the retainer in advance. Imagine the case, for example, of a young man injured in a farming accident. His family did not have tens of thousands of dollars to provide to a law firm in order to sue the manufacturer of the equipment that had caused the injury. The law firm was confident that they would eventually be successful and they, therefore, agreed to underwrite the litigation on behalf of the injured man, knowing that when they were successful, they would then be paid. The fee that they were paid when they won the case compensated the lawyers not only for the work that was done, but also for taking on the risk of the litigation, because there is always a chance that it will be unsuccessful. Contingency fees are, therefore, designed not only to compensate lawyers for the work done, but also for the risk undertaken on behalf of clients.

In the area of class actions, which can involve hundreds of millions of dollars, the courts have been careful in the use of contingency fees. There has been close supervision of the fees recovered by lawyers using contingency fee arrangements in successful class actions. In one case, I heard of a law firm that began to specialize in a particular form of class action. They were representing thousands of clients and the case involved millions and millions of pages of documents. It was necessary for that law firm to make an investment of nearly $100,000 in technology for their law firm in order to handle one case. They were pursuing that case on a contingency fee basis and, therefore, made that investment in technology in the expectation that someday they would be successful with the litigation and would recover enough in fees to reimburse themselves for the technology investment as well as for the time that they had spent on the case.

The contract used to hire a lawyer is, therefore, a special one, not just because we do not call it a "contract," but because you are hiring a lawyer to protect something that is important to you. It is, therefore, very important to not only pin down who is doing the work for you and exactly what your expectation is of the lawyer and what your expectation is in terms of costs. There is no point in hiring a lawyer and spending $25,000 on legal fees and disbursements to recover $24,000 in a judgment. Lawyers and clients must always work together to be mindful of netting the appropriate amount of money as the litigation proceeds.

In addition, lawyers are subject to solicitor-client privilege and we must keep all information delivered to us in absolute confidence. We may only release information concerning the work that we are doing on behalf of the client with their permission. We may breach our solicitor-client privilege only in circumstances where it would prevent the commission of a criminal offence or where we become aware of a genuine risk of child abuse. Lawyers cannot be forced to breach their solicitor-client privilege by way of court order.

Because of issues concerning identify fraud, law firms are now asking clients to produce photo identification at the time they sign contracts with the law firm. This is to ensure that we are opening files on behalf of genuine clients with genuine problems. This requirement for identification has been prompted mostly by the explosion in real estate fraud, where criminals used law firms to process mortgages using fictitious identification.

Make sure when you hire a lawyer that you incorporate all of the important terms into your contract.

Part 6 — Internet Contracts

In Section 1 of this chapter, we considered the basic components required for a contract—offer, acceptance and consideration. All of these elements can be achieved online and it is quite possible to form a legally binding contract on the Internet.

Most websites where you can make purchases will require a consumer to move through a variety of pages that have a box with "I Agree." By clicking on the "I Agree" button, the consumer is accepting terms of a potential contract. I have to admit, I have been guilty myself of making some hasty Internet purchases. Fortunately, to date, I have not been burned, but I have clicked through many pages on Internet sites without reading all of the terms and conditions. I have given my credit card number to companies in the United States and, keeping my fingers crossed, have never been disappointed by a product's not arriving. But what if it had not arrived? This is the problem with contracts on the Internet. Legitimate offers are made and legitimate acceptances given. Consideration may be passed by way of a credit card. The issue is often enforcement and, in dealing with enforcement, the issue becomes, where is the person with whom I have entered into this contract? Determining where a contract has been formed will dictate where a person is able to take steps to enforce it. It is quite conceivable that a person in New Brunswick could enter into a contract online with a person on the other side of the globe. If the product is not delivered, where does the disappointed consumer go for enforcement? If it is a product of small value and the consumer obtains a judgment in Small Claims Court in Saint John, that may not impress the owner of the website in India.

Canadians have taken to e-commerce like ducks to water, and while they initially were reluctant to reveal credit card information on the Internet, this has now become less of a concern and credit card numbers are readily given. I think, once people thought about the fact that they often give their credit card number to the pizza place at the end of the street or at gas stations, they realized that there is very little difference in giving that credit card number to someone on the Internet. If the number is stolen, it is stolen. The best advice that could be given to anyone dealing with Internet contracts is only deal with reputable companies who generally have secure websites with encrypted protection for your credit card information, with well-developed privacy policies and, more often than not, a consumer complaint department that can exchange a product if you are not happy.

But, do not think for moment that you cannot enter into a valid and enforceable contract on the Internet. It is being done thousands of times a day, every day, in Canada.

Part 7 — Unlawful Contracts

Is it possible to have a contract meet all of the essential components—offer, acceptance, consideration—but still be unenforceable? The answer is yes, because sometimes people enter into contracts for things that are not allowed.

Consider the following circumstances under which people entered into contracts and decide whether you would want the courts to enforce these agreements:

- Two people enter into a contract with terms that are designed to get around the provisions of the Income Tax Act, so that one of the parties to the contract pays less tax than they are supposed to.
- Two people enter into a contract, but the consideration that is given for the contract is illegal. For example, someone pays for a kitchen renovation with cocaine.
- Two people enter into a contract that results in one of the people being required to commit an illegal act. For example, one of them is required to smuggle guns across the border.
- Two people enter into a contract that is for something legal, but it will be done in an illegal way. For example, a contractor enters into an agreement to install electrical wiring, but will be doing it completely contrary to the Building Code.
- Two people enter into a contract to commit a crime or commit a civil tort against another person. For example, people enter into a contract to spread false and libellous rumours about a politician in exchange for money.
- Two people enter into a contract to mislead and defraud prospective shareholders about the value of assets in a company.
- Two people enter into a contract understating the price of a car in a Bill of Sale in order to reduce the amount of Provincial Sales Tax payable.
- A person tries to buy a contract of insurance to protect themselves against the consequences of criminal acts

that they commit, such as assault and drunk driving.

- People enter into a contract that is offensive to public morals or our sense of decency. For example, what if a person agrees to open a restaurant that would not serve Aboriginal people?

- A newspaper enters into a contract with a corporation to not publish negative stories about the corporation in exchange for the company's buying advertising space.

- An employee is required to sign an employment contract agreeing to keep information about environmental harm caused by the company secret.

- A victim of sexual abuse is required to sign a contract agreeing to keep a financial settlement secret.

- A person enters into a contract that amounts to an agreement to be a virtual slave to a religious cult.

- Someone signs a contract agreeing to be in a private army and to submit to a paramilitary lifestyle.

- Someone enters into a contract to smuggle generic drugs across the border for resale.

- Someone enters into a contract to sell supplies to a country that Canada is at war with.

- Someone enters into a contract to work with a group that is trying to overthrow the government of one of our allies.

- Someone enters into a contract to refuse to give evidence at a trial in exchange for money, or, vice versa, enters into a contract to give evidence and lie under oath for money.

- Companies enter into agreements to not compete against each other in certain territories and to fix prices.

As you can see from all of the above cases (which are real), people have tried to enter into lots of contracts that involved an offer, an acceptance and consideration, but the courts were not prepared to enforce them, for all of the right reasons.

Part 8 — Consumer Contracts

In this section, I want to alert you to the fact that in the area of contracts, provincial legislation and some federal legislation provides consumers with special protections for certain kinds of contracts that they may enter into.

As I have said above, each province has a different consumer protection law, but they tend to try to achieve the same goals of protecting consumers from unfair exploitation.

For example, the Ontario Consumer Protection Act sets out what are considered to be unfair practices and defines a long list of false, misleading or deceptive representations that a consumer can rely on to get out of a consumer contract. So, for example, if a business sells a product by making a representation that it performs a certain way or has uses that it does not have, or contains ingredients, benefits or qualities that are not truly a part of the product, then the consumer can get out of the transaction. The list of misrepresentations is so detailed that it even includes a prohibition against stating that a product requires a part, a replacement part or a repair that it does not need. Even exaggerating the benefit of a product is considered a misrepresentation. In addition, the legislation defines unconscionable representations, which are also considered to be unfair business practices.

The net effect of the statutory list of unfair practices is that if a contract is entered into (whether written, oral or implied) because of an unfair practice, the consumer has the right to rescind that agreement and obtain damages, if necessary.

The consumer protection laws of the provinces try to tackle the typical consumer problems around such things as memberships in health clubs, modelling and talent agencies, martial arts, sports and dance services and time-share agreements (see the discussion below in Section 9).

A good example of the way in which consumer laws are intended to work and help consumers can be seen in the way the law provides, for example, a "cooling-off period," during which time a consumer may, without any reason, cancel a contract into which they have entered. The "cooling-off period" is set by provincial legislation and can be used, for example, up to ten days after the contract has been signed.

So, while we have a general law of contract—offer, acceptance, consideration—some modern consumer laws allow those contracts to be cancelled or overridden in certain circumstances.

Internet shopping, telemarketing and even mail-order shopping come with risks for consumers, so consider the following tips when you are out in the marketplace entering into consumer contracts:

- Remember, stores are not required by law to take back goods that you do not want or that you think are defective. Most stores have a refund policy and an exchange policy. Make sure you understand that before you buy or try to return a product.
- The same is true with layaway plans. Once you put down a deposit and ask a store to hold something for you, they can hold you to that contract. Before you put down money on a layaway plan, make sure you want to carry through with the purchase of that particular product.
- Never make a deposit or partial payment unless you have a written contract and a receipt for your payment. Once you give them some consideration, you may be stuck with the contract.
- Exercise extreme caution when purchasing anything over the telephone. There have been some absolutely hair-raising horror stories of people being ripped off by tele-marketing fraudsters. Red flags should go up if the person you are doing business with over the telephone offers to send a courier to pick up your money or if they ask you to wire money to them. These agreements over the telephone are binding.
- Never give a person authority over the telephone to access your bank account.
- Never give out your credit card number, bank account number, social insurance number or other personal information to somebody over the telephone.
- If someone says that you have to pay shipping and handling in order to get a free prize, trust me, it is not a free prize.

- Consumer laws in your province or territory probably contain protections that allow you to cancel contracts entered into over the telephone. Make sure you know what those rights are before you start making purchases.

- When you start to hear comments like, "Sign now or the price is going up," "You have been specially selected…" or "You have won a prize," run in the other direction.

- Canadian interest in shopping on the Internet has grown by leaps and bounds, but this is the one area that you must be absolutely extra careful, because you may be giving your credit card number to somebody on the other side of the planet without any protection.

- Remember the old chestnut—"If it sounds too good to be true, it probably is too good to be true."

- Never respond to unsolicited email offers.

- Always read the fine print on your contract. Internet contracts can have some very small print, and avoid purchasing anything unless you are able to get a full hard copy of the contract off the seller's website.

- If you ever order anything over the Internet and give your credit card number, immediately check your credit card bill to make sure that only what you ordered was charged to the card.

- Some consumer laws provide for an opportunity to get out of contracts entered into on the Internet under certain conditions. Check your provincial law to make sure you have some opportunity to get out of contracts entered into on the Internet.

- Don't be bullied by telemarketing phone call thugs. If someone is being abusive and threatening on the phone about making payments or completing a contract that seems unfair, contact a lawyer or your Consumer Protection Bureau to get some help.

Part 9 — Time-shares

I want to deal with the concept of time-shares in the chapter on contracts rather than the chapter on real estate, because a time-share is a contract for time, a licence. With it, a person buys—not real estate—but the right to have time at a property.

This idea of time-shares has been around for a very long time. It actually started in Europe, and then it was made popular in the United States in the mid-seventies. It started out as a form of affordable vacation, whereby a person buys a licence or a right to use property for a specified week each year. The period of a time-share can be anywhere from twenty years to fifty years, and the time purchased can be anywhere from a week to a number of months. The beauty, of course, of a time-share is that there are minimal, if any, ownership responsibilities. The time-share owner pays a fee, and someone else does all of the work. The idea of building up equity in a time-share is unheard of.

Time-shares became much more interesting for many people when companies began to allow time-share owners to exchange their licences. One year your time-share licence can be used in the winter for skiing and the next year, presumably, for sunning on the beach.

My own experience with time-shares has been limited to suffering through a couple of brutal presentations while on vacation. The high-pressure sales tactics (and virtual abduction of people who have unwittingly stumbled into the time-share presentation) can be quite intimidating. I never took the bait, but many do. These tactics have, in some cases, given the time-share industry a very bad name, and some provinces have moved to include time-share sales under the consumer protection legislation. For example, Ontario's Consumer Protection Act defines a time-share agreement as a consumer agreement and provides requirements for what will constitute a valid time-share agreement (for example: it must be in writing; a copy of it must be given to the consumer; and it must be made in accordance with a number of prescribed requirements). You will be relieved to know that there is a ten-day "cooling-off period" after signing up for a time-share. The Ontario legislation provides a ten-day rescission period, running from the time that a written copy of the time-share agreement is delivered to the consumer. There is also an additional right to cancel within one year after the date of entering into the time-share agreement if, for some other reason, the vendor of the time-share did not follow the rules and prescribed requirements set out in the Consumer Protection Act. Check your provincial law before buying a time-share. (Of course, outside Canada, you are on your own.)

Related to the idea of time-shares is the idea of "points," whereby points are given a monetary value. A purchaser with a fixed number of points at a certain value may use the points to purchase time at a resort in a unit that is made available by the time-share operator. Consider the following example, where a particular resort development sells points at $150 per point, but there is a requirement that there be a minimum purchase of 100 points. This would translate into a $15,000 investment for a consumer that would generate an opportunity to use the total number of points purchased on an annual basis. The points have to be used within the year of purchase and cannot be carried forward. The owner of the points acquires no equity ownership in any properties but still pays a maintenance fee associated with the number of points that have been purchased. The bottom line is that it is a "time-share on points," but it comes in the form of points rather than a licence to use a particular unit for a particular period of time.

Time-shares and point systems are not for everyone, and I deal with them in this section concerning contracts because I have met more than one person who admitted (rather sheepishly) that they had succumbed to the pressure of a time-share presentation and purchased either a time-share or points. Unfortunately for them, their investment did not translate into more vacations at exotic locations around the world. It simply translated into an obligation to pay maintenance fees annually. If you go into this area, go in with your eyes wide open. No doubt some people have had success with their time-share—I've just never met one.

Part 10 — Payday Loans and Criminal Interest

On February 5, 2007, the Calgary Provincial Court convicted a pawnbroker after it was discovered that the pawnbroker had been gouging a couple living on a disability pension. This couple had gone to the pawnbroker to post their collection of jewellery in order to make ends meet while the husband underwent treatment for cancer. They borrowed $2,000. How much interest do you think that they paid for borrowing that money for six months? Would you believe $6,000? The judge called the actions of the pawnbroker "deplorable" and "an oppressive abuse of the law." He was fined $7,500 and ordered to make restitution to the couple. I am not very good at math, but news reports calculated that the rate of interest on that loan was 207,000%.

The Canadian Criminal Code states, in Section 347, that it is a crime to charge interest at a "criminal rate." The section defines criminal rate as "an effective annual rate of interest calculated in accordance with generally accepted actuarial practices and principles that exceeds 60% on the credit advanced under the Agreement."

The couple who pawned their jewellery had a contract with the pawnbroker. Similarly, Canadians who use "payday loan companies" are also entering into contracts to borrow money for what is expected to be a short period of time. Unfortunately, there have been some unpleasant situations where payday loan companies have exploited borrowers.

It may surprise you to know that the payday loan industry has really exploded since the mid-nineties, and that one estimate places more than 1,300 retail outlets across Canada. It is also estimated that nearly two million Canadians per year make use of these payday loan services. The payday loan industry has even done surveys to determine who, in fact, are their customers and learned that 53% of their customers are women and 47% are men. The typical payday loan is, on average, about $280 and it is borrowed for ten days. If you look at the web pages for payday loan companies, you will note that it is possible to borrow money online, provided certain rules are met. Proper identification must be provided and access to one's bank account must be provided. The way some payday loan companies operate is to obtain a direct withdrawal authorization from a customer's bank account. Money is borrowed for a fixed period of time. After that time expires, the loan company withdraws the money directly from the borrower's bank account. So far, that may sound quite innocent. If people want to borrow a small sum of money for a short period of time, that is their own business. If they want to give somebody authority to repay the loan directly from their own bank account, I guess that is their business too, but that is not where it ends. What if the borrower cannot pay the amount back on the date that it is due? This is where a borrower can start to get into trouble, because payday loan companies are more than happy to grant extensions, *provided fees are paid to obtain the right to an extension*. When one adds the interest rate being charged by the payday loan companies and adds the fees for extensions, some borrowers have found themselves in a situation similar to that couple in Calgary who made the mistake of going to the pawnbroker.

Quite a battle has broken out over the issue of payday loans. The Consumers' Association of Canada has urged the federal government to enforce the Criminal Code. In other words, if people charge more than 60% annual interest, then they should be prosecuted under the Criminal Code. The Consumers' Association reports instances where a $300 loan for two weeks (with interest rates and charges) exceeded 1,000% per annum in interest.

Payday loan companies have been unable to organize themselves into one association. There seem to be some "good players" and some "bad players," and some of the so-called "good players" have organized themselves into an association and have called on the federal government to bring in regulations. A number of provinces have expressed interest in setting up their own method of regulating the payday loan sector, but cannot do so, as long as the federal government has a Criminal Code provision setting interest at 60% in Section 347. The Payday Loan Association has proposed that the provincial governments set maximum allowable charges and fees for payday loans at $20 per $100 that is borrowed. They say that that amount—$20 per $100 that is borrowed—will allow them to break even on their loaning operations.

The United States, the United Kingdom and Australia have all developed rules and put them in place to protect consumers,

so why Canada cannot get its act together and de
regulatory structure is a mystery. Legislation has
at the federal level to amend the Criminal Code. T
appear willing and able to protect their consumers,
the Payday Loan Association wants rules. However, ~ majority of payday loan companies are not a part of that association
and, in the meantime, they continue to charge consumers very
high rates of interest—likely in violation of the Canadian
Criminal Code—and very onerous administrative fees.

A number of class actions have been started against payday
loan companies. One seeks $555 million on behalf of con-
sumers who were overcharged. Stay tuned for more fighting in
this area.

If there is an area of contracts that you want to avoid, it is a
payday loan problem. After I read about the sentencing of the
pawnbroker in Calgary, it reminded me that we used to call that
kind of lending "loan sharking." Beware.

Conclusion

Making and breaking contracts, whether for the purchase or
sale of land, employment or getting out of a time-share purchase, can involve some fancy legal footwork. I hope the above
sections give you some insight into the basics of contractual
obligations. Don't forget, if you have a concern about a contract
that you may have signed or that you may need to break, it never
hurts to spend a few minutes with an experienced lawyer for a
little guidance. I offered you some information; you accepted
it—what's missing? Good luck!

... why Canada cannot get its act together and develop a similar regulatory structure. A two-tier... legislation has been proposed at the federal level to amend the financial code. The provinces ... willing and able to protect their consumers, and at least the ... Revised Uniform ... (Government the major ...

... comprising loan companies, attract a part of the education one of the ... insurance. ... continue to charge consumers ... with tens of interest... itself in a position of the Canadian Consumers ... and very onerous significant fees.

... A number of class actions have been started against payday loan companies. ... one for $135 million on behalf of only... alleging ... were too much risk... they should not been taking in this area ...

... If there is any line of contracts that you want to avoid, it is a payday loan problem. After I read about the case going to the Supreme Court in Calgary, it occurred to me that we used to call that kind of lending "loan sharking." Beware.

Conclusion

... Meeting and making contracts, whether on the telephone or face to face, employment, or getting out of a mess: these can involve some fancy legal footwork. I hope the above sections give you some insight into the issues of consumer obligations. Don't forget: If you have a consumer obligation that you may have signed or that you may need to break, it never hurts to spend a few minutes with an experienced lawyer for a little guidance. I offered you some information, but don't pay do what's coming? Good luck.

Chapter 7

10 Things You Absolutely Need To Know About Real Estate Law

Canadians really love their real estate whether it's in the form of their home, cottage, farm or condominium. Real estate investments involve the opportunity for financial gain, but they can also involve a great deal of risk and other assorted challenges. These purchases are among the most important and serious investments made by Canadians. In this chapter, I hope to demystify the top ten things you need to know about real estate law in Canada.

Part 1 — Buying and Selling a Home

For most of us, this is the biggest and most expensive purchase or transaction we will ever enter into. It can certainly trigger more than a few sleepless nights the first time we go through the experience. Most of these transactions occur with the help of a real estate agent, but that is not mandatory. A wide variety of methods of buying and selling property, with and without real estate agents, are now available. If you are selling a piece of real estate with the help of a real estate agent, it will be necessary to enter into a contract whereby you, the vendor of the property, agree to give the real estate agent a percentage (usually between 3% and 8%) of the purchase price if they sell the property. The amount of the commission is usually related to whether the property is listed on MLS (Multiple Listing Service), or whether it is an exclusive listing with that particular agent.

Any agreement to buy or sell land must be in writing if it is to be enforced. An oral agreement to buy or sell property is therefore not enforceable, and lawyers regularly meet clients who are frustrated and unhappy because they thought they had "an understanding" with someone else to buy or sell a piece of property. "Understandings" are not enforceable. Only written agreements are enforceable when it comes to land.

The job of the real estate agent is to find for the vendor of the property a purchaser who will then enter into yet another contract—an Agreement of Purchase and Sale. This form of contract is usually in a standard form prescribed by the local real estate board. Again, this is not a mandatory requirement, but the standard forms include many valuable clauses, and any Agreement of Purchase and Sale for a piece of real estate should use these standard forms. The Agreement of Purchase and Sale can go through many stages with offers and counter-offers being exchanged between the vendor and the purchaser. Usually each change is initialled by the parties to acknowledge how the agreement is evolving and what is agreed to or not agreed to. This can result in an Agreement of Purchase and Sale looking like a bit of a mess after several rounds of negotiations. If it has reached the point where it is becoming difficult to understand, insist that a fresh version of the form be prepared capturing the latest offer. This will avoid confusion and conflict at a later date.

The Agreement of Purchase and Sale, once concluded, will set out the key terms of the deal. These key terms include:

- the price, the description of the property and its dimensions;
- the size of the deposit (usually between 2-5%, although this deposit can be higher if it's a new home). This deposit is held in trust until the deal is concluded. The Agreement will provide what happens if the deal falls through (this usually means that the vendor will keep the deposit);
- fixtures and whether they are to remain with the property or be removed. This will deal with such things as hot water tanks, saunas and even satellite dishes.
- chattels, meaning things that can be removed without damage to the property. This might includes things like a fridge, or stove, but would not include a built-in dishwasher.

The Agreement will set out the date on which the deal is supposed to close. "To close" a real estate deal means to conclude it, whereby the money is exchanged for the keys, and the purchaser obtains possession of the property.

Other conditions will also be set out in the Agreement of Purchase and Sale. Typical conditions include: having a home inspection done, that the purchaser obtain financing or that they be allowed to sell their existing home prior to concluding the purchase. Another common condition might be that the purchaser determines whether they can assume (that is, take over) an existing mortgage on the property.

The Agreement of Purchase and Sale will also set out a date by which the potential purchasers must ask for (requisition) answers to any problems that their lawyers may discover with respect to the property. For example, there may be a concern about whether a garage was built within the property lines.

The Agreement also sets out a date that establishes a deadline for any complaints about defects related to the property.

There may be a requirement that the vendors supply a survey of the property if there is one available.

When buying or selling property, it is important to keep in mind that the cost of a real estate transaction not only includes the purchase price of the property, but also the legal fees and disbursements (that is, out-of-pocket expenses that are related to such transactions). Disbursements can include such things as Land Transfer Tax and photocopies of documents and, of course, GST is applied to any fees that are charged. There is also the possibility that the purchaser will want to buy what is called "title insurance," that is, insurance against any future defect with the title to the property that they have purchased, if discovered at a later date.

The bottom line in buying and selling real estate is to work with reliable professionals, real estate agents, lawyers, notaries, home inspectors and financial institutions—and you will have at least a few more restful nights.

Part 2 — Mortgages and Lines of Credit

Borrowing money to buy property is, in large part, what

makes it so stressful. It can be a lot of money that has to be paid back over a very long period of time. It's not uncommon for mortgages to be spread out over a twenty-five-year period. Most buyers realize that the financing of the purchase is more than simply finding the lowest monthly payment. Financial institutions have traditionally used mortgages as the way to lend people money to buy real estate. The mortgage is used to protect the financial institution's interest in the loan. More recently, mortgages are being replaced with lines of credit, where a homeowner uses a line of credit that is registered against their home, just like a mortgage. One of the differences between a line of credit and a mortgage is that the homeowner can continue to use the line of credit as they pay it off. So they may, for example, pay down their "mortgage" a little bit, discover that they have the ability to now borrow on that line of credit again and then access it, for example, to renovate the kitchen. The amount of the line of credit is capped, but the ability to borrow against the property floats up and down as the "mortgage" is paid off. This can be advantageous for some people, but for others, it may mean that they never pay off any of the principal amount borrowed because they keep accessing the line of credit secured against the equity in their home.

A common question on *Strictly Legal* is, "What happens if I can't pay my mortgage?" In some cases, a person has had an unexpected job loss or some unavoidable expense that blows the household budget. In some cases, a spouse has simply moved out and the family is going through a separation and divorce. The first thing you need to know if you are faced with this predicament is: don't panic—you have options. First and foremost, go see the bank or mortgage company and explain the situation. The bank can either allow you to defer a few payments or even rearrange your repayment schedule to make it more manageable. Remember—*the bank does not want you to fail in paying your mortgage or line of credit*. They want you to succeed, and they will often be quite flexible in keeping you afloat, depending on the cause of the financial problem. Doing nothing and letting a mortgage go into default, that is unpaid, is never an option, even though most banks won't jump on you for simply missing a payment or even two.

If the situation is serious, consult a lawyer about your next option. I know this seems hard to imagine because you are thinking, "Wait a minute, I can't pay my mortgage, but I have money for a lawyer?" Tell the lawyer your situation. They will, more often than not, understand and help you. You can always arrange to pay the lawyer later, perhaps out of the refinancing of the mortgage. Sometimes lawyers have contacts with mortgage lenders or mortgage brokers, and they can arrange a new financial solution for you.

A mortgage operates on a simple concept—the financial institution lends you money and if you don't repay the loan on a monthly basis or by whatever period you've agreed to, *the full amount becomes due and payable immediately*. If the full amount is not paid, then the financial institution may take the property. The financial institution will either keep it or sell it to pay the debt. If the sale price doesn't cover the full amount of the mortgage debt, the financial institution can then sue the homeowner for the difference (this is called "suing on the covenant"). All costs in doing this get added to your debt. And, by the way, there are a few other things that can trigger what a mortgage lender considers to be a default. These can include not paying your realty taxes, or not keeping the property insured.

The term "to foreclose" means to take the property in full satisfaction of the loan. This involves the financial institution or mortgage lender starting a legal proceeding. Foreclosure means that they can take the property in full satisfaction of the loan even if the property is worth more than the debt itself. To stop a foreclosure, the borrower can pay up what's owing on the mortgage (plus a penalty that is usually set out in the mortgage) and try to get the situation back to normal, that is, with regular monthly payments.

The borrower can also ask to pay off the mortgage in full (this is called "redeeming the mortgage"). This is usually what happens if you have a new source of funds from a new mortgage lender. You can also ask that the house be sold—either with or without the help of the court. If you do it yourself, you are more likely to get the right price. Under no circumstances should you leave that up to the mortgage company because they may simply go and sell the property under what is known as "power of sale." No legal proceedings need to be started. They have this power by virtue of the terms in the lending agreement (in the fine print). This means they can force you out of the property, take possession of it and then try to sell it on their own. You'll get notice of the sale, but this means you are not in the driver's seat and that they can sell your property at bargain basement prices.

The bottom line is that mortgage troubles are real hassles for people, and I expect that, if there is a decline in the real estate market, many Canadians will face problems paying their mortgages. The important thing to remember is to be proactive with the person who has lent the money to you. Work with a lawyer who will help you protect your property and your initial investment. This will save you grief and money in the long run.

Part 3 — Real Estate Fraud

As if Canadians didn't have enough on their plate looking after their families and their jobs and their busy lives, here is something new for property owners to worry about—real estate fraud. This has become a billon-dollar problem across North America.

How does real estate fraud happen? It happens in a number of different ways but primarily through what are known as "value frauds" and "identity frauds." A value fraud can occur when a potential purchaser with a criminal motive offers to buy a property for, say, $350,000 from a legitimate property vendor. After coming to terms, but before closing, the criminal sells the property again but to another crook for $500,000. Of course, the property is not worth $500,000, but the bank or lender does not know that, so they advance the mortgage money that is, in part, used to pay off Vendor Number One. After a few months of making mortgage payments, the criminal duo abandons the property. When the bank moves in to collect on its mortgage, it realizes that it advanced more money than the property was really worth. The criminals are long gone with the mortgage proceeds and the bank gets stuck with the loss.

The second type of fraud is called "identity fraud," and it occurs when the criminals simply forge their way onto title to your home. In some cases, they have forged your name off the property and put their name on. They then go to the bank with phony identification and get a mortgage. Once the mortgage money is advanced to them, they disappear with it. A few months later, the real homeowner gets a notice from a mortgage company asking about payments that have been missed. The financial institution then threatens to sell the property and waves around a mortgage that, lo and behold, is actually registered on title to your home!

Identity fraudsters have even gone so far as to create fake law firms and fake or steal legitimate identification of real people. In one shocking case in Ontario, the criminals faked a Power of Attorney and sold an elderly man's property to innocent buyers who had obtained a legitimate mortgage. Both the innocent buyers and the innocent mortgage company were left out in the cold when the crooks disappeared with the mortgage money.

Provincial courts and legislatures have been struggling with finding a way to protect the integrity of titled property and to put a greater onus on financial institutions when they lend money. There's no doubt that the ease with which mortgage money is being lent and the ease with which it is accessible online have contributed to some sloppy investigations by those lending money.

This problem has become so prevalent that alerts have been sent out to lawyers along with checklists to keep them aware of the patterns behind these frauds. Lawyers are now asking clients to produce photo identification. Real estate lawyers are scrutinizing transactions. If a client wants to purchase property for cash and then subsequently places a mortgage on the property, the real estate lawyer may see red flags. Lawyers are also being told to keep their eyes peeled for clients who jump from lawyer to lawyer on real estate transactions and to look at deals closely when there's no real estate agent involved. The list of clues to discovering a potential fraudster is almost three pages long, but this has still not stopped rip-off artists from slipping through the system.

Most homeowners want to know what they can do to protect themselves from these kinds of frauds. Unfortunately, there's not much that can be done. The onus is falling on the lenders of mortgage funds, banks and financial institutions. They need to be more cautious and do a more thorough investigation of the transaction for which they are lending their funds. Elderly people seem to be victimized because they are vulnerable and often have a lot of equity in their homes. Lawyers are also recommending title insurance whereby an insurance policy is purchased, often for less than $500, to indemnify the property owner against any mischief with their title, including fraud.

The bottom line is, while there may not be much that can be done, it may be worth having a word with your real estate lawyer at the time of a purchase (or refinancing) about the advisability of title insurance and making a quick check of title to your property.

Part 4 — Rights-of-way, Easements, Squatters' Rights and Restrictive Covenants

As the legal owner of property, you have the right to keep people from cutting across it or to stop people from just using it and taking it away from you, right? Well, not exactly. In certain limited circumstances, a person can lose control of their own property, or pieces of it, to people who are not owners of the property. These situations fall into three categories:

• Easements (or sometimes known as rights-of-way);
• Adverse possession (or sometimes called "squatters' rights"); and
• Restrictive covenants.

An easement can be written permission to go across a piece of land. This is used by the cable companies, telephone companies or gas companies who run cables and pipes under and over land. Most property is subject to that type of easement, and they are necessary to make modern neighbourhoods work with all the conveniences. Unwritten easements arise because someone makes use of a person's property without their permission for a long time, and the owner of the property doesn't stop them. Hikers or snowmobilers may cut across the back of farm property for years, or people may cut a path across a vacant lot to get from their home to a shopping centre. Homeowners often cross each other's driveways or properties. Crossing a neighbour's land is particularly common in cottage country where access to a remote lake or riverfront property is only possible by crossing over another person's land. If the use lasts long enough, the person cutting across the property may get a "right-of-way" over the property. Technically, it's not that the person cutting across the property gets the right to cross it, it's that the owner of the property *loses the right to stop them* from cutting across the property. The owner's rights to deny access to the property are prescribed. Hence, these are often called "prescriptive rights." How long does the use of the property need to continue? It's generally between ten and twenty years, depending on the province. How does a homeowner or property owner stop the unwanted crossing of their property? Lock it, put up signs or a fence prohibiting access. Use the trespass laws and take active steps to interrupt that ten to twenty-year period. In other words, get in the way and interrupt the period of time and the use of the property, and the easement will not arise.

Adverse possession sounds so much more civilized than "squatters' rights," but it means the same thing. Through adverse possession, someone can actually take control of a piece of another person's land. They may, for example, put their fence around a portion of another person's land. It is different from an easement, which arises because someone crosses land. Adverse possession arises because someone is actually taking control and excluding the true owner from their property. That's why the possession is called "adverse."

Adverse possession is not available everywhere in Canada and, for example, it cannot be used to obtain possession of land owned by the Crown (the government). So forget about trying to take over a part of a provincial park or a national park simply by putting up a fence. There are also different ways each province and territory keeps track of registering title to property in Canada. One system is called the Land Titles System and the other is called the Registry System. Adverse possession is not possible against land that is covered by the Land Titles System. However, it is possible to obtain adverse possession against land that is registered under the Registry System. You need to check with a lawyer in your province if you are worried that someone is trying to take control of your property.

Restrictive covenants are restrictions on the use or ownership of property, and they are registered on the title. A person may buy property and agree to abide by these restrictive terms. Your lawyer will discover them at the time of purchase when searching title to the property on your behalf. The lawyer may report to you that you can only paint your house a certain colour scheme to blend with the rest of the neighbourhood. This is a fairly modest and typical restrictive covenant. However, long ago some restrictive covenants dictated who, in terms of race or religion, could buy, or not buy, property in communities. It is not that long ago that we saw restrictive covenants that prohibited "Negroes" or "Jews" or "Turks" from purchasing property in particular neighbourhoods. The courts decided that these and other vile restrictions on ownership of property were contrary to Canadian public policy and struck them down, but lawyers still see these covenants when they search title. They're an ugly reminder of the past, but they're unenforceable.

The bottom line is that your control of your land is not to be taken for granted. Protect it from unwanted easements and, possibly, adverse possession. Restrictive covenants may surface during an attempt to buy property, and it is up to you to decide whether you want to accept them.

Part 5 — Condominums

Condominium sales are so different from regular real estate transactions that I thought it was worth including this separate section. Every province has a special law governing condominiums. This law sets the process that a developer must go through in order to register and make a condominium available for occupation. Condominium ownership is a special form of owning real estate, because the owner of the condominium has ownership of their particular unit but also owns (along with the other condominium owners) all of the parts of the condominium known as "common elements." Common elements might include such things as a parking garage, swimming pool, fitness facilities, tennis courts and, of course, the landscape areas around the building, and even the elevators. The entire condominium building is owned by a condominium corporation, and that corporation has responsibility for looking after all of the common elements. The individual unit owners are responsible only for their units, but they pay a monthly fee to the corporation to look after everything else.

Condominium corporations (and the condominiums they own) are based on two documents that must be registered with the province. These documents are the "Description" (which includes the final building plans and a survey of the property involved) and a "Declaration" (which is, essentially, a charter that will govern occupation, ownership and use of the condominium by the residents). Condominiums are governed by a set of bylaws and rules administered by a board of directors.

It is not uncommon for a condominium developer to delay construction until at least half of the units have been pre-sold. This means that purchasers of condominiums often plunk down a lot of money (by way of a deposit) based on a model suite and nothing more. Because this type of purchase can be so complicated, most provinces provide in their condominium law for a ten-day "cooling-off period," if the condo purchaser decides the deal is not for them.

The number of documents (and the way in which condo purchasers go through a different form of real estate closing) means that it is strongly advised to have a lawyer involved. Financing a condominium purchase can be tricky because, in some cases where they have been delays in registering key condo documents, the condo purchaser can move into a condominium without having received full legal title to the unit. But, generally, financial institutions will not advance mortgage funds to a condo purchaser until after the full condominium corporation is registered on title. Timing is, therefore, critical.

The good news is that if you pay attention to the details and buy a condominium from a company with a good reputation for completing the job, and you use an experienced real estate lawyer, all the complicated paperwork will be a distant memory by the time you are able to move into your brand new condominium. And oh, by the way, everything I just said applies to brand new condominiums only. Once the condominium is registered, the resale of units is much easier. But remember, with the resale there is no ten-day "cooling-off period."

Part 6 — Noxious Neighbours

Disputes between neighbours are so common that Canadian lawyers' associations put on continuing education programs every year with titles like "Noxious Neighbours" or "Nightmare Neighbours." Assuming that simply speaking with your neighbour about a problem you face has not worked, consider calling Municipal Bylaw Enforcement, particularly if the problem with your neighbour concerns noise, smells, animals or garbage. Many bylaws regulate these problems. If that has not worked, you may have a couple of options including, suing your neighbour for nuisance or simply using a little "self-help."

The three most common sources of disputes between neighbours are trees and their branches or roots, fences (where to put them) and the sharing of driveways. If you share a driveway and each of you has a right-of-way over the other person's half, there's not much either of you can do to force cooperation. One person cannot force the other to do repairs or to even shovel snow. Of course, it's impossible to force people to be considerate, and you're going to be stuck with a battle if you have an uncooperative neighbour and a shared driveway.

It can be a little better with trees and fences. In the case of trees that hang over a property, especially if they cause damage, a mess or shade, or if they have roots coming out of the ground ruining a foundation or patio, the homeowner experiencing the problem can take steps to fix or improve the situation. Branches? Cut them off at the property line. Roots? Cut or dig them out on your side. But in both cases, do only as much as is needed to solve your particular problem. Do not go overboard and, for example, kill the entire tree if that is not necessary. If the trees are on your neighbour's property and they have caused damage, then your neighbour may be responsible to you to pay for or fix the damage caused.

It is important when dealing with problems concerning trees to check with local bylaw enforcement officers first because many municipalities have now instituted restrictions on the cutting of trees. They may be part of a protected "urban forest." It is one thing to cut a few branches; it is another to cut down the tree. Even if a tree is completely on your own property, you may not be able to cut it down without a permit if it is over a certain size. And by the way, you might want to make sure that the tree you're trying to cut down isn't owned by the municipality.

Fences are supposed to make good neighbours—but that seems to be only *after* they have been erected. Deciding where a fence should go and who should pay for it can be painful for neighbours who do not know how to cooperate. The need for a fence may be more than simply decorative. If a pool is involved, local bylaws will require the erection of a fence. Sometimes it is to keep a pet from wandering, and in some cases, the fence is simply for our all-important privacy.

If you face this kind of problem involving a fence, step one is to make sure you have the property line identified accurately. This will mean checking an existing survey, or maybe even having a survey done. Once the survey is completed, stake the property line so that it is clearly identifiable. For the erection of the fence, the property line is generally the fenceline.

Who pays? Typically, neighbours should share the cost of the fence, regardless of whose idea it was to erect it. If you cannot agree on the location and the cost sharing, then call your local municipality and they will, in all likelihood, have someone come out to your property and settle both issues. If push comes to shove, you can even sue your neighbour to contribute to the cost of erecting the fence.

Bottom line: there are times in disputes between neighbours when it is simply not possible to grin and bear it, and it is necessary to involve the municipal bylaw enforcement officers, sue the neighbour, involve the police (see the section on criminal harassment in Chapter 3) and even employ a little self-help.

Your own personal safety is always the number one concern, but before you consider moving to avoid your noxious neighbour, look at the help that's available.

Part 7 — Keeping the Family Cottage

What greater pleasure can there be than enjoying a family cottage, particularly over a number of generations? The enjoyment can turn quite sour, however, if a family has to come to grips with things like "keeping it in the family" when a child's marriage is in trouble, or when Capital Gains Tax on the transfer makes it unaffordable to the children, or if disputes arise when two or more of a cottage owner's children cannot agree on how to share the place once it has been inherited.

Of course, if the cottage owner does not want the trouble of sorting these issues out, the property can simply be sold and the Capital Gains Tax paid and the net equity, if any, passed on by way of cash inheritance to children. They are then free to head off into the marketplace and buy their own recreational property, if that is what they want.

It is a little trickier when the family wants the cottage to remain in the family for a number of generations. It is not uncommon for parents to watch their children's marriages closely, not least because the last thing a parent wants to do is leave the family cottage to their son or daughter by way of their will or as a part of estate planning, only to find that the family cottage ends up being an asset that must be divided in that child's subsequent divorce. This can be avoided: the child whose marriage may be in trouble can ask the spouse to sign a marriage contract acknowledging that any inherited cottage will not be an asset for division in any subsequent divorce, but depending on the state of the marriage, this can be a tricky conversation. On the other hand, lawyers can explain to that couple that if the marriage contract is not signed, then there will be no inheritance of the cottage at all. An alternative solution is for the cottage owner to include a provision in their will that any asset left to a child of their marriage is not to be shared by that child in any subsequent separation and divorce. In other words, the parent leaving the cottage to the child can stipulate in their own will that this is a gift to the child that is not to be shared in the event of divorce. Obviously, speaking with an experienced estate planning lawyer is critical to achieve this goal.

If a parent owns a cottage and wants to leave that cottage to the next generation in their will, at the moment of death there will be a "deemed disposition" of the cottage property from the cottage owner to the owner's estate, unless some other steps have been taken to transfer that property in advance of death. One estate-planning device that is recommended in such circumstances is placing the cottage property in joint tenancy with the children, so that at the point of death of the parent cottage owner, title to the cottage property passes, by virtue of the rule of survivorship, directly to the children, outside of the estate. This effectively avoids any probate tax on the value of the cottage, although look at Chapter 3 on wills to see the future tax implications.

If payment of the Capital Gains Tax is the issue, it may be advisable for the cottage owner to purchase life insurance, the proceeds of which will pay any Capital Gains Tax accruing as a result of the transfer of the property.

Last, but not least, it is possible to transfer the property into what is called an "alter ego trust." In order to use an alter ego trust, the creator of the trust must be at least sixty-five years of age. The owner of the cottage property transfers it into the special trust without Capital Gains Tax being triggered. The creator of the trust can then maintain control of the property, and the children who are beneficiaries of the alter ego trust are able to use the property but inherit it on the death of the creator of the alter ego trust. In that way, Capital Gains Tax can be deferred until the beneficiaries want to sell the cottage, if ever. Again, it is important to talk to an experienced estate planning lawyer, as alter ego trusts require specialized advice.

If the issue for the family is disputes over co-ownership of a cottage property after the death of the owner of the cottage, the family may benefit from a co-ownership agreement that addresses responsibility for bills, repairs and even rotating possession of a cottage. These agreements can be quite comprehensive and should be drafted with the assistance of an experienced real estate lawyer who can advise the family on details that will assist them in avoiding conflict in future.

A family cottage is a valuable legacy in so many ways. A little advance estate planning can make sure that your grandchildren and great-grandchildren benefit from it as well, even if Canada Revenue Agency takes a bite along the way.

Part 8 — Marijuana Grow Houses are Coming to Your Neighbourhood

At least three Canadian police forces are publishing the addresses of busted marijuana grow houses. What? You haven't heard about the latest potential nightmare for home buyers and homeowners who rent their property? A marijuana grow house is a home that has been physically altered to facilitate the production of marijuana. The alterations include cutting into hydro power sources in order to steal the extra electricity needed to power the high-wattage lights that help the plants grow. The ventilation in the house is often reconfigured to remove the strange smells that are produced by the marijuana plants. Regular spraying of pesticides, fungicides and herbicides on the plants in very high concentrations also contributes to a chemical contamination of the premises. And, let's not forget that there is an awful lot of water used on those plants and the resulting moisture generally leaves the house with a serious mould problem.

Guess how many grow ops are in Canada? Well, the Canadian Real Estate Association estimates as many as 50,000 across the country, and climbing. These houses, and other premises, are purchased or rented by organized criminals who essentially trash the house for as long as they can get away with it and leave behind a property that may have no hope of being repaired. In some cases, the mould and structural damage is so extensive that the house must be torn down. In some cases, these criminals buy the property. In other cases, they rent or sublet from innocent people. In one case, a man had an opportunity to work abroad. He rented his home to a respectable couple who, in turn, (without the owner's permission) sublet the property unwittingly to grow op criminals. The homeowner returned from abroad to find his house ruined.

The profit is certainly attractive for the criminals. It is estimated that one residential grow op will house 1,600 plants and produce a $1.6 million profit in one year. Here are the shockers for the owners of the property: most homeowners' insurance policies will not cover the cost of repairing damage caused by this type of criminal activity, and the estimates from the Insurance Bureau of Canada suggest that the average cost of repairing a home that has been used as a grow op—if it can be repaired at all—is about $40,000.

How can you recognize a marijuana grow house? The following list is taken directly from the website of the Toronto Police (who, unfortunately, are extremely familiar with the grow house phenomenon). Consider the following:

- The house does not appear lived-in. Someone visits but only stays for short periods of time.
- Activity inside the house seems to take place at odd hours.
- The exterior appearance of the property, such as the lawn and small repairs, is neglected.
- People using the property often back into the garage and enter the home through the garage.
- Garbage is minimal and may contain used soil and plant material.
- Windows are covered.
- Bright light escapes from windows, and windows are often covered with thick condensation.
- There are sounds of interior construction.
- Timers are set inside the residence.
- There is a strong "skunk-like" odour coming from the property.
- Items being brought into the house include soil planters, fans and large lights.
- Garbage bags are not left for the regular collection, but are transported away from the property.
- In the winter, there is no snow on the roof even when other houses in the area are snow-covered.
- There are unusual amounts of steam coming from the house vents.

A surprising indicator that a property might be a grow op is not that it smells of skunk but that it smells too good. Criminals often overuse fabric softener in dryers and vents in order to mask the smell of the plants. So, an excessive or frequent smell of fabric softener in the air may actually be a clue that the property is a grow op.

The problem is so extensive that the Canada Mortgage and Housing Corporation has started to develop National Remediation Guidelines for rebuilding or restoring a property that has been used as a grow house.

Now, here is where is gets particularly frightening for potential homeowners—real estate agents do not always tell potential buyers that a property was used as a grow house. Unscrupulous real estate agents will ensure that the real homeowner, who is aware of the grow op problem, is never available to meet with potential buyers. The agent will profess that he or she has no direct knowledge of whether the property was used as a grow op and the homeowner, of course, is never around to answer questions. In a very active market, a potential buyer might be discouraged from making an offer that is conditional upon a home inspection. In haste to buy a house at a bargain price, the purchaser may find that they bought nothing but trouble. At least one Toronto real estate lawyer is recommending that any offer to purchase a resale home contain a clause whereby the seller of the property warrants and represents that the property was not used for the growth or manufacture of any illegal substances during their period of ownership, and that to the best of the seller's knowledge and belief, the use of the property, and the buildings and structures thereon, has never been for the growth or manufacture of illegal substances. If the vendor balks at putting such a clause in, you know that you are probably dealing with a grow house or a former grow house.

This brings us full circle to the fact that police forces are now publishing the addresses of busted grow houses. If you are in the market for property, you must beware. Check the police list: a house that seems to be a bargain may be anything but. In addition to having the seller warrant that it was not used as a grow house, insist on a building inspection by a certified home inspector. The people who are trying to unload former grow houses will slap on a lot of paint and plaster to cover up the mess that was left behind by the criminals. A certified home inspector will see right through it. If an agent or a vendor of property is rushing you to buy without a home inspection, alarm bells should be going off.

On top of turning the actual buildings into disasters, these grow houses are contributing a lot of cash to criminal activity in Canada. Their presence in a neighbourhood increases the risk of violence and residual crime. Their theft of electricity leads to higher utility bills. These properties are much more likely to have fires than normal homes, and the tampering with electrical power access can create electrocution hazards on the property. If all of that is not horrifying enough, police have found that some grow houses have been booby-trapped to injure or kill trespassers and emergency service workers.

If you suspect that there is a grow op house in your neighbourhood or you know of one, contact the police and let them deal with it. Remember, the people running that grow house are criminals and will do anything to ensure that they are not caught.

Part 9 — Construction Liens — Certificates of Pending Litigation

At least two things can tie up title to a person's property—a lien and a Certificate of Pending Litigation. These two legal devices are designed to protect people who may have claims against a piece of property. Their claim might arise because they did work on the property and want to get paid, or they improved it somehow and they actually want the property itself.

Construction liens are designed to give contractors and subcontractors security for work they have done but have not been paid for yet. Contractors (with whom you have a contract) and subcontractors (with whom you may not have a contract) can both put a lien on your property if they have done work to improve it. The lien is a notice to anyone who might be interested in the property. The lien is essentially saying, "Don't buy this property! Don't refinance this property! If you do, you will do so subject to my claim."

A homeowner whose property has a lien on it runs the risk of having to pay the subcontractors who have not been paid by the contractor. The way to ensure that this does not happen is to hold back a percentage of the total value of the contract for work that was being done as protection for unpaid contractors and subcontractors. Hold back amounts are set by provincial law and range from 7 - 20%, depending on the province. The set percentage is then held for a fixed period of thirty to sixty days, again, depending on the province. The period runs from the day the work is substantially complete. After that period, the hold-back money can be paid out or released to the contractor.

If you are going to hire contractors to do work, find out how much your provincial holdback amount is and how long you must hold it back. If a lien is registered, don't ignore it. Get a lawyer involved immediately, as it could affect your mortgage or your ability to refinance the property. Written agreements with contractors for renovations are an absolute must, and the written contract should deal with the requirement for holdbacks and obligations to subcontractors.

A Certificate of Pending Litigation is slightly different from a construction lien. Pending litigation notices do not just mean that the person who has registered it claims to have improved the property. The Certificate is designed to tell the world that the person claims *the property itself*. Once the Certificate of Pending Litigation is registered, no one will buy or finance the property until they have determined why the Certificate was registered. Again, you need a lawyer to get rid of the Certificate, and this should be dealt with as soon as possible. A situation in which a Certificate of Pending Litigation might be registered could involve, for example, a person who enters into an Agreement of Purchase and Sale to sell property to a person and then refuses to close that deal and instead, sells it to another person. The first purchaser of the property may want to enforce the Agreement of Purchase and Sale that they entered into with the vendor. They would then register it to ensure that the property cannot be sold to anyone else.

The bottom line is that construction liens and Certificates of

Pending Litigation can be registered on title in a number of circumstances. Being proactive is certainly the best strategy for dealing with this type of issue.

Part 10 — Forms of Ownership

These days it is not as simple as just "owning" some real estate. The options seem to grow by the day. Consider the following possibilities for owning land in Canada:

i) Joint tenancy;
ii) Tenancy-in-common;
iii) Condo ownership;
iv) Tenant shareholder in a corporation;
v) Co-ownership, including fractional ownership; and
vi) Life interest.

i) Joint tenancy

One or more people may own a piece of property, with each one having an identical interest and an equal entitlement to possession of the property. This is what is known as "joint tenancy," and it is characterized by a very important feature. If any one person dies, the remaining joint tenants automatically take over that person's interest in the property. In other words, it does not flow to the heirs of the deceased owner. It flows directly to the other co-owners (the joint tenants). This is called the "rule of survivorship," and it is what distinguishes a joint tenancy from all other forms of ownership. It is possible for creditors of any one joint tenant to make a claim against the property. The joint tenancy can be severed sometimes by simply trying to sell an interest in the joint tenancy without the permission of the others, or by trying to transfer the property to oneself. The advantage of a joint tenancy? It can be a great way to pass property after your death to avoid the need for probate, especially for a home or a cottage.

ii) Tenants-in-common

With a tenancy-in-common, there is no rule of survivorship. If one tenant or co-owner dies, the property share goes to their estate and beneficiaries. Tenants-in-common can have different types of shares in a property and need not necessarily have equal shares. A tenancy-in-common can be a good way of passing on shares in a family cottage through to different generations. Imagine the situation where a father has three children and wants to pass on the family cottage to them, and each of those children want to pass on their share of the cottage to their children at a later date. If the cottage was held as joint tenancy, as each of the children died, the surviving child would have the whole cottage. However, if the children's interests in the cottage were held as tenants-in-common, as each child died, their share would be passed on to their children, thereby maintaining another generation's involvement in the family cottage.

iii) Condo ownership

Condo ownership started many years ago in Europe but has rapidly become a feature of North American cities. Condos, lofts and other variations (such as townhouses) are all available. A condo owner gets title or ownership of the individual unit and has sole responsibility for maintaining that unit, but they also acquire an interest in the condo corporation that owns the common elements of the building or community. The condo owners pay a monthly fee to the condo corporation as their share of those expenses to maintain the common elements. Condo ownership can look easy, but the transaction is a little more complicated than a regular house purchase. For example, there are many documents that must be prepared and registered to ensure that the entire project—not just the one condo that may be being purchased—is legitimate under the provincial condominium laws.

iv) Tenant shareholder in a corporation

Cooperatives are popular too, and people who "buy" units in a co-op are actually buying a share in a corporation that owns all the co-op units. They are called "tenant shareholders." The corporation owns everything—buildings, land, parking lot and amenities. The co-op "owner" owns nothing except their shares in the corporation and has only a right to occupy a particular unit. The cooperative unit holder, or tenant shareholder, cannot sell without the permission of the condo corporation board of directors.

v) Co-ownership, including fractional ownership

A number of people can combine into a form of co-ownership. By doing so, they join together and, perhaps, buy a building with a number of units in it. Instead of splitting the property into individual units that are owned (like a co-op or a condo), the group enters into a contract to share the building. Each receives a long lease in the building for their particular unit. A recent variation of this idea is "fractional ownership," whereby a piece of property is split into time units. So, for example, a person may buy a number of "units" that translate into a period of weeks, during which the purchaser is entitled to use the property. This is a relatively new development, and some people have found that financial institutions have been a little slow to understand fractional ownership and have been reluctant to advance financing for this type of, more often than not recreational, property.

vi) Life interest

A life interest form of ownership entails giving a person the right to live in, occupy or use a piece of property for as long as they live. When they die, they lose any interest in the property. This type of ownership of real estate can be useful in a situation, for example, where a man wants to let his second wife use a property until her death, at which time it would go to his children from a first marriage. You can see how such an arrangement would keep everyone happy. The surviving second wife is able to use her husband's property until her death. The children of the man who has passed away know that their inheritance will flow to them after the second wife has passed away. In the interim, she cannot sell the property and she cannot mortgage it, although, in some circumstances (depending on the terms of the life interest), she may be able to rent it or share it with someone else.

The bottom line is there are lots of ways to hold property in Canada. Each has its advantages and disadvantages, particularly in terms of arranging financing. When buying property, make sure that you discuss with your lawyer the appropriate way of having ownership.

Conclusion

Real estate is an important part of Canadians' lives. A great deal of our wealth and personal well-being is tied up with our homes, our cottages and other forms of real estate. The key to success in real estate matters seems to come down to working with good professionals and understanding some of the basics. Be a smart consumer when it comes to real estate. I hope the foregoing has demystified the area, even just a little bit.

Chapter 8

10 Things You Absolutely Need To Know About
Employment Law

After our families and our homes, what could be more important than our jobs? In this chapter, I want to demystify a number of aspects of employment in Canada and consider some of the challenges facing employers and employees over the next few years.

Part 1 — The Workplace

As a starting point, I want to set out some basic considerations in the area of employment law. First and foremost, there is a big difference between working in a unionized workplace and a non-unionized workplace. I do not mean job satisfaction or simple things like hourly wages and benefits. I mean the kind of protections, rights and methods of protecting those rights available to employees and employers. In a unionized workplace, employees and employers have signed a collective agreement. That agreement governs the working relationship, and it is intended to be a total package. The union represents the employees in negotiating the collective agreement, and then it works to ensure that the employer complies with that agreement. I do not have space in this chapter to discuss the ways in which unions are formed or dissolved, but it is important for you to understand the significance of a collective agreement, as it establishes the rights of employees in their workplace. This collective agreement will cover everything from wages and benefits to vacations and holidays, occupational safety and the way in which employees may be laid off or fired. In this latter respect, the collective agreement deals with circumstances in which the employer may have "just cause" for dismissing an employee. The collective agreement will set out the process by which employees may complain about their treatment (called a "grievance"), and it will set out the process (usually an arbitration) by which any grievances are resolved.

Non-unionized workplaces do not have collective agreements, and the rights and responsibilities of employees and employers are typically resolved in the courts. If someone thinks they have been fired without cause, they sue. If someone thinks that their privacy in the workplace has been invaded, they sue. The courts have developed guidelines over the years to assist employees and employers in the non-unionized workplace environment. So, assuming you are an employee, if you are unionized, your collective agreement will be of great assistance. If you are not unionized, case law that has evolved over hundreds of years will be used by lawyers and judges to determine your rights and obligations.

Now, what if you are working in a workplace but you are not an employee?

Over the last few decades, we have seen an increase in the number of "independent contractors" in Canadian workplaces. Employers do not always want to take on all of the responsibilities that come with having employees. Federal and provincial laws impose a long list of obligations on employers. There are workers' compensation obligations, tax remittance obligations, Canada Revenue Agency commitments, and so on. There are also obligations to employees at the time of dismissal that some employers simply want to avoid, hence the rise of the independent contractor. Independent contractors have few, if any, rights beyond what is in their contract.

So, when considering rights and obligations in the workplace, we must first determine whether the person in question is an independent contractor or an employee. Employees work in the employer's workspace. The employer provides them with any tools or supplies that they require to do the job. Their hours are set by the employer and they receive direct supervision or training from the employer. Independent contractors, on the other hand, may or may not work in the employer's place of business. Independent contractors provide their own tools and supplies in order to complete the job that they have been assigned. Independent contractors do not generally work under the direct supervision of an employer, and they do not receive training from the employer.

This has not stopped some employers from trying to characterize employees as independent contractors in order to avoid all of the obligations that go with having employees. Instead of simply paying the employee a weekly or monthly wage, an employer will ask the "employee" to invoice the employer and the employer then pays the invoice as if the employee were a contractor. However, an employer who tries to avoid provincial employment laws in this way may find that the courts are more than happy to simply re-characterize what he or she thought was an independent contractor as an actual employee—along with all those obligations the employer was trying to avoid.

So, when looking at the workplace, two key questions must be asked at the outset:

• Is it a unionized or non-unionized workplace?
• Is this person an employee or an independent contractor?

Virtually all rights and obligations in the workplace flow from the answers to those questions.

Part 2 — Hiring Employees — The Right Way

Everyone in business wants to hire the right employee— someone with the right skill set, at the right wage, and someone who will fit into the company's existing workforce. On the other hand, potential employees want to know that they got—or did not get—the job for the right reasons. Hiring employees calls for sensitivity, discretion and some smarts about Canadian employment law. At the time of hiring, an employer is not allowed (by virtue of our provincial human rights codes and laws) to ask questions that might lead a prospective employee to believe that there was discrimination at work in denying them the job for which they applied. What kinds of questions might lead a person to conclude that the employer is discriminatory? Consider the following:

- Questions that are designed to determine the race, ethnic origin or even citizenship of the potential employee;
- Questions that may suggest the employer is interested in the religious practices or religious background of the potential employee;
- Questions that demonstrate an interest in the gender or sexual orientation of the prospective employee;
- Questions that suggest interest in marital status, or pregnancy, or whether plans to have a family may have an impact on the hiring decision;
- Questions that concern political preferences, such as support for a particular political party;
- Questions about age, and physical or mental disabilities;
- Questions about whether prospective employees have a criminal record for which they have received a pardon.

If a prospective, but unsuccessful, employee is asked a question in the above categories, they might conclude that they did not get the job because of their race, ethnic origin, age, sexual orientation or the fact that they had a criminal record. This could, in some cases, lead to the employee making a complaint to the provincial human rights commission. That, in turn, would trigger an investigation and possibly an order that the employer compensate the prospective employee or even pay damages, if the question was discriminatory.

At the same time, asking some of these questions is necessary to hiring an employee with the right skills. An employer, for example, may need to know whether the prospective employee is legally entitled to work in Canada. The employer may need to know whether the employee has a criminal record for which they have not received a pardon because the position involved requires the employee to be bonded. The employer may need to know whether the employee has the strength or physical capability to perform strenuous activity, and so on. These questions, which are designed to determine whether the prospective employee can *do the job*, are different from questions designed to *discriminate* against an employee on the basis of where they are from, what religion they practice or their sexual orientation.

In other words, it's what a person can *do*, not who they are, that an employer is justified in determining through questions at an interview.

As will be seen in the sections below, hiring the right kind of employee is good for business. Bringing someone into your workplace can be very positive or a very destructive. Human rights legislation is designed to protect Canadians from discrimination, and there is no reason why a smart employer cannot ask the right questions and determine whether this particular individual can do the job regardless of their race, ethnic origin, religion, sexual orientation, marital status, political beliefs and so on.

Part 3 — How to Fire an Employee

Shhh…The following is based on a top secret memo written by a lawyer who represents employers. The employer, in this case, wanted to fire employees, but did not have "cause." In other words, they did not have a good reason to fire the employees. In Canada, employers can fire their employees, for the following reasons: if they have good reason (eg. theft or violence); or if they give them reasonable notice (varies with the job); or if they give them reasonable pay instead of notice. If the employer does not do that, it can be considered "wrongful dismissal," and the employee may have a right to sue the employer to obtain, not only compensation for not having received reasonable notice, but also damages, if they suffered mental distress or if the employer was particularly mean-spirited in the way they did the firing.

The employer's lawyer sent a memo to the employer with the title "How to Minimize Your Liability and Expenses When Firing Employees Without Cause." What follows is an excerpt of that memo.

• Remember that the Supreme Court of Canada has ruled that employers have a duty to treat their employees fairly throughout the employment relationship *and* when their relationship ends.

• Try to make the firing stress free. Arrange for the employee to meet with their manager in a neutral place. Pick a private room, at a time of day when other employees are not around, such as first thing in the morning, at lunch time, or late in the day.

- Don't leave the firing until Friday afternoon. Do it early in the week.
- If you fire somebody on a Friday afternoon, they can't do anything about getting a new job until Monday. This means that they just fume through the weekend and take it out on their spouse and kids. This may just make them angry and send them into a lawyer's office on Monday morning.
- Don't fire people close to the holidays, just after they have had surgery or on their birthday.
- If you're firing somebody who has a senior job, arrange for an outplacement support to be available immediately. Get them focused on finding a new job instead of complaining about your firing them. This will show that you are caring and compassionate.
- If the employee is being fired on the spot, make sure you sever access to their computer immediately before (or while) the interview is taking place. Never let them have access to their computer again. They may seek revenge!
- Have a box available so that they can clean out their desk and remove their personal belongings.
- If the employee doesn't have a car, pay for them to take a taxi home and make arrangements for their box to be shipped, or make it easy for them to take it home. Make sure they don't take any company property, particularly client lists or any sensitive corporate insider information.
- In the termination meeting, make it short and painless. Don't give them the impression that there is any benefit to rehashing the past. Make sure they understand the decision is final. Don't simply ask them to sign a release. Make sure they understand that there is some form of package being offered to ease them into their new employment—which they should start looking for right away.

- Give them a little bit of time to think about it. This way, you won't look like you are being unfair. Give them a little bit more than the minimum standard or severance that is called for by provincial employment standards legislation. This will make you appear generous when they take it to a lawyer for an opinion.
- Another reason to make the offer a little more generous is if the employee rejects it and decides to go to court, you may be able to get your costs recovered if the employee's lawsuit is dismissed.
- When deciding whether to make, and how to make, a reasonable offer to the employee, keep in mind their age, their length of service, what they have done for the company and their ability to find a new job. This is no time to be penny-pinching, if they have been a good employee.
- The Supreme Court of Canada and other courts have hammered employers recently for being unfair to employees at the time of dismissal. The courts have recently ordered employers to pay punitive damages and to provide extraordinary amounts of notice to compensate employees.
- In a couple of cases in Canada, employers have been ordered to pay hundreds of thousands of dollars in punitive damages because they fired employees that the courts considered to have disabilities, harassed pregnant women on the job, or used what one judge described as "scuzzy behaviour"…

So, there you have it. That is the kind of advice that employment lawyers are giving companies. Now you know how to fire someone properly, and if you are an employee, now you know the warning signs and what can happen.

Part 4 — Non-Competition, Non-Disclosure and Non-Solicitation Clauses

Employers are often worried about hiring an employee, training that person, giving them access to the company's secrets and the company's client list and training them to work in a particular territory, only to watch the employee walk out the door after several months, wander down the street and either open their own business in direct competition or work for a competitor.

In one case a staffing agency hired an employee, provided him with insider knowledge about the business and then watched that same employee leave and go to work for two of its top competitors—this despite having signed a non-competition clause. The company sued to enforce the agreement.

The courts refused to enforce the non-competition clause because it was too unreasonable and too restrictive on the person who had left. The courts seem prepared to enforce non-competition clauses only if they are reasonable and if they restrict future competition just enough to protect the employer. The courts focus on ensuring that the employer has an actual proprietary interest that is entitled to be protected; on whether the non-competition clause is too broad and whether the restriction on competition is against any competition generally or is limited to non-solicitation of the former employer's customers. Canadian courts seem to like the marketplace to be competitive and dislike non-competition clauses.

This offers little comfort to employers. So, what can they do if they need to protect confidential corporate information from their competitors? After all, we want companies to be able to share key information with their employees, don't we?

An alternative approach is for the employer to ask employees to sign employment contracts that have the employee agree to a non-solicitation provision. This provision would prohibit an employee from either contacting or soliciting other employees, or the employer's clients, for a specific period of time after the employee left the company. The courts are willing to enforce that kind of reasonable restriction. Secondly, the employer can ask an employee to sign an employment contract that includes a form of confidentiality provision, by which the employee agrees not to disclose certain types of information that the employer wants to keep confidential. Again, the courts are prepared to enforce that kind of reasonable restriction.

So, employers are well-advised to have new employees in critical positions sign employment contracts. In these employment contracts, they should include:

- Reasonable restriction on non-competition if the employment arrangement does not work out.
- A term by which the employee agrees not to solicit former employees and clients of the former employer.
- Agreement to keep confidential information confidential from future employers.

If all of these provisions are reasonable, and do not render the employee (upon leaving) utterly unemployable, then the courts will enforce those agreements.

At the same time, an employer may want to include in the employment contract an acknowledgment that intellectual property created by the employee during the course of their employment belongs to the employer. It is a popular misconception that the employer owns every idea or invention developed by an employee during the course of their work. This is not true. An employer should have contracts requiring their employees to assign exclusive ownership rights to any inventions conceived or developed while in the employ of the employer. This is particularly important in what is known as "the new economy," where innovative ideas are the real assets of companies.

Part 5 — Surveillance in the Workplace

I have some bad news—privacy in the workplace is just about dead in Canada. Cameras are popping up all over the place—street corners, shopping malls, the corner store, banks, condo hallways, parking garages, and ATMs. And if that isn't bad enough, they are only going to become more prevalent. The reason for cameras becoming so common is that employers need to protect their business from thieves—both inside and outside the company!

Neither the Canadian Constitution nor the Charter of Rights and Freedoms gives Canadians a right to privacy. Our courts are struggling to protect people in the workplace from invasions of their privacy, but it is getting more and more difficult. Is the employee entitled to a reasonable expectation of privacy? Well, it depends. For example, if the employee is the receptionist at a financial institution and she has five cameras pointed at her workspace, does she expect privacy? I hope not. What if she goes into a hallway to speak to a colleague privately about a personal matter and a camera records it? Does she have privacy? Maybe. But, maybe not, if the camera is in plain sight and the employees have all been told about the cameras. What if she is in the washroom inside a cubicle? Does she have privacy there? I sure hope so. These are the questions being considered every day. Employers are putting cameras up to deter criminals and, in the process, everyone around them loses their privacy.

The large signs that we see posted near these cameras say things like, "Premises are Monitored by Camera." These signs are designed to remove any reasonable expectation of privacy. These signs warn customers in the hope that they will be deterred from criminal activity and remove the privacy rights of employees who are working in that same space.

Courts will also support an employer who puts cameras in the workplace to catch employees who are suspected of theft or other criminal activity. Recently, I watched an employer's black and white videotape of an employee working at a counter and handling cash receipts. The tape was being used to justify the termination of a woman employee suspected of theft. Did she know the camera was mounted over the work area? Yes. Did she still put her hand in the till? The tapes don't lie.

Another way that employers are ensuring that they will not be accused of invasion of privacy by their employees is to have employees acknowledge at the time of employment (sometimes in the form of an employment contract) that the employer has the right to monitor activities in the workplace, either by way of camera, audio monitoring or otherwise. We have all phoned some large institution and been placed on hold. One of the first things we hear is a message that says, "This call may be monitored for the purposes of quality control." This is a warning to the caller and to the employee that neither of them has a reasonable expectation of privacy during the telephone conversation.

So, it is not just cameras that are a concern for privacy in the workplace. It is also audio recordings and, lately, the ability of an employer to monitor keystrokes on computers and visits to unauthorized websites. It is possible for an experienced computer investigator to determine precisely which keys were struck on a particular computer, the time of day and, of course, in what order. The investigator will determine the length of time each web page was open and even include a record of all text input by an employee on a chat site. Gulp. In other words, an employer can reconstruct what an employee did at their computer virtually all day long. Is it an invasion of privacy, given that the employer owns the computer? The courts do not seem to think so. In fact, lawyers and judges have been required to read all those steamy emails that forensic investigators have retrieved from employee computers. You thought they were deleted? Think again.

Companies have complained recently that office computer systems often strain in the middle of the day and over the lunch hour, as employees use the computers to access the Internet for personal reasons. Some employers block access altogether or permit only very limited personal time per day. Porn is always a "no-no." If an employer prohibits access to the Internet for personal purposes during the day, and the employer has disciplined an employee for making improper use of the Internet, can the employee complain? No. In fact, they may find themselves fired. It is advisable for an employer to tell their employees that computer use is being monitored and that they have no reasonable expectation of privacy when using the company computers. It is advisable, but it is certainly not mandatory.

Some lawyers have called terminations of employees for abuse of the employer's computer "e-cause." These are the new electronic reasons for firing people. Porn and other illicit material on the employer's computer system can lead to dismissal. Just ask the Canadian woman fired from a gas company because obscene emails were found on her computer. Or, consider the fellow who worked for a Quebec company and was fired for spending more than 300 hours surfing porn sites in a five-month period on the employer's computer. Not only was it offensive, but the arbitrator who heard the case considered the employee's activities "theft of the employer's time and resources."

The Canadian Criminal Code contains numerous provisions concerning invasion of privacy. Almost all of them relate to interception of telephone communications and are designed to ensure that Canadians are not intercepting private communications between private citizens. However, the bottom line, again, is (at least in the employment context), does the employee have a reasonable expectation of privacy when using company phones for personal business? Apparently, less and less.

Last and not least, of course, is the fact that an employer is quite free to search any property that is a part of the employer's premises. This includes the employee's desk or workstation, locker rooms, bathrooms and even personal change areas. Personal searches are frowned on, but employers usually get around this by asking employees to voluntarily submit to personal searches. Those who refuse may find themselves in search of a new job.

As I said at the beginning of this chapter, it is mostly bad news in the area of privacy in the workplace. The emphasis seems to favour very much the employer monitoring the workplace for criminal activity and employee wrongdoing.

Part 6 — Take This Job and Sho... Quitting Time!

The old country and western song makes quitting a job seem downright fun—almost cathartic. But real life is often quite different. Few people quit their job on a whim, but for those who do quit, there are some rights and responsibilities that go with it.

When can an employee just walk out and not worry about the employer taking steps to sue them? Actually, the circumstances make common sense when you think about it. If your boss asks you to do something that is illegal or immoral or dangerous for you or for your co-workers, you are entitled to quit on the spot and no court will ever find fault with your decision. For example, every province in Canada requires employers to provide a safe workplace, safe equipment for employees to use and safe tools to do the job. Every province has occupational health and safety legislation. These laws allow employees and workers to refuse to work in conditions that they honestly believe are unsafe. In Ontario in 2004, 100 people were killed on the job and nearly 100,000 were injured seriously. Every province also maintains a workers' compensation insurance system, whereby employers pay a fee into a government fund. Employees who are injured on the job are able to make a claim for compensation. Not every business is covered by these compensation schemes, but a quick check with your provincial ministry of labour will tell you whether you would be entitled to such compensation, if you were injured on the job.

What happens, though, if an employee is not being asked to do something illegal, immoral or dangerous to themselves or co-workers? What if the reason for quitting is that a better job has come along—but it starts tomorrow?! Can an employer do anything in a situation like that? In fact, they can. Just like an employer cannot fire an employee without cause or reasonable notice, an employee cannot quit without cause or without providing reasonable notice. Provincial employment standards law sets out a minimum period of notice that should be given by employees who quit. This period does not usually exceed two weeks, but an employee would be well-advised to check with the provincial ministry of labour prior to walking out on a job with anything less than two weeks notice, if there was no good reason for quitting. Employees who quit without cause and without adequate notice may find themselves being sued by their employer. If the employee's departure on short notice prevented the employer from finding someone to replace the quitting employee and that harms the employer's business, the employer may be entitled to damages. In one Saskatchewan case, the employer sued the employee for more than $2,000 spent on training the employee.

There is an important overlap between wrongful dismissal and quitting, because sometimes an employee quits when the situation at work has become intolerable. The employer is not asking them to do anything illegal, immoral or dangerous, but the environment in the workplace may have changed. The employee may find that they have been demoted or, perhaps, embarrassed in front of their co-workers for nothing. They may find that their pay or benefits have been reduced. In one case, an employee was passed over for an obvious promotion and found themselves squeezed into a menial job for which they were clearly overqualified. The writing was on the wall from the employer: "I'm not going to fire you, but I sure hope you quit." In a situation like that the employee may be facing what is known as "constructive dismissal."

In one shocking Saskatchewan case, an employer flew into a rage because an employee had, in his view, mistreated a heifer. The rage included the employer questioning the employee's intelligence and insulting his French-Canadian background. The rage escalated into a physical altercation that involved the employer chasing the employee with a large pair of tagging pliers. He grabbed the employee by the throat with the pliers and reportedly said, "I know I'll go to jail, but I'll have the satisfaction of killing a stupid Frenchman." The employee felt he could not return to work after such an outburst and the court agreed that that was a constructive dismissal, because the work environment was hostile. No kidding.

It is important that employees act quickly in such a situation. If any of these circumstances have arisen, and you feel squeezed out of the workplace, it is imperative that you speak with a lawyer quickly if you wish to preserve your right to sue for constructive dismissal. A constructive dismissal is the same as a wrongful dismissal and can be compensated through damages and, in some cases, punitive damages.

More often than not, there is a lot more to quitting than simply telling the boss to, "Take this job and shove it."

Part 7 — Whistle-blowing

Imagine being in one of the following situations:

• You are hired for a summer job driving a truck and need the money for university tuition. Your boss tells you to fill up the holding tank on your truck with waste oil and other chemicals, and then drive around on remote country roads, draining the tank to get rid of the waste "for free."

- You work for the provincial government, and you find that your boss has been faking invoices and steering work to a company owned by his brother-in-law, who is charging double the normal price for services.
- You work for a union and you discover one of the supervisors is double-dipping in his salary payments and in reimbursement for auto expenses.
- Your boss asks you to climb inside a piece of malfunctioning manufacturing equipment to clean some blades that are stuck. You are reluctant to do so because the machine could restart, and it looks dangerous.
- You report one of the above situations to your superiors and find that you are suddenly being disciplined and harassed. Your employment file is suddenly filled with warnings and threats of dismissal. You feel that it is obviously related to what you know and what you reported.

What can a Canadian do when faced with such situations?

All of these examples touch on the area of whistle-blower protection laws. Provincial laws across Canada, and now the Canadian Criminal Code, offer some protection for employees who report dangerous workplaces, environmental harm, theft or corruption and other wrongdoing in their workplace.

These laws prohibit what are known as "employer reprisals"—demotions, reduced pay, a poisoned work environment, suspension and sudden probationary periods. Over the years in Canada, prior to whistle-blower protection, employees who were close to the front line and saw wrongdoing were reluctant to speak up because it would mean their job and their ability to earn a living. Gradually, provinces and territories introduced protection for these potential whistle-blowers.

In one Saskatchewan case, a woman working for a trade union caught one of the officials in the union double-dipping. She reported the double-dipping to one of her supervisors and was promptly fired. When she went to use the whistle-blower protection, the union that had fired her took the position that she should have reported the wrongdoing to a lawful authority, not one of her supervisors. I know, that is a bit of a head scratcher and it went all the way to the Supreme Court of Canada, where the Supreme Court agreed that reporting to her supervisor was the same as reporting to a lawful authority and she deserved whistle-blower protection.

In Ontario, the Environmental Protection Act and the Environmental Bill of Rights both contain whistle-blower protection provisions for employees who do not want to choose between protecting the environment and keeping their job. Under the Environmental Bill of Rights if an employee has reported environmental harm and believes that an employer has taken reprisals against them, the employee can contact the Labour Relations Board and trigger an investigation. If that investigation does not lead to a settlement of the matter, then the Board can order the employer to stop or fix the action of which the employee has complained, reinstate the employee or compensate the employee for lost earnings. Similar provisions exist in the labour relations legislation for employees who wish to report labour problems and in the occupational health and safety legislation, which is designed to protect employees from dangerous situations in their workplace.

There have been two recent major developments designed to protect employees who become aware of wrongdoing in the workplace. The Ontario government passed a law in December 2006 giving employees of the provincial public service whistle-blower protection if they reveal government wrongdoing. The province's Integrity Commissioner will investigate allegations made by public servants and then report to the public and to the legislature. This type of legislation has become popular as a result of the "Sponsorship Scandal" that engulfed the federal Liberal government back in 2004. Public service employees who spoke up found they had few friends inside government. Many were hounded out of the public service and embarrassed in the media. A part of the response to the "Sponsorship Scandal" was to introduce laws protecting whistle-blowers, hence the Ontario law, which will likely be copied in other provinces and territories across Canada.

The Canadian Criminal Code also contains a provision that

makes it an offence for an employer or a person acting on behalf of an employer to take disciplinary measures against an employee with the intent to compel that employee to abstain from providing information about wrongdoing pursuant to any federal or provincial law or regulation. This provision in the Criminal Code covers not only actual retaliation, but threats of retaliation communicated directly or indirectly to the employee. The penalty, if someone is convicted, is as much as five years in jail, if the Crown Attorney proceeds by way of indictment.

If you are in a situation where you are concerned about illegal activity in your workplace, consider speaking confidentially with a co-worker. If you are in a unionized workplace, speak with your shop steward. If you have no one to speak with, consult with a lawyer to ensure that you proceed properly and obtain the maximum protection under whistle-blower laws. If the situation is an emergency, if harm to the public or to the environment is imminent, or if you are being placed in a dangerous situation, you are within your rights to refuse to follow your employer's instructions. Always err on the side of caution and your personal safety, and consult with a lawyer immediately. The laws, and our courts' interpretation of the whistle-blower law, err on the side of protecting the whistle-blower.

Part 8 — Violence in the Workplace

It seems like not a year goes by without some horrific workplace shooting. Would you believe that in the United States more than one thousand people die each year as a result of violence in their workplace—that's twenty people a week! Canada has not been immune to this type of workplace violence either. In Ottawa, just a few years ago, an employee of the local transportation company came to work with a gun and murdered co-workers. Similarly, in Toronto, a contractor killed a manager and seriously wounded other employees in a workplace shooting.

These incidents are, of course, as much a matter of mental health as anything else, but they do provide insights into what is going on in certain workplaces. For example, the Ottawa employee claimed to have been a victim of workplace harassment and bullying. These allegations are never an excuse for murderous behaviour, but employers and employees need to be aware of any simmering pot of frustration and what may push that simmering pot to the point of boiling over.

Sexual harassment has been the subject of a great deal of analysis and legal attention over the last few decades. Office codes of conduct have gone a long way to calming down the workplace—they have not eliminated sexual harassment, but companies are dealing it with very actively. Other forms of harassment are now emerging, however, and employers and employees must deal with them as well.

Can employees be fired for harassment and bullying of a non-sexual nature? Can employees who quit because they chose not to suffer the bullying complain to the courts of constructive dismissal? Canadian courts have answered yes in both cases.

In an Ontario case, an office administrator felt forced to quit after trying to tolerate a co-worker's daily verbal abuse. The harassment and bullying included swearing, yelling and threats. She quit and sued for wrongful dismissal. In Saskatchewan, a man working on a farm was called "a liar," "a bastard" and suffered other forms of harassment by his employer and felt forced to quit. He sued for constructive dismissal.

Employers have been faulted for not providing a workplace conducive to the well-being of their employees. How could someone competently perform their duties in a workplace filled with profanities, bullying and threats? They couldn't, so the court supported their claims for constructive dismissal.

Employers have to watch these bullies and not let them poison the workplace. If they do not pay attention or are not prepared to take steps to provide a safe and harassment-free workplace, they may find themselves on the receiving end of complaints under occupational health and safety legislation, which requires employers to provide a safe workplace. So, step one: identify bullies and harassers and deal with them quickly.

Step two is a little more complicated. What happens if the bully loses control, is dismissed (justifiably), but then threatens to return to the workplace for revenge? Obviously, if the threat is an active one, the first call is to the police, but often these employees do not verbalize their threat, they simply go away and then return unexpectedly. If a workplace has experienced such bullying, some suggestions for maintaining a safe workplace would include controlling access to the office. No one, whether a stranger or a former employee, should be able to simply wander into an office without some scrutiny. It is not uncommon for former employees to arrive at their old workplace and simply walk in to chat with their buddies. This should not be allowed to happen, as it endangers staff when former employees (who return disgruntled) walk into the workplace and engage staff in arguments or violence.

In some offices, depending on the level of difficulty in the past or the type of work in which they are engaged, panic buttons may be necessary so that staff can sound alarms if situations are out of control. Many law firms have panic buttons installed for their receptionist, so violence in the reception area can be dealt with immediately.

Aside from trying to make sure that these bullies are not in the workforce to begin with, the way in which they are fired can have a profound effect upon their level of hostility. If a bully is fired, a detailed exit strategy should be developed. If there is a possibility of violence, the police should be involved. If threats have been made, a visit from the police to that employee may discourage the person from acting on their anger. There should be counselling for troubled employees who have been fired.

It is far better for employers to be proactive in making sure they do not hire these bullies to begin with, but if one ends up in your workplace, get rid of them quickly and effectively. If the employer does not act quickly, they are putting their business and their other employees at risk. Those employees may very well say that they have had enough, quit and sue the employer for constructive dismissal. One bad apple really can ruin an entire company.

Part 9 — Mandatory Retirement

Wow! Some days that sounds great. Imagine being forced to retire! Sign me up. I am just kidding, of course. The reality is quite different for many Canadians. They want to keep working after the age of sixty-five. They enjoy their jobs and, in many cases, they need the money, particularly older women who may have entered the workforce late because of having children. They may need to be in the workforce longer, in order to catch up with their earnings and savings. Despite this desire to work and the need to work, until recently many Canadians were forced to retire when they reached the age of sixty-five. Provincial laws did not protect them from mandatory retirement policies and they were forced out of the workforce.

Now, our society is aging very quickly. For example, as of 2005, 13% of the population was over the age of sixty-five, and within a couple of decades it is estimated that the number of Canadians over the age of sixty-five will be 20%. Imagine that, one in five over sixty-five! In Canada, we are also faced with a shortage of skilled workers and this is going to become even more dramatic as the baby boomers become eligible to retire in the hundreds of thousands each year. It is no coincidence that the arguments for forcing people into retirement—arguments like, "Oh, young people need to move up the ladder," or, "There aren't enough jobs to go around"—are suddenly replaced with statements such as "Maybe we need to keep your skills around a little longer," or, "We would like you to work part-time," "We would like you to stay on call and do special projects," and so on. Many Canadian companies are finding that they need older employees to hang in there. As a result, the idea of mandatory retirement is quickly becoming a thing of the past.

Mandatory retirement policies are now illegal and are considered discriminatory on the basis of age, as a result of amendments to provincial human rights codes. As of December 12, 2006, Ontario joined Alberta, Manitoba, Quebec, PEI, Nunavut, the Yukon and Northwest Territories in banning mandatory retirement policies. Other provinces are looking at similar changes. However, the federal level of government still takes the position that it is not a discriminatory practice to terminate someone's employment because that person has reached the "normal" age of retirement for employees working in similar positions. So, in certain circumstances, at the federal level (that is, companies that are regulated by federal law), mandatory retirement is still permitted.

Even though mandatory retirement has been prohibited in many provinces, there are some circumstances in which discrimination based on age is permissible. This is where there are legitimate reasons for the particular occupation to have a younger person, as opposed to an older one. So, I suppose, if a person over the age of sixty-five applies for a job as a skateboard tester, they may find their resume ignored!

Mandatory retirement is gone and that means that the estimated 6% of Canadians over the age of sixty-five who want to work can still go for it—just take it easy!

Part 10 — Misconduct During Non-Working Hours By Employees — Grounds for Dismissal?

In a recent US case, a female teacher was drummed out of the high school at which she taught when it was discovered that her previous employment included making a number of porn movies. How this came to be known and how she was ultimately recognized is a subject of speculation, but most people assume that a former lover was seeking revenge and leaked her unseemly history to school authorities. The case raises an interesting question—what impact can an employee's activities outside of work have on their employment?

There have been a number of Canadian cases over the years which considered this type of problem. How would you handle the following?

• An employee carries on an affair with a fellow employee's wife.
• A fireman carries on an affair with a neighbour's wife and brags about it non-stop at work.
• A manager of a "family business" has sexual relations with several of his female staff outside office hours while married to the daughter of one of his bosses.
• An employee has numerous sexual encounters with female staff, including nude swimming, attending strip clubs and a "Roman tub incident" and creates a sexualized work environment.

- A female employee begins an affair with a convicted sex offender who was receiving counselling from the company for which she works.
- An employee assistance counsellor begins an affair with the wife of a man he is counselling.
- A manager becomes less tolerant of an employee's insubordinate behaviour *after* their affair has ended.
- An employee assaults a female colleague when she breaks off their affair.
- An employee tells a colleague to "f—- off" in front of the colleague's four-year-old child.
- A schoolteacher expresses his racist views outside of the classroom.
- A teacher makes porno movies on her own time after class.
- An employee makes porno movies on her employer's school buses.

Should any or all of these individuals be fired because of their activities? Over the years, the Canadian courts have taken a less moralistic view of romantic activities outside of the workplace and slowly evolved an approach that focuses on the impact of the extra-curricular activity on the employee's performance in the workplace and its effect on other employees in the workplace. For example, if the employee who carried on affairs outside of the office with female subordinates sexualized the workplace to the point that staff felt they had no choice but to engage in sexual behaviour, then this may qualify as sexual harassment. It could result in, at a minimum, a warning for the employee, but more likely in other employees complaining of constructive dismissal for sexual harassment.

The woman who became involved with the convicted sexual offender could not claim that she was wrongfully dismissed and the court, in reviewing her conduct, felt that she had made a series of errors in judgment, which amounted to a fundamental breach of her commitment to the company.

In such situations, in order to justify dismissing an employee, a company would need to establish such things as (a) the conduct of the employee has harmed the company's reputation or product, (b) the employee's behaviour has rendered them unable to perform their duties satisfactorily, or (c) the employee's behaviour has so effected the workplace that other employees refuse to (or are reluctant to) work with him or her, (d) the employee has been guilty of a serious breach of the Criminal Code and damaged the reputation of the company and (e) the conduct made it difficult for the company to properly manage that employee's behaviour.

The activities of teachers tend to attract a higher level of scrutiny, presumably because they are role models for students. Their extracurricular activities can reflect not only on the teaching profession, but the entire school system itself. So, the schoolteacher who made pornographic films after-hours could not complain about being wrongfully dismissed, nor could the employee who made pornographic movies on the school bus.

The bottom line is that an employee's conduct in non-working hours must damage the employee's ability to perform their job or undermine their credibility in the workplace to such an extent that it is not reasonable for them to continue.

It is an interesting issue, if only because of the nerve shown by some dismissed employees: "I should be able to make pornographic movies and still be employed as a schoolteacher." With nerve like that, she should be flying a fighter jet, not teaching high school.

Conclusion

In the above sections, I have reviewed some of the challenges that employers and employees face in the Canadian workplace. I hope that these insights contribute in some small way to creating a more peaceful and happy workplace for you.

Chapter 9

10 Things You Absolutely Need To Know About
Intellectual Property

Sometimes we are watching TV and we see an advertisement for a new product. Maybe it is a new kind of exercise machine or something for cutting vegetables. After the demonstration, we see a note at the bottom of the screen telling us that the "patent is pending." Other times, we may find ourselves calling products by their brand names rather than by generic terms. So, instead of saying tissue, we call it "Kleenex," and instead of copying, we call it "Xeroxing." Maybe on the way to work we decide to grab a coffee at a place we identify simply by the unique Starbucks logo instead of the actual name of the outlet. Just recently, there was newspaper coverage about Microsoft's successful lawsuit against a company that infringed its copyright on some software. The Federal Court of Canada awarded Microsoft the largest award ever, $500,000 against a Quebec company. All of these issues concern intellectual property. Patents, trademarks and copyrights—they are intangible expressions of some creative brainwave that a person has had, and from which they hope to profit. And that is really what intellectual property is all about—protecting an idea for a period of time so that the person who created it has an opportunity to profit. This aspect of law can be a little complicated and changes day by day, particularly with developments in technology. In this chapter, I hope to demystify some of the basic concepts around intellectual property and how it affects our lives and businesses.

Part 1 — Patents

Patents are for inventions. This can be the invention of a new machine or some unique manufacturing process, or it can even be an improvement on an existing device. As long as it is novel, has some utility and is not an obvious process, the inventor of it can obtain authority from the government protecting their right to that invention for up to twenty years.

In order to protect the invention, the inventor must register the design with the Canadian Intellectual Property Office. Over the next eighteen months to two years, public servants will review the application and decide whether it meets the criteria of being novel, of utility and not obvious. If the application is successful, the inventor will receive a grant of a patent. This grant will provide the inventor with the exclusive right to the use of that invention for up to twenty years. While the patent application is being examined, the would-be inventor can start to make immediate use of the idea, and guess what the inventor tells the world—patent pending!

Inventors need to be aware of these issues:

- Getting a patent is very specialized and you will definitely need to hire either a patent lawyer or a patent agent to assist with the preparation of the application, its filing and its processing.
- It is expensive, so if you hope to profit from the invention, make sure that the idea is so worthwhile that you will eventually recover the expense of processing the patent application itself. Few people have the resources to patent unprofitable concepts.
- The patent is only good for Canada. If you need protection in other jurisdictions, it will be necessary to file further patent applications.
- If someone infringes your patent and starts to manufacture, use or sell something based on the inventor's design, the onus of protecting the patent falls entirely on the inventor. In other words, the government does not go and protect your patent for you. You have to invest more money in hiring a lawyer to sue the person who is infringing the patent.

Part 2 — Trademarks

As I was finalizing this section, it was reported on the news that two business giants had settled a ten-year long trademark dispute. Apple Computers (with the famous logo of an apple with a bite out of it) and Apple Corps (the famous green apple logo of the Beatles) came to terms over who is infringing whose trademark. It is a good example of the importance of these identifying symbols to business.

A trademark is a word, a symbol, a picture or a combination of those things that is used to identify a product or a service in such a way as to distinguish it from other products or services. Our lives are bombarded with trademarks and most school children would be able to name ten right off the top of their head. For example, the famous Nike "swoosh" or checkmark logo and the three stripes on an Adidas product are trademarks, and they come in three varieties:

- An ordinary *trademark*, which is the basic word or logo. So, for example, the Starbucks' circular logo is a trademark, as is the name Starbucks. (I think I used Starbucks here because I drank a lot of coffee during the writing of this book.) The logo is a design trademark and the word is a word trademark.
- A *certification mark*. This type of trademark is used to alert the consumer or a purchaser to the fact that the product meets a certain standard, either in quality or content.
- A *distinguishing guise*. This kind of trademark concerns the shape of the product or the packaging in which it arrives. It has its value in ensuring that a consumer recognizes the product from the very shape, without ever needing to see a name or a logo, although they are usually used in conjunction. The Volkswagen "Beetle" is an example of this.

Although there is no legal obligation to register a trademark, it is a good idea because if you end up in a dispute over whether you actually have the trademark, the registration is excellent proof that you came up with the trademark first. Once registered, the owner of the trademark will have the exclusive right to use that trademark for fifteen years. The good news is that the protection can be renewed for a further fifteen years and a further fifteen years after that, and so on, indefinitely.

Just as in the case of a patent, there are some painful realities:

• It can be expensive to register a trademark.
• It can be slow while the Intellectual Property Office and your trademark agent ensure that someone else does not already have a trademark that is the same or similar.
• Even once registered, the trademark is only effectively protected in Canada.
• If someone decides they are going to infringe your trademark, once again, the onus falls on the owner of the trademark to police it. This means hiring a lawyer and suing the person who is infringing the trademark. So, the next time you see a small ™ or an ® beside a logo or name, you will understand that someone has taken the time to create a trademark, and that they have the exclusive right to use it (at least in Canada) and at least for fifteen years at a time.

Part 3 — Copyright

Do you want an excellent example of copyright? This book is copyrighted! That means that I have the right to produce or reproduce this book or any material from it. If someone else photocopies the book or, say, scans it into a computer, that is illegal, unless of course they get my permission in advance. Similarly, BNN TV owns the copyright to *Strictly Legal*, the television program. If someone copied the program, that would be a breach of BNN's copyright, and if there were a radio program based on *Strictly Legal* and someone copied the radio program, then that would be a breach of copyright again.

Copyright is designed to protect works that are, like this book, written, artistic (so, for example, drawings and illustrations can be copyrighted), dramatic (so, for example, a play could be copyrighted) or musical (both musical notes and lyrics can be copyrighted). At the beginning of this chapter, I mentioned the recent case of Microsoft suing a company successfully for

$500,000. That case concerned copying of software programs and they, too, are protected by copyright. A computer software program is simply an electronic version of writing.

Unlike patents and trademarks, there is no need to register a copyright with the Canadian Intellectual Property Office. It is possible to register it, but there is no legal requirement. Why? Because the copyright entitlement arises the moment an original work is created. It does not even have to be published or made public in any way.

Unlike patents and trademarks, copyright protection is available for citizens of countries (hundreds of them) that have signed the international treaties designed to protect copyright.

The copyright on this book will last for my entire lifetime and then for fifty years after my death. From the moment I create an original work until the day the copyright expires (many, many years from now, I hope), I need do nothing to maintain that copyright. No fees have to be paid. No renewal notices must be filed. During that time, if someone infringes my copyright, it is up to me to hire a lawyer to pursue the person and recover any damages related to their breach of my rights.

If I want, I am free to licence or assign the copyright to someone so that they can reproduce the work and profit from it. Even if I do authorize someone else to profit from this work, I still retain what are known as "moral rights." This means that I can insist that the person who has been given the right to use my work not alter it or distort it in some way, unless I agree. An interesting example of this type of enforcement of moral rights arose around an artist's work being displayed in the Eaton Centre in Toronto. The artist, Michael Snow, had prepared a number of sculptures of Canada geese. These geese were suspended from the ceiling of the Eaton Centre and depicted, beautifully, a flock of geese in flight. One year, at Christmastime, the owners of the Eaton Centre decided that it would be a nice "Christmassy" touch to add red bows to each of the geese. The artist took exception and even though he had sold the sculptures to the Eaton Centre, he retained the moral right to insist that the sculptures not be distorted or altered. A court agreed and the bows were removed.

So, if you are sitting there writing "the great Canadian novel" or "the great Canadian play" or "the great Canadian computer program," there is no need to incur any expensive filing fees to protect it, as it is copyrighted the moment you create it. However, you may see from time to time a © beside a work, indicating that it has been copyrighted by the person whose name appears beside the small ©. There is no legal requirement to put the symbol there, but it is a good way of alerting the public to the fact that this material is copyrighted and owned (© Michael Cochrane).

Part 4 — Plant Breeders' Rights

I know what you are probably thinking: Plant Breeders' Rights?! I'm not kidding. It is possible in Canada to, in a sense, patent certain forms of plants. There is actually a Plant Breeders' Rights Act. If a person has developed a new plant variety, the Plant Breeders' Rights Act gives them an opportunity to protect that new variety, the same way that someone else might protect the patent for a new machine. An application is completed and filed with the Canadian Intellectual Property Office and the Canadian Food Inspection Agency. In order to be protected, the variety must fulfill certain requirements. It must be new, uniform (in this context, this means that all plants within the one variety must be the same) and it must be stable (it cannot be a one-time version of the plant). Once the plant breeder is granted protection, that individual is entitled to control the reproduction and sale of the seeds for up to eighteen years.

There have been some interesting court cases in Canada over plants and seeds. The case of *Monsanto v. Schmeiser* went to the Supreme Court of Canada over a situation where a farmer (Percy Schmeiser) had been collecting and using seeds patented by the company Monsanto. The seed was known as "Roundup Ready" and is designed for growing canola. Mr. Schmeiser claimed that he had segregated these seeds, saved them and then planted them. Through his efforts, he was able to grow over 1,000 acres of "Roundup Ready" canola, essentially for free. Had he purchased the seeds from Monsanto, it would have cost him about $15,000. The Supreme Court of Canada held the farmer liable for collecting and using the seeds in breach of the company's patent. While the case was controversial (as some critics felt that it placed commercial interests ahead of the traditional agricultural practice of farmers' collecting seeds for future crops), others felt that it was simply a recognition that this company had invested millions of dollars in developing the seeds and that someone could not come along and simply replicate the seeds without paying for them.

Part 5 — Trade Secrets

Trademarks, copyrights and patents are all about protecting a creative moment by telling the world: "Hey, I invented this. This is mine. I wrote this." But, what if you do not want anyone to know? What if the secret of your success needs to stay a secret?

This can be a challenge. There is no legal requirement to register what you consider to be your trade secret. If you can keep the information (for example a special process you developed for baking a product or your famous "Grandma's Secret Sauce") a secret, then it may never need to be revealed, but in this day and age, with corporate espionage rampant, a truly valuable trade secret will not stay secret for long.

I heard recently of a businessman who sold a manufacturing process system to a foreign company and shipped it to them, but when he arrived to assemble it, the company had spread the entire system out on the floor of a huge factory warehouse. In another room, dozens of women at computers were copying everything from the screws to the paint colour. He had a patent in Canada and some trade secrets within the process, but what was he supposed to do now? Trade secret? Not anymore.

It can be the same with your grandma's secret sauce. There is nothing to stop someone from breaking it down to determine the ingredients and then replicating it. Now it is their secret sauce.

More often than not, the source of the leak may be an employee. In the US, an employee of a large corporation was recently caught peddling their "secret formula" on the Internet. To prevent this kind of thing, companies in such a position have a few ways of protecting their trade secret:

- Limit access to the information and track closely who knows what and when they learn it.
- Have employees sign non-disclosure/confidentiality agreements as a part of their employment contracts. These contracts must be specific and spell out the potential consequences of a breach of the confidentiality, for example, immediate dismissal and being sued for damages caused by the disclosure.
- In addition to keeping a lid on access to the secret information, and in addition to confidentiality agreements in employee contracts, senior Canadian lawyers have recommended including non-competition clauses and non-solicitation covenants in employee contracts. This inhibits employees from leaving one company to join another company and taking the information with them.
- Develop corporate policies to promote the protection of information, the policing of information assets, as well as maintaining regular surveillance and monitoring of the use of information. Companies should consider developing a "code of conduct" regarding the use of confidential information by their employees. This, along with training for employees (stressing the importance of maintaining confidentiality), should help.

There has been some discussion in Canada of trying to use the Criminal Code to prosecute employees who breach a company's trade secrets. The idea would be to treat the breach of the secret as a theft of information. However, the Supreme Court of Canada, in a recent case, decided that confidential information is not capable of being stolen and that information is not property, for the purposes of the theft provisions of the Criminal Code. In the United States, they have passed an Economic Espionage Act that criminalizes the theft of trade secrets. We should expect that Canadian lawmakers will look at a similar provision in the future if enough corporate secrets are pinched.

Part 6 — Inventor Rip-Offs

I am fascinated by the small ads in newspapers and magazines, particularly the ingenuity and entrepreneurship so many people demonstrate with their interesting product developments. It seems like millions of people are working on a better mousetrap, their own secret sauce or clothes for dogs. Mixed in with these ads by people trying to sell their products, are ads that offer a service: "We Will Help You Bring Your Invention To Market!" "Help For Inventors!" "Got A Great Idea? We Can Help!" Some of these ads prey on people who may not know what to do with their "Next Great Board Game for The Whole Family" (which, by the way, is a very hard product to bring to market), or their invention of a new golf ball that is impossible to lose (I pray that someone is working on that right now). These individuals may not have the know-how or the capital to develop their idea and bring it to market, and they need help.

The answer is not to give the idea away to complete strangers who advertise in newspapers and magazines. Those strangers had their own great idea — "Hey, I have no ideas, so I'll advertise and get other people to send me theirs!" Do not do it. If you have a great idea, keep it secret. Go see an intellectual property lawyer. They will listen and are, of course, required to keep the information confidential because of solicitor-client privilege. The lawyer can then assist you with advice about how to bring your product forward, including obtaining financing for the development of a prototype and for developing a patent, if that is recommended. Intellectual property lawyers have experience with the needs of inventors and enjoy the excitement of seeing someone's great idea come to fruition.

If you give your idea away to a stranger, it is gone, and there will be little that you can do about it.

Part 7 — Inventing on the Job

Who owns the invention conceived by an employee while at work? The answer seems obvious: the employer pays the employee to come to work, and if the employee has a brain wave while being paid, well that should belong to the employer, right? Actually, it is not that cut and dried, and this is creating problems for some businesses, particularly those that are part of the burgeoning knowledge-based economy, which is based on creativity and the development of innovative ideas.

Canadian courts have been asked to grapple with this problem, and the old approach that the employee who invents on the job holds that invention in trust for the benefit of their employer is less useful today. Without a specific written contract that states that the employer owns any inventions created by the employee, there is a strong likelihood that the employee is going to get to keep the invention. Let's look at a couple of scenarios and see if there are some guidelines:

- An employee is hired to invent things, but the employee has not signed a contract that has an express provision for ownership of inventions that are developed. In this case, the employer will probably own the invention because the employee has been specifically hired to invent and that is their job on behalf of the employer. So, the employer, in all likelihood, will be able to keep the invention in the event of a dispute.
- An employee is not hired specifically to invent or develop ideas but, while on the job, invents something outside the scope of their employment relationship. In addition, the employee has not signed an employment contract with an express provision giving the employer ownership of inventions. In this scenario, the employee, in all likelihood, will be entitled to retain ownership rights and will be accorded any benefits derived from the invention.
- The employee is not hired to invent or develop innovative ideas but, while on the job, invents something inside or outside the scope of the employment relationship. The person has signed an employment contract expressly providing that the employer will have ownership of any inventions created by employees. In this situation, the employer will be able to enforce the contract and retain ownership rights and be accorded the benefits derived from the invention.

The Canadian courts are sending businesses a clear message. Employers must enter into contracts requiring their employees to assign exclusive ownership rights in their inventions to the employer. Inventions and innovations are the critical assets of the new economy, and failure to protect these assets could be a big mistake if the employee decides that there are greener pastures for their invention elsewhere.

Part 8 — The Internet and Your Intellectual Property

I have a website (*www.michaelcochrane.ca*), and on the site I have posted a variety of things, including articles, short stories and comments. The website does not say that the material is copyrighted and there is no small © beside all of the material. If someone visits my website and likes it so much that they copy it, or they like one of my short stories so much that they decide to download it and use it, have they breached my copyright? In other words, have I done enough to protect my right to copyright on the Internet?

There is a popular misconception that copyright, trademarks and other aspects of intellectual property law do not apply to the Internet in the same way as they do to other forms of media, such as print, television or radio. This could not be further from the truth. The same laws that apply to those media apply to the Internet and Canadian courts have supported a person's entitlement to copyright for things published on the web. There are only two exceptions to this right: material can be reproduced if the author of it gives permission, or if the only reason the material was taken in the first place was to do so some research. In those two situations, a court will not find a breach of copyright.

So, if you publish on the Internet, you will be protected by copyright. If you encounter other people's writings, drawings or other intellectual property on the Internet, they are not in the public domain and simply there for the taking, so exercise caution and do not be tempted to steal simply because the material has been published to the entire world on the Internet. The author still has copyright. And remember—that copyright lasts until fifty years after the person who wrote it has passed away.

Considering that the Internet is still relatively new, it is a long time before anybody is going to lose copyright.

Part 9 — Creative Commons

At the other end of the spectrum of protecting intellectual property, there is a movement afoot to increase access to information through the Internet. For a completely different take on the copyright law, consider Creative Commons, which is an international non-profit organization. Its website enables copyright holders to grant some of their rights to the public so that the public can access otherwise copyrighted information for free.

Professor Michael Geist at the University of Ottawa has edited a book entitled, *In the Public Interest: The Future of Canadian Copyright Law*. The 600-page book has numerous articles written by a variety of Canadian academics and is published by Irwin Law Inc. Professor Geist is a recognized expert and holds the Canadian Research Chair in Internet and E-Commerce Law at the University of Ottawa. Professor Geist and his publisher are allowing the entire book to be downloaded free of charge. In the event that there are any royalties from the publication of the book, they are being donated to Creative Commons. The book is available at *www.irwinlaw.com/books. aspx?bookid=120*.

There is a bit of method to the seeming madness in giving a 600-page book away for free. Professor Geist surmised that, given the length of the book, not many people could afford to download and print the book in its entirety, as it would be cheaper to buy the book pre-printed and bound by the publisher. Professor Geist's guess was that free access to the information in the book on the Internet would increase interest in the book and thereby generate sales of the printed version.

The jury is out on whether the idea of licensing the publication of a book in the Creative Commons will catch on for anything more than academic interests, but it is certainly a generous and creative way of placing valuable information about copyright law in the hands of the public. Go, Professor Geist, go! Go, Creative Commons, go!

Part 10 — Can We Patent Life?

Over the last decade, the news has been filled with stories of cloning sheep, DNA breakthroughs and what has been referred to as the "Harvard Mouse." These are all discussions focused on scientific advances, and even though numerous countries have banned research that could lead to human cloning, and even though many groups have denounced the very research itself, it seems impossible to deny that somewhere in the world this scientific research continues. We know for a fact that Scottish scientists did clone a sheep, and we know for a fact that scientists at Harvard genetically altered a mouse for cancer research purposes. Why is this of interest in the area of intellectual property? Well, the Harvard Mouse received patent protection both in the United States and in Europe. The Canadian Supreme Court refused to accept a patent claim, but our jurisdiction recognizes patents from the United States and Europe. It seems to be a widely held view that US patent law is broader than Canadian law, and it seems inevitable that more variations on the Harvard Mouse idea will emerge. If a mouse can be patented, why not an entire human? Lawyers, scientists and ethicists have started to struggle with the blurring of lines between humans and other life forms. If a particular animal is used to grow an organ for a human, and that animal is then patented, how long can it be before the organs that are transplanted into humans are patented and the human being itself becomes the ultimate patent?

In one super-bizarre twist, someone speculated that if a person becomes patented, then perhaps that person giving birth to a child could be interpreted as patent infringement. In the meantime, apart from these lawyers' parlour games, for the purposes of Canadian law, our courts are not prepared to allow Canadian patent law to be applied to life forms, human or otherwise. In the rest of the world, though? That is another question. Patents on life forms may be piling up by the minute.

Conclusion

As you can see from the above sections, the law of intellectual property is a fascinating but complicated intersection of a number of fields—science, the arts, literature, medicine, health and ethics. It is one of the most dynamic areas of law and will, no doubt, produce some wild controversies in the very near future.

Chapter 10

Ten **Really** Interesting Things You Absolutely Need to Know About Canadian Law

In the previous nine chapters we have looked at specific areas of law under some general headings. One of the great things about law is that real life doesn't necessarily get conveniently pigeon-holed into a particular area, and certainly many of the calls and emails that I have had at *Strictly Legal* don't fit neatly into any of the categories above. There are lots of interesting things that happen to people and lots of interesting questions that arise just as a part of our ordinary lives. In this chapter, I have selected ten miscellaneous areas and looked at them individually. For example, on TV we see a great number of programs concerned with forensics, and certainly that subject has come up on *Strictly Legal*, so I have included a section that looks at DNA and its impact on the law. After the Conservative government did an about-face on income trust law, callers to *Strictly Legal* wanted to know if they could sue politicians if they didn't keep their promises. There have been some cases of that in Canada, and in this chapter I take a look at the prospects for lawsuits against politicians who don't keep their promises. Issues concerning animals, parental responsibility for children, sport injuries, golf course liability (you read that correctly: golf course liability) and even people suing each other because of lottery winnings and other curious twists and turns in the law are considered in this chapter. Everything you are about to read about has really happened to someone in Canada.

Part 1 — DNA and Its Impact on Canadian Law

TV shows focusing on forensic investigations seem to be all the rage right now. Somehow, I really doubt that police forces across North America have such beautiful and sophisticated labs for their criminal investigations. However, there is no doubt that scientific breakthroughs have had a huge impact on the way our law works. In particular, DNA has had an effect, not only on the criminal law in linking people directly to crime scenes, but also the law of estates, family law and even the reunification of children with birth parents and other siblings.

DNA stands for deoxyribonucleic acid. Ninety-nine per cent of the DNA in humans is identical, but that 1% of our DNA that is unique is what is used to allow biological identification of a particular person. Samples of DNA can be obtained from tissue, blood (even dried blood), bone marrow, tooth pulp, saliva and hair samples. If a direct sample is not available from a deceased person, DNA samples from known living relatives, such as a brother or sister, can be used to establish a DNA pattern for a deceased person. If there are enough samples from enough relatives, inferences can be drawn about a person's DNA.

Before the breakthroughs around DNA, lawyers were restricted to looking at the results of blood tests, but now we are seeing situations where fathers take hair samples from their children on access visits to do secret testing for DNA. These are men who are suspicious about whether they are actually the father of the child in question. In other cases, lawyers are asked to get court orders to obtain blood and tissue samples from hospitals in order to do testing. Teeth are examined, and in some situations, bodies have been exhumed to produce bone or tooth samples.

In the family law context, DNA is most commonly used with respect to paternity disputes. Blood samples are also used, and in fact, in some provinces the legislation speaks only of blood samples being obtained for paternity investigations. However, DNA is much, much more reliable. The sequence of events is usually that a child is born, the mother sues for child support, and the father questions the paternity of the child. In order to resolve the question, the courts will order paternity testing and that, more often than not, is conclusive. However, we are now seeing situations in which fathers question the paternity of a child long after the child has been born and even long after the family has been separated. Lawyers have met men who have discovered that the child they raised as their own is in fact not biologically theirs. In some cases, this bombshell goes off just as the child is about to head off for university! In most cases it does not diminish the parent's love for the child, but it certainly can have an impact on the issue of child support. In addition, we are also seeing some parents claim paternity fraud. Paternity fraud might arise where a mother seeks child support from a man who she knows for a fact is not the father of the child in question. The courts are asked to consider whether the father should be reimbursed for the child support that he has paid or whether some form of damages or costs should be ordered against the mother. In one Ontario case, a woman who had been raped by one man told another man that she was involved with that he was the father of the child born as a result of the assault. Years later, the man determined through DNA that he was not the biological father of that child.

A second area in which DNA has had a huge impact is in determining if someone is the child of a deceased person. If so, they may be entitled to make a claim against the estate. It is not uncommon now to see someone surface after a death claiming to be a child of the person who has died, all of this coming as a shock to the deceased's traditional "family." DNA testing can be used to answer the question, and often the person's story is true—they are indeed an illegitimate, secret child of the deceased person. In some cases, people have actually left blood samples with a DNA bank. The sample can be used in such circumstances to prove who is and who is not a child of the deceased person. There have been situations in which lawyers have asked for tissue samples and blood samples in the event that further testing is required.

Another interesting question that arises is: who may authorize DNA testing on the remains of a deceased person? Not every person has the foresight to attach a direction or an authorization to their will or to leave a sample of their DNA. In the absence of some specific authorization, it would appear that the executor or estate trustee has the authority to make decisions regarding the body of the deceased. This could include asking that the body be exhumed for DNA testing.

Canadian provinces have also been easing the laws with respect to reunification of adopted children and their birth parents. This has led to circumstances in which the adopted person and the supposed birth parent seek confirmation of their biological link at the point of reunification. Sometimes the birth parent has passed away, but other siblings can be located. With enough testing of individuals, DNA links between child and birth parent can be confirmed even if the birth parent has died and there is no DNA sample.

In questions of paternity, a little jurisdictional competition has arisen in the area of DNA testing. Some labs in European jurisdictions have profited by inviting parents in other jurisdictions to send DNA samples by courier and have the results delivered by return courier. Mouth swabs or as few as ten hairs from an individual can be used to do reliable DNA testing. On this last point, reliability is critical. In some cases, the competition between labs has been so fierce that price-cutting has led to a decline in standards. There have even been stories of fake DNA testing reports and of individuals' being paid to deliver the "correct results." This means that anyone preparing to do DNA testing should use a reliable lab. There are a number of good ones in Canada.

It was recently alleged that Michael Jackson is not the father of his two children. His partner, Debbie Rowe, who is definitely the children's mother, says that he is not the biological father, but that the children were conceived using a donor from a sperm bank. DNA will give us the answer someday soon.

Part 2 — Damages

In this section, I want to take a few minutes to explain how damages are calculated when a person is successful with a lawsuit and also to explain some of the related concepts that may increase or decrease the amount of damages recovered.

There are three forms of damages—general, special and punitive. Sometimes they have other names attached to them. For example, punitive damages are sometimes called aggravated or exemplary damages. Special damages are sometimes referred to as "out-of-pockets," but the basic idea behind the types of damages is easily understood. General damages are intended to compensate a person for pain and suffering or damage they have suffered as a result of some harm. Special damages are intended to reimburse an injured person for specific, quantifiable items that are lost. So, for example, if an injured person makes specific expenditure for a van that can be operated by a paraplegic, then that may be a specific item for which the individual can be compensated. Punitive damages are also damages, but they are not ordered to compensate an injured person. They are ordered to punish the person who caused some damage. It is a way for the court to send a signal that one of the parties to the litigation has behaved unfairly. Punitive damages have been awarded, for example, against insurance companies that insisted that an insured person had committed arson when there was no evidence to support such a serious allegation.

Damages that flow from a breach of contract and a civil wrong (or what is known as a tort) are similar, but they are not necessarily calculated in exactly the same way. For example, in the case of breach of contract, the contract itself may have some provisions that govern the calculation of damages if a breach occurs. Some contracts even set out an amount that is payable if there is a breach, almost like a fine that is paid because everyone knows exactly what the cost of a breach will be. In tort cases, such as negligence or assault and battery, the calculation of the damages can be quite a feat, depending on the severity of the damage caused. The object, generally, in awarding damages is to try and put the injured person back in the position that they would have been in had nothing bad happened to them. That can be impossible if someone is severely injured or scarred. The Court will often look at extensive medical evidence and opinions to determine exactly how much money it will take to restore that individual from the harm that they suffered.

Sometimes you will hear the expression that damages are "too remote." This means that the damage that is claimed is far too distant from the actual act that caused the initial injury. For example, let's say someone was driving to the airport, and they were in a car accident, and they were injured. As a result of the injury, they cancelled a vacation. Clearly, they would be compensated for their injuries and for the monies lost as a result of the missed vacation, but what if the person who was injured claimed that had they been able to go on the vacation they would have had a chance to go to a party and at the party they would have had a chance to win a valuable prize. At a certain point the damages become too remote to expect anyone to compensate the injured person. The Court always makes sure that the claims for damages are reasonable.

On *Strictly Legal* I talked about the concept of "*novus actus interveniens*." This is the idea that after someone has been injured, another event occurs that perhaps makes the injury worse or different in some way. The person who caused the initial injury will state that he or she cannot reasonably be expected to compensate the injured person for the harm that was caused after the intervening act, the "*novus actus interveniens*". A good example would be a situation where someone was injured in a ski accident and broke their leg. If that person was then taken to the hospital, and a doctor negligently dealt with the injury, and the leg had to be amputated, the person who caused the initial ski accident injury cannot be held responsible for the increase in suffering and harm and damages after the doctor's negligence.

Another concept that is mentioned in calculating damages is the "Thin Skull Doctrine." It is a general rule of damage calculation that when you injure somebody, you take that victim as you find them. In other words, if the person you harm has some particularly high sensitivity to injury, that is not going to be an excuse for you to not pay their damages. If they were predisposed to injury, you will be responsible for the consequences of harming them. For example, imagine if you harmed a person who was a hemophiliac. You would have no way of knowing that when you injured them, but certainly their propensity to heal much more slowly than a normal person is something for which the person causing the injury will be responsible. The only time that the "Thin Skull Doctrine" is not applicable is if the injury suffered is completely off the scale of what would be expected to happen to somebody in those circumstances. So, for example, imagine being in a car accident with someone who is injured and later, as a result of their injuries, becomes depressed and, as a result of their depression, develops an addiction to gambling. Those damages may be too remote or they may not be payable because the person who was injured had a "thin skull."

Sometimes the person injured also sues for economic loss. In other words, as a result of their injuries, they not only experienced pain and suffering, but they lost some economic benefit; they lost their job, they lost their home, they lost their business. These kinds of economic losses are recoverable as a part of damages provided they're direct and reasonable.

Family members also are affected when someone is injured or damaged, and family members must often take time off from work to care for an injured person or to assist them in recovery. Perhaps they provide daycare for their children or bring the injured person into their home for 24-hour care. This type of claim on behalf of family members who have also suffered a loss of enjoyment of life or a loss of companionship can be joined in a lawsuit and recovered at the same time the injured person recovers their damages.

Lawyers have a dark "joke" about being involved in an accident, suggesting that if you're going to be in an accident, make sure that you kill the person because the damages will be less. This is based on the fact that if a person is killed as a result of an injury, the pain and suffering component ends, and it is no longer compensable. However, the loss of income component for the surviving family and the deceased individual's estate may still be considerable. Trust me—there is no benefit to killing someone as opposed to merely injuring them. If the injured person dies while the litigation over their injuries is underway, there will be some procedural changes because the deceased person's claim will now be taken over by the estate, and there will be a recalculation of the damages being claimed, including a recalculation of loss of care and companionship for children and other family members.

Another word that comes up from time to time in the area of damages is "mitigate." It is said that a person who is injured has a duty to mitigate or lessen their losses. In other words, a person who has been injured cannot sit back and just let as much as dam-

228 — Michael G. Cochrane

age as possible happen to them, hoping that they are going to be compensated for everything that flows from the original event. So, for example, if an individual's basement was flooded, and he just decided to leave everything in the basement without removing anything to try to dry it out and save it, his overall damages would be reduced because he failed to mitigate. The onus is on the person being asked to pay the damages to prove that the person claiming damages failed to mitigate, however.

Sometimes a person being sued for damages will state that the injury to the victim involved contributory negligence. In other words, the injured person caused some of their own injuries. The most common example of this is where someone is in a car accident that has clearly been caused by one of the drivers, but the injured person's injuries are much more severe because they were not wearing a seat belt. This is called "contributory negligence."

Another concept that comes up from time to time is "*volentia non fit injuria,*" which is just a fancy way of saying "voluntary assumption of the risk." If you've ever taken a minute to read the opposite side of a ticket for a hockey game or a sporting event, you'll notice that there's a release there stating that spectators are voluntarily assuming the risk of the possibility of an injury. For example, if a spectator is hit by a puck, that is a foreseeable consequence of being at a hockey game. Similarly, spectators at a golf course watching a tournament can expect to run the risk of being hit by an errant golf ball. When someone sues for damages, a defendant who is being asked to pay those damages may state by way of defence that the injured person voluntarily assumed the risk of the injury and should not be compensated. (For information about this issue see Sections 6 and 7 below concerning sports injuries and golf course liability.)

The way in which damages are calculated is often tailored to the type of claim that is being made. So, a breach of contract is different from negligence, and fatal accidents are different from non-fatal accidents; damages for assault and battery are different from damages for slander or libel, and so on. Each case needs to be tailored to its own specific facts and the people involved.

Part 3 — Suing Politicians to Keep Their Promises

On more than one occasion on *Strictly Legal* I have received telephone calls asking whether a politician can be sued for breaking a promise. If one believes the rhetoric we hear from some Canadian political leaders, keeping a promise "is a badge of honour." Election campaigns are rife with statements amounting to, "re-elect me because I did what I said I was going to do!"

So, how can citizens hold politicians accountable for the promises that they make and then break? In some situations, citizens actually have sued to get a judge's opinion on whether there should be some accountability in a courtroom rather than just a number of years later at the polls.

The two most interesting cases come from British Columbia and Ontario. The British Columbia case concerned the infamous "fudget budget." The lawsuit, which was initially framed as a class action, was later reduced to a claim by three representatives who purported to speak on behalf of voters in their constituencies. They alleged that the NDP party in British Columbia and the MLAs seeking re-election made statements about the 1995/1996 and 1996/1997 provincial budgets, knowing the statements were false. The voters claimed that had they known that representations about the budget were untrue, they would not have voted for the NDP. They sought a court order overturning the election of thirty-nine NDP MLAs. The case was important because if the voters had succeeded in overturning the election of even a handful of NDP MLAs, the majority of the NDP in the legislative assembly would have been turned upside down. Ultimately it was conceivable that the government could fall and trigger another election. The voters were not successful in overturning the election of the MLAs, but the court took a long hard look at relationship between the courts and politics. Those who have spent time looking at the "fudget budget" case have concluded that it set a precedent that will very likely bring more political controversies into the courts for review.

The second case, from Ontario, concerns a written promise made by Liberal Premier Dalton McGuinty during the 2003 election campaign. Promising not to increase taxes without the expressed permission of voters was a key commitment in garnering credibility for the Liberals during the election campaign.

The then Premier of Ontario, Mike Harris, had passed a law known as the Taxpayer Protection Act. Mr. McGuinty, who was at that time hoping to replace Harris as premier, signed a written promise to abide by the Taxpayer Protection Act and to not raise taxes if he was elected. The Liberals were elected but in their very first budget they introduced a "health care premium" which qualified, of course, as a tax. The Canadian Taxpayers Federation then sued to have the law introducing this new tax declared invalid. They also sued Mr. McGuinty, who was now Premier, for breach of contract and for negligent misrepresentation in promising not to raise taxes.

The matter was dealt with in a court in Ontario in 2004 and the judge, after reviewing all the facts, stated "few people would consider that all of the promises made and pledges given constitute legally binding agreements between the candidate and the elector or electors to whom these promises or pledges were made." It was also the judge's conclusion that to have a proper, functioning democracy, candidates and parties should do their best to follow through on their promises, but it is not the role of the courts to police politics on behalf of voters.

A number of callers to *Strictly Legal* asked whether a class action (see Section 9 below dealing with class action) against the Conservative Party of Canada and the Prime Minister, Stephen Harper, would be possible after the change to the rules for taxation of income trusts. This change was alleged to cost investors millions of dollars, and threats of lawsuits continue to be made. Anyone planning to undertake such a lawsuit has at least two previous rulings from Canadian courts to guide them. However, until a judge rules that politicians can be held accountable in a courtroom, voters will have only the ballot box and a chance to vote differently in the next election. We will see how this area evolves in the next few years.

Part 4 — Animals

Legal problems concerning animals typically come up in four general areas:

i) Divorce and separation, and in particular who gets the
  pets?

ii) Dog bites;

iii) Abuse of animals; and

iv) Wills—is it possible to provide for an animal after the
  owner's death?

i) Divorce and separation

When it comes to separation and divorce, the question of
who gets the pet can be quite emotional. When a legally married couple divorces, their pets can get caught in the crossfire as
quickly as some children in a custody dispute. In fact, some
people carry on about their pets as if they *were* children. In the
eyes of the law though, while pets are life forms and should be
respected and loved, they are in the final analysis simply property. This issue has gone as far as to the Ontario Court of
Appeal, and the learned justices there have confirmed that
courts cannot make custody orders with respect to pets. They
are to treat them simply as property to be divided in the regular
course in divorce or separation proceedings.

As we know from Chapter 2, dealing with family law
issues, the value of property is to be divided at the time of separation and divorce for legally married couples. The trouble
with pets is, there is sometimes no clear owner, or the ownership
is joint, or the value of the animal in question cannot be easily
determined. It can be a lot more complicated than simply who
gets the dog, the cat or the horses?

In some cases, spouses have been forced to bid for their
pets. This amounts to one saying to the other, "Do you really
want Blackie? Well then, what's he worth to you?" Other couples share their pets post-separation almost as if they had a
"joint custody" arrangement for the animal.

Certainly, if someone brought the pet into the marriage then
they will leave with that pet. If the pet was a gift made by one
spouse to the other during the course of the relationship then it
will not be shared, as gifts are exempt from sharing. If the children are attached to a pet (or the opposite—the child can't be
near the pet because they are allergic), this can have an impact

on who ends up caring for Fido. Otherwise, the regular rules for property division apply, and a value will need to be obtained for the animals in question. The values of the pets are put into the property division calculation, and then generally a bidding war begins in the context of separating property. Some couples are forced to negotiate over the pets the same way they negotiate over the contents of their homes. If a couple can't decide and they leave it to a judge, it's guaranteed that only one person will be happy.

Common-law couples may be in a different position because, as we saw above in Chapter 2 dealing with family law, provinces treat the division of property at the end of common-law relationships differently than marriages. With legally married people, it's an automatic pooling of the value of assets acquired between the date of marriage and the date of separation. With common-law couples, you are presumed to take out the items that are in your name (this is, of course subject to some of the new property division schemes that are being developed in provinces like Manitoba, British Columbia and Nova Scotia where couples have an opportunity to opt into property sharing even though living common-law). Common-law couples can get just as emotional as legally married couples about their pets, and yes, judges themselves have pets, but that doesn't stop them from making tough decisions when it comes to dividing pets at the time of separation.

ii) Dog bites

This can be one of the more scary situations for people, especially parents of small children. As I was writing this book, a small boy on a reserve in Western Canada was killed by a pack of dogs. Every year, there is more than one pitiful story of a child being disfigured by a dog's bite to their face, arms or torso. When it happens, there is a lot of trouble. Consider the following possibilities.

- The dog may have to be destroyed. Legislation in a number of provinces allows for the seizure and destruction of an animal considered to be dangerous. In particular, in Ontario a law was passed recently concerning pit bulls. These dogs are now banned, and in an interesting twist, not only pit bulls themselves are banned but also dogs *that look like pit bulls*. In terms of destruction of an animal, there have been some incidents recently where police have been forced to shoot animals in order to restore calm when the animal has attacked an individual.

Another, less serious, consequence of a dog biting is the possible requirement that the dog wear a muzzle. For example, in the City of Toronto, if a dog bites an individual and there is a complaint to animal bylaw enforcement, then the likely response from the city will be a requirement that the animal wear a muzzle when in public.

The statement "every dog gets one bite" is an absolute falsehood. Every dog is, and every dog owner is, responsible for every bite. If your dog bites or has a propensity to bite, not doing something about prevention could unleash a horrible sequence of events for you and the dog.

- The owner of the dog may also be charged with a variety of offences. Every municipality has bylaw restrictions with respect to animals, in some cases requiring licensing, leashing and fencing, and there are even limitations with respect to the number of animals permitted on property in some jurisdictions. Provincial laws also have offence provisions in very serious cases where someone has been reckless or has deliberately used their dog, for example in an attack on a person. Charges can be laid that will result in serious fines and jail sentences. If a dog bites, it is possible that three separate sets of offences may be triggered: there may be charges under municipal bylaws; there may be charges under provincial laws, and even the Criminal Code can be used depending on how serious the bite is and on the owner's track record in managing the animal.

- Owners are responsible for any harm caused by their animals. So, for example, if a dog is running loose and bites a child, the owner of the dog can expect to be sued

234 — Michael G. Cochrane

for general damages (see Section 2 in this chapter), which are intended to compensate the injured person for pain and suffering and perhaps for the expenses of private therapy for a child who has been traumatized. In addition, the court could order punitive damages to punish reckless behaviour by the owner of the dog.

Let's be clear about one thing, the fact that it is a dog that caused the injury will not change the consequences if medical treatment is required. In other words, if someone's face is disfigured by a car accident and they require plastic surgery, the damages can be considerable. If the same type of disfigurement has been caused by the bite of a dog, the owner will be just as responsible as the person who caused the car accident. Few, if any, people carry insurance for such an incident. At least if you hit someone with your car, there is a likelihood that the insurance policy will cover you, so you don't have to pay the damages and the legal fees out of your own pocket. An uninsured dog owner could lose their home just paying legal fees not to mention the damages that would be awarded in defending such a case.

An exception might be where the dog attack occurs on the dog owner's own property and then house insurance or tenant insurance may be used to cover the claim. It is important to check the terms of the policies however to see if such a claim would be covered or if it is specifically excluded.

• The owner of property on which the attack occurred (if they are not the dog's owner) may also be sued. In other words, if someone takes their dog to someone else's home, and the dog is allowed to run around in the yard and while in the yard it bites someone, then the homeowner—in addition to the dog owner—may be required to compensate the injured person.

In such circumstances, if you have an applicable insurance policy and you are able to use it to cover the claim, the insurance company will provide a lawyer to defend the case. This, in itself, can be a huge financial lifesaver. Lawyer's fees can rapidly reach into the tens of thousands of dollars when defending personal injury cases, and don't forget there is virtually no upside in such a lawsuit for the owner of the dog. It is extremely unlikely that you will be on the receiving end of any money, and very unlikely that you will receive any reimbursement for any legal fees incurred. When you defend such a lawsuit, even if you win you may still walk away with very high lawyer's fees if you don't have insurance in place. The bottom line here is that if you have animal that may bite, either take steps to minimize the likelihood of that incurring or ensure that you have some kind of insurance in place to protect you.

iii) Abuse of animals

Municipal bylaws, provincial law and the Canadian Criminal Code all provide laws for the prevention of abuse to animals. These rules are designed to protect wildlife, pets owned by Canadians, and even animals in zoos or circuses. If you witness a situation of animal abuse, the starting point is the municipal bylaw enforcement agency. If there is no authority readily availability to intervene, the next stop is the local police station where you will no doubt receive the attention of sympathetic police officers. It is a curious fact about animal abuse that authorities tend to keep a watch on individuals accused of cruelty to animals. It is considered to be evidence of an individual who may escalate their violence into violence against people. Many serial killers had a history of animal cruelty when they were young, and this just makes them extra creepy.

iv) Wills and estates and pets

Yes, you can leave everything to your cat! Many people are concerned about what will happen to their pets after they themselves have died. The best way to ensure that an animal is cared for is to leave a sum of money to the executor of your estate or to a trustee to care for the animal. In some cases, the person making the will has left a certain some of money to an animal shelter to care for the animal. An individual will then administer the funds to ensure the particular animal's well-being.

Related to this question is what happens to a person's pet when that individual has passed away. So much attention is focused on the person who has died that pets may be forgotten. Someone may need to intervene quickly to ensure that the pet has a good home or that it is at the very least taken to a local animal shelter where it can be adopted or—as an absolute last resort—humanely put down if no one steps forward to care for it. That last part may sound harsh, but it is not uncommon to have a family member or even the executor of someone's estate arrive at the deceased's home to find several animals that are no longer being cared for. If you were in that person's shoes, could you find a home for several pets on short notice? If you are an animal lover, and you have pets, you may want to consider providing some guidance for who will care for your pet in the event of your death.

Animals are certainly an important part of the lives of Canadians. They can be responsible for a great deal of grief if a couple splits up, or if the animal bites someone, or if for some reason if the animal is not cared for or abused. If you are a pet owner or you know someone who has pets, it is worth taking a moment to think about all of these issues and I don't just mean the value of having insurance in place if a dog bites a child. Just ensure that your animals are accorded the love and respect that they deserve no matter what happens.

Part 5 — Parents' Responsibility For Their Children

A number of Canadian provinces have passed laws making parents responsible for damage caused by their children. As we saw in Chapter 4, a child under the age of twelve cannot be charged with a criminal offence. Children from the ages of twelve to eighteen, however, are treated as young offenders and if they get into trouble, that may not be the end of it for either them or their parents.

Both children and their parents can be held responsible to pay damages for harm caused by the child. In one Ontario case, a five-year-old boy was playing with his mother's cigarette lighter in a bedroom closet at 7:30 a.m. while his mother slept in her bedroom. A fire started, and it damaged multiple units in the apartment building in which they lived. The owner of the apartment building and an adjoining tenant sued the mother on the basis that she was negligent for failing to secure the cigarette lighters and failing to supervise her child. A part of the testimony at the trial involved a neighbour saying that the night before the fire, he had seen the woman's children playing with matches and had told the mother about this. The result was that the mother was responsible for all of the damages resulting from the fire. Let's hope she had insurance.

What if the harm caused by the children is actually a result of criminal activity? In one case, children who were fourteen and ten years of age broke into houses and stole more than $20,000 worth of jewellery and other valuable items. The victims of the break-in sued the parents of the children, and the issue arose at the trial as to whether the children were being properly supervised. The older boy had been asked to babysit the younger one and was being paid $2 an hour; a regular schedule of check-in times with the parents had been arranged with telephone calls and a schedule of activities. Despite that plan, the children, under the leadership of the older boy, still managed to get into trouble by breaking into houses. In that case, the victims of the break-in relied upon the Parental Responsibility Act, which is the law that many provinces are adopting. It defines a child as a person who is under the age of eighteen, and it states that where a child takes, damages or destroys property, the owner may bring an action in a Small Claims Court against the parent of the child to recover damages. The parents have a defence, however, if they can prove to the court that they were exercising reasonable supervision over the child, and reasonable efforts had been made to prevent or discourage the child from engaging in the kind of activity that resulted in the loss. A long list of considerations is also set out in the act so that the court may consider such things as the age of the child, prior conduct of the child, the potential danger of the activity, the physical or mental capacity of the child, any kinds of physical, psychological or medical disorders, the kind of direct supervision that the child was under at the time and, interestingly, the court will even consider whether the parents have sought to improve their parenting skills by attending parenting courses. That last one may seem a little redundant after there has been trouble and damage caused. In the particular case of the young burglars, the parents were not held responsible for the damage caused by the children because the judge thought they had taken adequate steps to control the children during the day and had not been careless.

This has become an issue in another very dangerous and deadly context—street racing by young people. Ontario, British Columbia and other provinces have all experienced some horrific fatalities involving young people racing cars. In the Greater Toronto Area alone, twenty-nine people were killed in a six-year period directly as a result of street racing. Children under the age of eighteen, who somehow get access to an automobile and street race with fatal consequences, may find themselves charged with Criminal Code offences. They may also find that their parents are being sued for damages.

There are many young people coming to Canada to study. When they do so, they require a custodian in Canada if their parents are not here to care for them. All minor applicants wanting permission to live and study in Canada must supply a declaration signed by their parents or legal guardians as well as by their custodian in Canada. This declaration states that arrangements have been made for the custodian to act in the place of a parent. People who enter into these "custodian arrangements" should appreciate that if the minor child causes damages, they too may be held responsible, the same way a parent would be held responsible for the harm caused by their children. If you are in a situation where your child may be at risk of getting into trouble and causing damage, or if your child is going to be left in charge of a particular situation, such as babysitting, keep in mind that their actions, and any damages that flow from them, may be traced directly back to you and your wallet.

Part 6 — Sports Injuries

Concerns about sports injuries arise in two general situations: when someone is injured as a spectator at a sporting event and when someone is injured as a participant in a sporting event.

Attendance at any North American sporting event that involves the purchase of a ticket includes implied acceptance of the conditions that appear on the reverse of that ticket. I would hazard a guess that very few spectators actually read the conditions that are attached to the purchase of their ticket, but they are quite comprehensive. Essentially, a spectator at a sporting event is agreeing to accept the reasonable risk that injuries may occur. Pucks may fly into the crowd, baseballs may be hit into the stands, players may fall into the laps of spectators, and so on. If these types of things happen while we watch a sporting event and we are injured, barring some unusual circumstances, we will not be able to sue to recover damages for these injuries. When we attend the event, we are voluntarily assuming the risk that something like that may happen. I say "barring some unusual circumstances" because there are always exceptions. For example, if a spectator deliberately bought a seat in a section that was protected by netting or protective glass—as is typical at the end of most hockey arenas—and for some reason the netting or glass is not maintained, and a puck gets through the net and injures a spectator, then there may be liability for the owner/operator of the sporting event. In other words, if the owner/operator of the arena offers these seats as protected areas, then there will be a higher responsibility to ensure that they are in fact protected.

These releases and limitations on liability do not extend to every conceivable injury that can occur. The spectator is consenting only to the types of incidents that reasonably occur as a part of such sporting events. In British Columbia's Vancouver Stadium the roof recently collapsed, and in Montreal the infamous stadium built for the 1976 Olympics is now crumbling at certain points. If a chunk of concrete fell off a stadium and struck a spectator, the owner/operator of the arena or stadium could not rely on the release on the ticket. Spectators do not reasonably accept the risk of such injuries. Similarly, if an elevator or escalator broke and people were injured at a sports facility the limitation of liability on the ticket would not apply.

If deliberate acts occur, the limitation and release of liability may not apply. So, if a football player or a baseball player deliberately throws a piece of equipment into the stands and injuries occur, fans do not accept the risk of such behaviour. If hockey players carry their brawl into the stands, and spectators are injured, the releases on the tickets will not apply.

Our liability to each other for injuries suffered during the course of a sporting event *in which we are participating* is similar to that of spectators. Participants in sporting events are consenting to a certain amount of risk of injury. Hockey players in a contact league know that they will be bodychecked from time to time. If the players, however, are in a non-contact league, and a player delivers a bodycheck deliberately and another player is injured, the injured player did not consent to that level of potential harm and a lawsuit could follow.

Canadian courts see cases every year of young people being injured in hockey games. In one case in British Columbia, a player in a midget hockey league for players between seventeen and nineteen years of age was checked head first into the boards by another player who was considered to be the biggest player in the league. The smaller player broke his neck and was rendered a C4 quadriplegic. Checking from behind in such circumstances is banned in the league rules. The judge ruled that the check was thoughtless, and that the player who hit from behind was duty-bound to avoid contacting the other player from the rear in that way. In other words, if the player had administered a normal bodycheck and the other player had simply fallen to the ice and broken his neck, no liability would have flowed from that because that is a part of that which we consent to as a participant. By breaking the rules and checking from behind, the player went beyond what the other player was reasonably consenting to.

This type of issue was canvassed extensively in the incident involving Todd Bertuzzi and Steve Moore. Bertuzzi punched Moore blindly in the side of the head, knocking Moore unconscious. Bertuzzi then fell forward, and with his momentum, drove Moore's head into the ice, breaking three vertebrae in his neck, giving him a grade three concussion, ligament damage and facial cuts among other injuries. Moore and his parents are suing

Bertuzzi in civil court as a result of that attack because, even though these players are professional and hockey is a rough sport, there's no reasonable possibility that Moore would have consented to that level of violence against him in a hockey game. Bertuzzi was also convicted of assault causing bodily harm and was given a conditional discharge and one-year probation.

A variation on this theme of liability for injuries suffered while enjoying sporting events concerns the relationship between the participant and those who are responsible for the activity. For example, the use of waterslides, ski hills and other facilities.

In one Ontario case, a man broke his ankle at a water park. He had used the slide two or three times that day but on one occasion when he stepped into the entry tub at the top of the slide, he slipped and came down hard on his ankle. He sued the owner/operator of the water park. Their defence was that the injured man had voluntarily assumed the risk of such injuries when he came to the park. In that particular case, the judge concluded that the defendants had not proved the voluntary assumption of risk and said that the mere enjoyment of the slide, for which a fee had been charged, did not amount to abandonment of his legal rights. He was compensated for his pain and suffering.

Other interesting cases in this area deal with ski resorts, which have on the back of their day tickets and season passes extensive releases of liability for injuries suffered. The injuries range from skiers being killed in avalanches to skiers being run over by snowmobiles, but in each and every case, owners of the resorts have relied upon the release of liability on the ticket. In one case, involving a ski resort in British Columbia, a season's pass holder collided with a snowmobile being operated by an employee of the resort. The resort was successful in relying upon their release, and the judge found that it is usual and customary to find snowmobiles being used to transport maintenance and lift personnel about the mountain, and that the injured person was very familiar with the presence and operation of the snowmobiles on the trails at the resort. Result: no liability for the resort.

The cases reported in Canada cover just about every type of sporting event from motorcycles to horseback riding to ball hockey and more. If you are a spectator, you are consenting to reasonable possibility of injury being caused by some aspect of that sporting event. In other words, errant pucks and foul balls are not going to give you the right to sue unless it is a very unusual circumstance. If you are a participant in a sport, you are also consenting to a risk of injury, provided the activities are reasonable and within the rules of the game. If you are using facilities provided by someone, such as a water park, a hockey arena, a ski hill, and so on, your activity may be subject to limitations on liability and releases that form a part of your contract to use that facility. These releases and limitations on liability must be in writing and must be brought to your attention. That is why they are printed on the back of the ticket. If you suffer an injury, and the cause of that injury is some activity that is a reasonable part of what occurs at that location, you may not be successful in your claim for compensation.

Part 7 — Golf Course Liability

I've become a bit of a golf nut over the last few years and love nothing more than to spend a day on the course with my buddies. After witnessing a particularly scary incident involving a golf cart one day, I decided to do some research on golf course liability. There are literally dozens of cases across North America of golfers and golf courses getting involved in law suits. The claims tend to fall into the following categories:

i) Golfers injuring spectators;
ii) Golfers injuring other golfers;
iii) Golfers suing golf courses for negligent design;
iv) Adjacent property owners suing golf courses because they are causing a nuisance.

i) Golfers injuring spectators

When a spectator attends an event at a golf course, the ticket or pass that they purchase has a release or a limitation of liability on the reverse side (see Part 6 in this chapter dealing with Sports Injuries). Spectators at golfing events consent to the possibility that they may be struck by an errant golf ball. In other words, this is a part of attending such an event. Spectators typically line the fairways, stand near tee boxes, and crowd around golfers at every turn in the golf course. Spectators are often hit by golf balls, but they cannot sue successfully for damages because they have voluntarily assumed the risk of that type of injury when they attended the event. Once again, the voluntary assumption of risk extends only to activities that are normal for a golf course, and within the rules of golf. An errant tee shot is one thing but a ball struck in anger and without thinking of the crowd, or a club tossed that strikes a spectator is not the kind of behaviour that a spectator is willing to assume the risk of. Bottom line: if you're attending a golf tournament, keep your eyes open, and don't expect to sue anybody if you get hit in the ordinary course of play.

ii) *Golfers suing other golfers*

If you are playing golf, and you are following the rules, and your shot happens to strike another player, there will be no liability. Just like other participants in sporting events, all golfers willingly assume the risk of these types of injuries when they are on a golf course. If you shank a shot and it hits someone on another tee box or fairway, liability is very unlikely. This is the case regardless of how bad the shot is. Judges have said specifically in court decisions that no one expects golf shots to always go where they are intended to go. That is what makes it golf. The tricky part is injuries that are caused by golfers *who are operating outside the rules of golf.* For example, in one case a golfer was the last one in his foursome to tee off. His tee shot appeared to go into the woods. The other golfers in his foursome began to walk to their golf carts. The golfer on the tee box however, teed up what became known as "the unannounced mulligan" (basically taking his shot over). Without saying anything to his partners, he proceeded to hit what he considered to be a second drive. Unfortunately, the second ball went from the heel of his golf club to the cheekbone of his playing partner, fracturing it. His partner sued him successfully for the injury because the unannounced mulligan is not a part of the rules of golf, and his playing partners had no reasonable expectation that he would simply tee up another ball and hit it without a warning.

A similar result occurs when other, more obvious, misconduct occurs. Golfers who throw clubs or hit clubs on ball washers and so on will be responsible for any injuries caused by their outbursts. This is the case whether the injured person is a part of the golfer's foursome or on another part of the course. If you follow the rules you'll be fine. If not, you'll be liable.

iii) Golfers suing golf courses for negligent design

When I describe this type of liability to most golfers they laugh at the possibility that someone could consider a golf course to have been negligently designed. We may say a lot of other things about the layout of a course, but negligent? The way these types of claims arise, however, makes perfect sense. Consider for example, the situation of a golfer who tees off and hits his drive a modest 200 yards down the centre of the fairway. He arrives at his ball and looks at the scorecard to determine his yardage to the green on the par four. The card says 175 yards. He makes a club selection and strokes his second shot 165 yards, hoping to roll it onto the green. When he arrives at the green, he finds a golfer in the foursome ahead of his lying unconscious on the tee box for the next hole. It is then that he realizes that the layout of the golf course had been changed, but the yardage markings for the card had not been updated. He had selected too much club in the circumstances and, instead of landing the ball in front of the green, drove it onto the next tee box. That is negligent design.

These types of claims have arisen in connection with cart paths, yardage markers, sightlines and the like. Golf course owners, managers and superintendents need to be aware of these types of dangers, which are not ordinarily accepted as a risk of playing golf. The injured golfer in the situation I mention sued the golfer whose shot passed the green; that golfer in turn sued the golf course to pass on the liability caused by their negligence.

iv) *Adjacent property owners and golf courses*

There is growing litigation against golf courses and driving ranges in connection with the effects of errant golf balls on adjacent properties. In Toronto, there was a recent case against Islington Golf Club in connection with errant shots on the third hole. (Been there; done that!) These shots ended up in the backyard of a homeowner who had constructed his home after the construction of the golf course. He complained that the design of the course facilitated golf balls hitting his property to such an extent that it was a nuisance. The court agreed and the golf course was forced to change the layout of the hole and to take steps to alleviate the problem of balls landing in that homeowner's yard.

In one Alberta case, homeowners who lived adjacent to the driving range portion of a golf course obtained an injunction against the golf course to stop golf balls from coming into their yard. Golf courses will be forced to erect nets or change the layout of courses if the errant shots of golfers fly onto adjacent properties or roadways to such an extent that they cause a nuisance.

It is not uncommon for cars that pass by golf courses to be struck by golf balls that have left the playing area. Drivers are not expected to accept the risk of that type of damage to their vehicle and a quick stop at the pro shop of the golf course in question should be made to register a complaint and request for compensation. At one golf club in Toronto, members who hit shots off the golf course property into the residential area (whether a home or roadway) follow an honour system of reporting their shot and the type of ball, in case there is a claim of damage.

For these and other reasons, I think it's always important to invite a lawyer to play golf with you.

Part 8 — Lotteries — Litigation

I probably could have written an entire book about lotteries and the difficulties people can get into—when they win! The only good news is that, despite my hunch that no one actually wins lotteries, the amount of litigation over lotteries suggests that a few people out there are winning—and fighting about it.

The problems that arise I categorize as follows:

i) Lottery winners suing their co-winners;
ii) Divorcing/separating couples fighting over lottery winnings;
iii) Lottery winners fighting lottery corporations, Canada Revenue Agency and trustees in bankruptcy.

Some of the conduct in these cases is not pretty. As one judge said, "Lottery won, friendship lost."

i) Lottery winners suing their co-winners

Problems arise between co-winners primarily because of a lack of certainty about who paid for the ticket and who was to share it if there was a win. In one case, a group of women contributed to the purchase of a "group" set of tickets each week. This went on for some time until one week one of the women did not contribute because of a lack of money. Guess what? That is the week they won. She got nothing, but she felt she should have because of their long-standing habit of chipping in and sharing. She claimed that there was "an understanding." Lack of clarity about what is supposed to happen is really what these cases are all about. Some people photocopy the ticket and everyone who has paid gets a copy—no copy, no participation in the winnings. That is how group play should work.

In another case, two women were in the same bowling league for many years. They shared raffle tickets fifty-fifty; sometimes they won, most of the time they did not. Sometimes they shared the winnings if they were both present on the evening of the win. Sometimes they did not share if only one of them came to the bowling that night. Then came the *Cash for Life* lottery tickets at a Christmas party one year. One friend picked up the other lady's ticket for her since she could not attend that particular Christmas party. Guess what? One ticket won, one ticket did not. Was there a contract between these two ladies to share all winnings in the lotteries? Answer—no. Was there a trust arrangement where if one won the lottery she would hold it in trust for the other? No. No clear agreement for sharing meant no sharing of the winnings.

A family that had emigrated from Poland in 1989 was torn apart when "they" won $450,000 in the *Lotto 649*. Was it a family ticket? Gee, they all posed with the ticket and said that it was going to be shared pursuant to a "household understanding." The judge in that case came just shy of calling them outright liars. (Some of the evidence that they gave during the trial was described as "preposterous.") The essential point is that confusion arose because nothing was in writing. And that probably describes the situation for most families, where everyone throws a dollar into a pot and someone drives to the corner store to pick up the ticket. There is never any trouble until someone wins.

There are many more cases about group fights, but the surefire way to avoid them is to formalize the group's understanding of what happens, who buys, who shares and so on. If you're in a group at your office, send the following message around by email or copy it on the ticket and distribute copies to everyone: "The guy who wrote *Strictly Legal* says we should pin down our agreement to avoid fights when we win." Here are the rules:

- No contribution to the ticket, no participation in the winnings.
- Share equally; if the agreement is otherwise, spell it out.
- Whoever does the buying should keep track of where and when they bought it and how much they spent.
- Clarify what happens with "extras." Problems have arisen where the person who went to buy the group ticket also bought a few extra tickets for themselves, and the extra tickets were the winners. Make sure it is clear which tickets are for the group and which tickets are not.
- Photocopy the group ticket and tell everyone: "If you have a copy of that ticket, and you've made your financial contribution to its purchase, you are going to participate in the winnings."
- Avoid situations where someone says, "Well, I put in four dollars instead of two last week, but nothing this week, so I should share."

It is interesting that you never see cases of people suing each other over lottery winnings when they have it all written down...lesson learned.

ii) Divorcing and separating couples

There are many cases involving married, separated, separating and long-divorced couples suing each other over lottery ticket winnings. The winning ticket is relevant to at least three issues: property division, child support and spousal support.

Whether the money was won before or after the separation, it will be relevant when a winner has a support obligation. In other words, if you are paying support and you win the lottery, it is going to be relevant to the amount of child or spousal support that you pay in the future. (Interestingly, if you are the payer of child support, it will likely increase the child support obligations, but if the recipient of support wins a lottery, it has no impact on the amount of monthly child support.) For spousal support it will have an impact possibly for both the payer and the recipient. If the payer's winnings are considerable, it may cause the amount of spousal support to go up, and if a recipient's winnings are significant, it may cause the amount of spousal support paid to that person to go down.

Property division is a little trickier. It should depend only on when the ticket is purchased. If it was purchased before the marriage ended, then it will go into the pot for sharing. If it was purchased after separation, then it should not be divided because post-separation property is not supposed to be in the pot. However, this has not stopped a few judges (in Alberta particularly) from bending the rules and forcing winners to share, because in one case "the couple had an agreement to share any winnings." The wife was old and she was ill, and as a result the law was bent. The husband was ordered to give 25% of his post-separation winnings to his wife.

In another case, the wife wanted a credit at the time of separation for spending all of her lottery winnings on the family. The court's answer? "No way." If you use your lottery winnings for household expenses and to benefit your spouse and children you are not going to get a credit for it if the relationship breaks down.

In another case, the husband did not disclose the money he had received from a big lottery win. Instead, he spent the money and in the matrimonial proceedings said it was a "gift" from the lottery corporation. If it was property characterized as a gift, then it would not be subject to division. This argument didn't fly very far, and he ended up losing half of the matrimonial home as a result, because that was the only asset he had left to reimburse his separating spouse her share of the winnings.

If you and your spouse have some understanding that you are *not* going to split the winnings equally, then write it down because that seems to be the presumption that is going to operate—particularly if the ticket was purchased before separation. The exception is common-law couples. As we have seen in Chapter 2, they do not generally share property at the time of separation. However, I have to stress that *the law is different in each province and territory*. Some provinces are extending property division rights to common-law couples under certain situations. For example, in Ontario it is very unlikely that a common-law couple would be required to share a lottery ticket winning in the name of one of the spouses. In Manitoba, they probably would have to share it. I know—the law of common-law property division is getting crazier by the minute. If you are separating and you win the lottery, talk to a lawyer immediately in confidence. A lot will depend on where you live, and the circumstances of your case in determining whether you will be required to share your winnings.

iii) Lottery winners versus lottery corporations, Canada Revenue Agency and trustees in bankruptcies

If winners don't have enough to worry about with co-winners and spouses coming after them, they may have to fight other authorities as well.

In an Alberta case, a woman had the winning ticket stolen from her purse while grocery shopping at the local Safeway. (It is not clear why she hung onto that winning ticket for almost ten months and kept it in her purse.) Thank goodness she had made a photocopy of the winning ticket. When she presented that to the lottery corporation, the question arose: Is a photocopy good enough? She had to sue the Western Canada Lottery Corporation to get those winnings because the rules of the lottery said vaguely that an original ticket must be presented. When the court looked at the ticket and determined that it was in fact an accurate copy of the winning ticket, the court said, "Pay her."

A winner of the Ontario *Cash for Life* lottery was a little disappointed to learn that the $1,000 a week for life was actually only for twenty years, and it was also an annuity from a life insurance company. However, it was the winning ticket in a lottery, so the question arose: "Is it taxable?" Since 1972, lottery winnings in Canada are supposed to be tax-free. Not in this case. An annuity is a stream of income and, as such, it's taxable.

The last case I want to touch on concerns a man who went bankrupt. He worked with a trustee in bankruptcy and came up with an arrangement whereby he would make various modest payments with the hope that he would soon be discharged from bankruptcy. He didn't live up to the agreement that he had reached with the trustee, and as a result he was not yet discharged. Guess what happened? He won the lottery, and the question arose: "Should his creditors get paid?" The court ruled, "Absolutely."

Most of us assume that lottery winnings are a cause for celebration. For many people, they are not, and that's because the circumstances under which they enter into group purchases or have household understandings end up creating more trouble than they solve. If you are doing these group purchases, get something in writing so that there is no misunderstanding. If you don't, and you win the lottery, count your blessings, but you're probably going to end up having to argue to hang on to those winnings as they will certainly be relevant to child and spousal support and may be forced into the pot for division even if you are already clearly separated. The best reason to get a Separation Agreement immediately after separating is that there are releases in Separation Agreements that would block such claims being made against lottery winners.

I don't know about you—there's a lot of litigation out there, but I'm still buying lottery tickets.

Part 9 — Class Actions

Sometimes when reading the paper, you may see large advertisements concerning class actions. These lawsuits concern failed consumer products, frustrated investors, people injured as a result of a large accident such as an airplane crash or a subway crash and many other types of injuries that affect a large number of people.

A class proceeding is a court action that is brought on behalf of, or for the benefit of, numerous people who have suffered a common injury. It is a procedural mechanism. In other words, it is a way of suing people—it is not something that you sue for. Most normal claims made in court are launched by one or two people against one or two other people, but a class action can involve tens of thousands of people. The basic idea behind this procedural mechanism is to provide an efficient way for all of the people who have been injured to have their claims dealt with in one lawsuit. The alternative would be to have perhaps tens of thousands of people suing because they bought a defective product. A class action lets them all join in one lawsuit that is binding on the person responsible for the damages. It is better for the people who have suffered a loss, it is better for the person who caused the loss, and it is better for the justice system because it is much more efficient.

We have not always had class actions. In fact, there is no national class action procedure in Canada, although there has been some discussion about drafting one. Each province has the ability to pass a provincial class action law. Ontario has done so, as have Quebec and British Columbia. Other provinces have the procedure under consideration.

Before the class action procedure was brought to Canada, if a group of people suffered a common injury they would all have to join together, hire a lawyer, put their names on the claim and serve the defendant who had allegedly caused the injuries. This was very cumbersome, and the result of the case would only be binding on the people who were named in the claim. If someone else came along the next day and said that they had suffered the same kinds of damages, they could start the lawsuit all over again, duplicating costs and use of court time. The beauty of a

252 — *Michael G. Cochrane*

class action is that it allows two people to represent everyone who has suffered the loss. Those two people are able to hire a lawyer, issue a claim in the provincial court, serve it on the defendant and then ask for certification of the court action by a judge. Certification means that a judge looks at the type of claim and decides whether a class action procedure is the best way of dealing with it. The judge is not concerned with whether the claim will eventually succeed. The judge only looks to see if it is a good way to pursue these damages. If the case is certified, the two representative claimants have the authority to speak on behalf of everyone who might be affected by the litigation. They have an obligation to make sure that other people who are interested in the claim get notice. That's why we see the ads in the newspaper. Representative claimants are publishing notices in the paper to tell other claimants that a class action has been certified on their behalf. Sometimes the ad in the paper will tell everyone that the case has been settled and how to go about claiming their money.

Class actions are being used in Canada for such things as product liability cases, or situations of mass injury or loss, including environmental claims. But they've also been used in the situations of institutional sexual abuse, where we have seen lawsuits brought by large numbers of students, for example, sexually abused or physically abused at training schools or residential schools.

What if you don't want to be in a class action? I recently received notice in the mail, telling me that I was a member of a class action against a credit card company. I had no idea that somebody had started the case. I am happy to participate in it. If I didn't want to, I would send in a notice to the class action claimants telling them that I wish to opt out. If I opt out, I reserve the right to sue the defendant on my own, or I can simply abandon the case.

As the case proceeds through the courts, the judges will be interested in resolving the one issue that is common to all participants. For example, was the subway being operated in a negligent way when it was involved in an accident? If the answer is yes, then that common issue is determined for the benefit of everyone who has been injured and they can each submit their individual claims for compensation. One of the special features of class action litigation is the ability of lawyers who represent the class to act on behalf of them by way of a contingency fee. This means that the lawyers take on the risk of doing all the work and paying for all of the litigation without any contribution from the clients until the point at which they are successful. If they are eventually successful in the litigation, the lawyers will get a fee to compensate them for their time and energy and personal investment in the litigation. If the case is unsuccessful, the lawyers get nothing.

We will see more and more class action litigation in Canada, particularly as it concerns frustrated investors, consumer complaints about defective products, and environmental damage.

Part 10 — Sexual Abuse Claims

There has been an explosion in litigation over sexual abuse claims in Canada. These claims are with respect to sexual abuse of both children and adults. When these claims arise in the context of institutions, such as residential schools, training schools or schools for the deaf and blind, they are often grouped as a class action. However, there are many sexual abuse claims that are advanced on an individual basis. These claims arise from childhood sexual abuse and the consequences that adults suffer from as they grow older. In addition, litigation on behalf of children who have been sexually abused is also becoming common.

In 2003, a report was published about the economic costs of child abuse in Canada. That report concluded that in 1998 alone the estimated cost of child sexual abuse was over $1.3 billion. Personally, I consider that to be a conservative estimate.

Lawsuits in connection with sexual abuse of children must be launched with the assistance of a litigation guardian, in other words, an adult who is starting and conducting the case on behalf of the child. These claims are not only against the actual abuser, whether that person is a father, brother, aunt, uncle or neighbour, they are also commenced against individuals who may have been in a position to stop the abuse from occurring. So, for example, we now see children suing, not only the parent who abused them, but the parent who did nothing to prevent the abuse.

One concern about bringing a claim for damages related to childhood sexual abuse is the amount of time that has passed between the abuse and the making of the claim. If the abuse occurred when someone was, for example, twelve years old but they don't bring a claim to court until they are forty years old, should the court refuse to deal with those kinds of claims? The answer is no, and the courts have been quite willing to ignore the traditional limitation periods that would cut off litigation after a fixed period of time. Limitation periods generally do not affect children's rights. Limitation periods do not affect the rights of someone who is unable to assert their rights because of some mental deficiency, and the courts have been prepared to ignore limitation periods where there was a special relationship between the child and the abuser. This special relationship is called a fiduciary relationship, and it means that the person who abused the child was in a position of trust that was then misused.

We therefore see claims in our courts by people who were abused many years ago. The defendants who are alleged to have done the abusing complain that evidence has disappeared, witnesses are unavailable and that they are not able to properly defend themselves. Courts have been prepared to work with those concerns and scrutinize evidence and attempt to weigh the veracity of the claims. If you have a claim, do not sit back and wait. Gather your strength and get some support. If you expect to recover compensation or have some accountability, you must come forward and speak out or run the risk of losing the right to do so.

This litigation is often conducted in private, with the parties frequently agreeing to go into mediation or arbitration (see Chapter 1: The "System") to ensure total privacy. In that process it is not uncommon to see the person who was abused being asked to sign a confidentiality agreement in exchange for a settlement. The abuser purchases their silence?

An alternative approach is to go to the police and investigate whether criminal charges can be laid against the alleged abuser. If a conviction is obtained, or at the very least if charges are laid, it may be possible for a victim to approach the Criminal

Injuries Compensation Board, which is available in each province. The Board assesses the claim and then makes an award to the abused person. Generally these awards are much less than what would be obtained in a court. It is also necessary to await the outcome of the criminal proceedings before proceeding with Criminal Injuries Compensation Board claims. This can add years of delay to what may already be a very painful situation for the victim.

If you are a victim of sexual abuse, or if your child has been a victim of sexual abuse, you have an obligation to consult immediately with a lawyer to determine first if there is already a class action lawsuit underway that may be protecting your interests, and in which you can participate. You also have an obligation to ensure that the abuser is reported and not a danger to other children. Each provincial government has special programs available for victims of child sexual abuse and consultation with the provincial Attorney General or the ministry responsible for children's issues will direct you to confidential resources. Doing nothing is rarely an option.

Conclusion

There is a lot more to Canadian law than contracts, wills and estates and family law. Life is complicated. Even good news can make our lives complicated—lottery winnings, time on the golf course, going to a hockey game, taking the dog for a walk—and things can take an unexpected turn. I hope this chapter has not only demystified some unusual areas of the law but also shown you how Canadian law is woven through our lives.

Conclusion

Why I Wrote This Book

Well, we certainly covered quite a bit of legal ground in the foregoing ten chapters. It's legal ground that I think Canadians—new and old—need to be familiar with, things such as:

- How to handle lawyers;
- The rise of paralegals;
- The perils of self-representation;
- The mysteries of judges and juries;
- Suing and being sued and new alternatives like mediation and arbitration;
- Evidence and how it is used;
- Costs and legal fees;
- Family law, from divorce to property division and support;
- Wills and Powers of Attorney and guardianship of children;
- Organ donations and funeral arrangements;
- Criminal law and dealing with police;
- Common offences;
- Art theft;
- Criminal records and pardons;
- Business law, corporations and franchises;
- Employer/employee interests, including hiring, firing and quitting;
- Workplace privacy;
- Contracts—legal and illegal;
- Payday loans;
- Buying and selling a house or a condo;
- Real estate fraud;
- The marijuana grow op that might be next door;
- Violence in the workplace;
- Whistle-blowing;
- Trademarks, patents and copyright;

- Protecting inventions;
- DNA and the law;
- Suing politicians;
- Animals and the law;
- Sports injuries (and even golf course liability,) and much, much more.

This book includes hundreds of useful tips and insights on Canadian law. This is law you can use to protect yourself, your family, your property, your job and your company.

Why do I think it's so important for Canadians to understand the law? Because the Canadian justice system is based on a very profound and, to me, beautiful concept—the "rule of law." All of us are under one law, enforced impartially for our collective benefit. The success of that concept is what separates us from other parts of the world that seem to be tearing themselves apart. The success of the rule of law is what creates our civil society, a society that I truly believe is a model for the world. I know Canadian society is not perfect; there is much that we can improve. But, you know what? It works, in large part because of the rule of law.

But as rosy as that sounds, I am worried. I am worried that the core principle is in danger. Our justice system is no longer accessible to many, many Canadians. It has become too expensive to use. It has become too slow to have meaning. It has become too mysterious and too opaque.

I know this from the questions people ask me on *Strictly Legal,* and I see it in the faces of people I meet when speaking to the public and in the faces of clients who sit across from me every day. I am worried that Canadians are losing touch with Canadian law at the moment they may need it most.

This book is *not* legal advice. It is *not* a legal encyclopedia. It is some legal information designed to penetrate the wall going up around justice. Justice should not be mysterious. It should be understood. Canadians should not fear lawyers, judges and our courts. We should not fear financial ruin because we have a legal problem. If we do, then the rule of law and our civil society will erode.

The justice system needs help right now. This is my small contribution.

— Michael G. Cochrane

"LawyerSpeak©"

Ab initio
Definition: From the beginning
Example: His lawsuit had no chance ab initio.

Ab ovo usque ad mala
Definition: From eggs to apples or from beginning to end.
Example: The witness's evidence was unbelievable ab ovo usque ad mala.

Acceleration clause
Definition: Clause in mortgage that accelerates the maturity date so principal sum falls due.
Example: I missed two mortgage payments and now the whole thing is due because of the acceleration clause.

A contrario sensu
Definition: On the other hand
Example: A contrario sensu, the jury may be hung.

Ad hoc
Definition: For a particular or special purpose.
Example: His approach to the trial was ad hoc.

Ad Idem
Definition: To the same thing or to the same result. Meeting of minds in agreement.
Example: I think we are ad idem on the terms of the contract.

A justitia, quasi a quodam fante, omnia jura emanant.
Definition: From justice, as a fountain, all rights flow.
Example: As the judge said at the end of her judgment, a justitia, quasi a quodam fante, omnia jura emanant.

Bona fide
Definition: With good faith
Example: Her intentions in mediation were entirely bona fide.

Brownfields
Definition: Lands on which industrial or commercial activity took place in the past, and which may need to be cleaned before redevelopment.

Example: I'm not purchasing those brownfields because remediation will be too expensive.

Causa sine qua non

Definition: The cause without which the occurrence would not have happened

Example: His shanked drive was the causa sine qua non of the broken nose.

Caveat

Definition: Let him beware. A document used to register a challenge to a will.

Example: Uncle Bill was pressured to sign that crazy will, so I filed a caveat to challenge it.

Constructive dismissal

Definition: Form of wrongful dismissal when an employer puts the employee in a position where they feel forced to quit due to a change in duties, pay or benefits.

Example: I couldn't take the verbal abuse. I had to quit. I'm suing for constructive dismissal.

Contributory negligence

Definition: An injured person has done something to contribute to their own injury.

Example: His refusal to wear a seat belt made his injuries worse. He was contributorily negligent.

De facto

Definition: In fact, actually

Example: He had no custody order, but he had de facto custody of the children.

Escrow

Definition: Delivered into the hands of a third person to be held until certain conditions are met.

Example: The lawyer held the documents in escrow until the inspection was completed.

Ex officio

Definition: By virtue of office

Example: As president of the company, he had access to the vault ex officio.

Ex parte

> *Definition*: On one side only. No notice given to the other side of a court appearance.
>
> *Example*: It was an emergency, so the motion had to be ex parte.

Ex post facto

> *Definition*: After the fact
>
> *Example*: The impaired driver had many regrets ex post facto.

Fee simple

> *Definition*: The highest estate or right in real property. Total ownership.
>
> *Example*: There were no limitations on the property, so he purchased it in fee simple.

In camera

> *Definition*: In private
>
> *Example*: The judge met with the child in camera.

Intestate

> *Definition*: To die without a will.
>
> *Example*: He died intestate because he didn't get to sign his will.

Legally separated

> *Definition*: To cease living together as husband and wife
>
> *Example*: Even though he only moved out of the bedroom and not the house, they were still legally separated.

Lis pendens

> *Definition*: A suit or action pending in court.
>
> *Example*: The vendor refused to complete the sale of the property, so I registered a lis pendens on title to it.

Marriage of convenience

> *Definition*: Fraudulent marriage entered into in order to facilitate immigration, not to produce a true marital relationship.
>
> *Example*: She paid him $12,000 to enter into a marriage of convenience for her immigration to Canada.

Mens Rea — guilty mind
Actus Reus — guilty act
> = Guilt for criminal conviction
> *Example*: When he carried out a premeditated murder, he demonstrated both a mens rea and an actus reus.

Non est Factum
> *Definition*: It is not his deed.
> *Example*: I didn't know I was signing a deed. I thought it was a will. It's non est factum.

Novus actus interveniens
> *Definition*: A new act intervening.
> *Example*: The doctor's improper setting of the leg the driver broke in the accident was a novus actus interveniens.

Onus probandi
> *Definition*: Burden of Proof
> *Example*: The plaintiff had the onus propandi of showing a breach of contract.

Quantum meruit
> *Definition*: As much as he deserved.
> *Example*: Based on quantum meruit, he should recover reasonable value for the services rendered.

Quid pro quo
> *Definition*: What for what. This expression is meant to describe a situation where something is given in exchange for something else—a form of mutual consideration.
> *Example*: Let's do it quid pro quo. I'll lend you my car, if you mow my lawn for a month.

Res judicata
> *Definition*: A matter adjudged or settled by judgment. The issue has already been determined by the court.
> *Example*: The court already decided that I wasn't negligent. The matter is res judicata.

Uberrima fides
> *Definition*: The most good faith. This applies to life insur-

ance, which is a contract depending on the utmost good faith in disclosure and representation.

Example: He lied about his health on the application and the policy is void since it was a matter of uberrima fides.

Ultra vires

Definition: Beyond Powers. An act may be beyond the powers of a corporation or legislature.

Example: The provincial legislature's new law dealing with national security was ultra vires.

Index

A Little Background on the Author
Michael G. Cochrane, B.A., LL.B. -

Michael Cochrane has been practising law in Ontario for more than twenty-seven years in both the public and the private sector. He is a partner with Ricketts, Harris LLP in Toronto and was a senior policy lawyer in the Ontario Attorney General's Office. His practice has an emphasis on family law, estates law, mediation, civil litigation and public policy law. He has appeared before all levels of Court, including the Ontario Superior Court of Justice, the Ontario Divisional Court and the Supreme Court of Canada.

Mr. Cochrane is the host of BNN's *Strictly Legal* and has appeared as a legal expert on numerous television and radio programs, including CTV's *Canada AM*, *Jane Hawtin Live*, CBC's *counterSpin*, TVO and *MoneyTalk*.

He is the author of several books, including *Surviving Your Divorce: A Guide to Canadian Family Law,* now in its fourth edition from Wiley; *Surviving Your Parents' Divorce: A Guide for Young Canadians*; *For Better or For Worse: The Canadian Guide to Marriage Contracts and Cohabitation Agreements*; *Class Actions: A Guide to the Class Proceedings Act*, and *Family Law in Ontario for Lawyers and Law Clerks*, published by Canada Law Book, and he was the co-editor of the *Annual Review of Civil Litigation*, published by Thomson Carswell, from 2001 to 2004. He is also a regular columnist for magazines and newspapers.

In addition to being trained in Negotiation and Advanced Negotiation at Harvard Law School, Mr. Cochrane was a Fellow at the National Association of Attorneys General in Washington D.C. He has lectured in law at the University of Ottawa, Law Faculty, in the areas of Legal Institutions, Property and Wills, at Osgoode Hall Law School in the area of Public Law and at Ryerson University in the area of Environmental Law. He is a frequent speaker on legal issues across Canada.

Mr. Cochrane can be reached at Ricketts, Harris LLP in Toronto at (416) 364-6211; mcochrane@rickettsharris.com and through the Ricketts, Harris website at *www.rickettsharris.com*. For more information about Mr. Cochrane, visit his website at *www.michaelcochrane.ca*.